CINEMA BEFORE THE WORLD

Cinema before the World

THE GLOBAL ROUTES OF THE LUMIÈRE BROTHERS

Michael Allan

FORDHAM UNIVERSITY PRESS   NEW YORK   2026

Fordham University Press gratefully acknowledges financial assistance and support provided for the publication of this book by the Oregon Humanities Center.

Copyright © 2026 Fordham University Press

All rights reserved. No part of this publication may be reproduced, stored in a retrieval system, or transmitted in any form or by any means—electronic, mechanical, photocopy, recording, or any other—except for brief quotations in printed reviews, without the prior permission of the publisher.

Fordham University Press has no responsibility for the persistence or accuracy of URLs for external or third-party Internet websites referred to in this publication and does not guarantee that any content on such websites is, or will remain, accurate or appropriate.

Fordham University Press also publishes its books in a variety of electronic formats. Some content that appears in print may not be available in electronic books.

Visit us online at www.fordhampress.com.

For EU safety/GPSR concerns: Mare Nostrum Group B.V., Doelen 72, 4831 GR Breda, The Netherlands, gpsr@mare-nostrum.co.uk

Library of Congress Cataloging-in-Publication Data available online at https://catalog.loc.gov.

Printed in the United States of America

28 27 26   5 4 3 2 1

First edition

Contents

Introduction. Microhistory: Envisioning Ellipsis   1
A Flashback to Cinema's Elsewhere, 5 • Microhistory: Excess as Method, 10 • Illusions of Index, or the Ethnographic Mirage, 13 • Conceptual Cartography, 17 • A Preface to Prehistory: A Potential Future of Cinema, 20

1   World: The Labor of Representation   23
On Atlases and Adjacency, 26 • An Archive of Potential Worlds, 31 • Iteration and Empire, or the Labor of World Cinema, 35 • Afterimages of Future Pasts: Glass and Bricks, 39

2   Location: Locating Looks in World Cinema   43
Mirror: A Local History of World Cinema, 47 • Window: A World History of Local Cinema, 51 • (The Postcolonial) Pivot: Unlearning Imperial Enchantment, 56 • Portal: Beyond the World Picture, 60

3   Frames: De-Centering Orientalist Optics   62
A Frame Story, 65 • Enframing the Unpredictable, 70 • Beyond Icon and Index, or a Prayer for Mimesis, 72 • An Expanded Field, 75 • The Photorama, or a World without Frames, 80 • De-Orientalizing Optics, 82

4   Sovereignty: Iterations of Cinematic Statecraft   85
Serial Sovereigns, 88 • The Khedive's Two Bodies, 91 • Sovereign Cuts, 95 • Sovereign Afterlives, 99 • The Sovereign Image?, 103

5 History: The Duration of Myth   105
   Perfecting Place, 108 • Picturing the Past, 110 • The Image of Duration, 114 • Cinematic Futures, 119 • The Cinematic Event, 122

6 Tracks: Tracking the World in/as Cinema   124
   Placing Perceptual Paradigms, 129 • Middle East Trains, 132 • World in/as Motion, 138 • Arriving at a Farewell, 140

7 Scale: The World as Close-Up   145
   The Figure in the Carpet, 148 • The Close-Up at a Formal Distance, 151 • Looking and Masking, 158 • Zoom Out: Facing the Globe, 162

Epilogue. Planet: Otherworldly Futures   167
   Toward a Planetary Cinema, 169 • Planetarity, 173 • The Promise of a Future Planet, 176 • A World beyond Compare, 178

ACKNOWLEDGMENTS   181

NOTES   187

BIBLIOGRAPHY   215

INDEX   231

CINEMA BEFORE THE WORLD

INTRODUCTION
Microhistory
Envisioning Ellipsis

In 1925, when Georges-Michel Coissac published *Histoire du cinématographe de ses origines à nos jours*, he included a reference to the travelogue of Monsieur Alexandre Promio: "Our readers will certainly read with interest the travelogue [*carnet de route*] of M. Promio."[1] Offset with indentation and an accompanying photograph, the travelogue flashes back to a moment in film history before the emergence of film culture. The framing of the account reveals that during the first months of 1896, soon after the invention of the cinematograph, Promio undertook a voyage from France across the globe as part of his collaboration with the Lumière Brothers. Promio's travelogue lists the various countries he visited, including Spain, England, Italy, Germany, Turkey, and the United States. At each stop, Promio used the Lumière cinematograph to record 50-second animated views, and he demonstrated the wonders of this newly patented device to local audiences. The world captured on Promio's cinematograph was a world prior to the conventions of film spectatorship, acting, and editing that would arise years later. And even though painters, photographers, and writers had long documented global travels, Promio helped to capture scenes in motion and in time, recording monuments, parades, ports, trains, and everyday life, and projecting the vision of the Lumière cinematograph to admiring audiences around the world.

But Promio's story contains a curious ellipsis. For all that he reveals about his time in England and the United States, he is remarkably abrupt when describing his travels across the Middle East. In fact, apart from a brief reference to his time in Turkey, Promio leaves unsaid that he traveled to those countries now known as Algeria, Tunisia, Egypt, Lebanon, and Syria:

> I have little to say about my trip to Turkey, apart from the great difficulty I had to introduce my camera [*appareil de prise de vues*]. At that time, in Abdul Hamid's Turkey, any instrument with a crank [*muni d'une manivelle*] was suspicious; it was necessary to call in the French embassy and then even a few coins skillfully forgotten in the hand of some official, to obtain unhindered entry. At last I was able to operate in Constantinople, Smyrna, Jaffa, Jerusalem, etc.[2]

His brief mention of a trip to Turkey (about which he has "little to say"), followed by "Constantinople, Smyrna, Jaffa, Jerusalem, etc.," raises questions about his cognitive map of the world he traveled. His use of "etcetera" effectively elides many locations now understood to be part of the global spread of the cinematograph, and missing from his account altogether are the trips he took across North Africa. What Promio does recall has more to do with conditions of his entry—Abdul Hamid II, the French embassy, and bribery—than it does with the locations he visited or even the audiences he met.[3] At the time of Promio's trip in 1897, the region he describes as Turkey in his travelogue was the seat of the Ottoman Empire. Abdul Hamid II oversaw a model of statecraft quite different from the governance that would emerge after the first World War, enough so that the historical gap between Promio's films in 1897 and his travelogue in 1925 attests to two different geopolitical worlds. In Promio's curious ellipsis, then, is a fundamental transformation, a visual archaeology of a social world that his films capture more vividly than his limited remarks.

I am drawn to the ellipsis in Promio's travelogue—though a seemingly minor detail—for all that it reveals about the dynamic geography connecting past, present, and future. The challenge of world cinema of this period is not simply that film had yet to be understood as it would years later, but that the nature of the world—those social, legal, and political formations that came to be understood as the natural order of things—was not quite as it seemed. And so, when Promio suggests, "I have little to say," he introduces a distinction between what he *says* as a camera operator and what his various films *reveal*. This gap in Promio's account helps draw our attention to a situation where his words fall short of the visual archive he leaves behind. The landscapes depicted in the films evolve with the passage of time, and the titles used in the catalogue attribute different names to locations shown on-screen, dependent on shifts in the political order. What does remain of Promio's voyage is a visual trace in nearly one hundred films from the countries now known as Algeria,

Tunisia, Egypt, Palestine, Lebanon, Syria, and Turkey shot in 1896 and 1897.[4] These films forge an emergent framework for world cinema situated at the intersection of an ellipsis in a travelogue and the transformation of a region known as North Africa and the Middle East.

I take the ellipsis in Promio's story not to assert a more proper telling of the origins of cinema, nor to produce North Africa and the Middle East as a supplement to film history. Rather, by engaging the interplay between the sites captured on camera and the projections of the world on-screen, I question the grounds that inform when, where, and how to see cinematically. World cinema is not a matter of here and elsewhere, the local and the foreign. It is, as this book will suggest, predicated on the estrangement of the world that the cinematograph provides. All are foreign to the technology that Promio circulated on his voyage in 1896–1897, and a projected film is never present to the situation in which it was initially captured. I point to the disjuncture between saying and seeing in Promio's travelogue in order to grapple with the dynamics of what we might call a potential history of world cinema. I borrow in this endeavor from Ariella Aïsha Azoulay's proclamation that "potential history is not an alternative account of this already historicized world, but rather a deliberate attempt to pulverize the matrix of history, to disavow what was historicized by making repressed potentialities present again within the fabricated phenomenological field of imperial history."[5]

At the intersection of film theory and film history, *Cinema before the World* draws from the archive of Promio's North Africa and Middle East films to reveal the fundamental ambivalence of the moving image—that is, its ever-unsettled grounds, between past and future, here and there, filming and projection. Across seven chapters, the book extends the critical afterlife from Promio's ellipsis in the travelogue to the global visions animated in the interplay of light and shadow in Algeria, Egypt, and Ottoman Palestine. How do North Africa and the Middle East take place in this early history of film? What are the conditions of location for a medium contingent on projection? What does it mean to be rendered visible as a region in the cartography of world cinema? The answers, I suggest, rest between empirical slips of a written archival record and the visual excess of what is projected on screens. In every projected film is less a motif of capture than one of saturation—the cinematic world is not one of scarcity, but abundance.[6] What follows, ultimately, is the story of how an ellipsis (a verbal blackout, *un trou de mémoire*) leads us to the surplus of the global archive, or how we move from what goes unmentioned, forgotten, and unspoken to a vision (recorded, projected, and reiterated) of a potential history of world cinema.

As a scholar of cinema and comparative literature, I find myself drawn to Promio's place in the catalogue of Lumière Brothers films on account of the resonance it poses for transnational cultural analysis. I have been trained to take seriously the importance of research in original languages and national cultural traditions. This leads to scholarly projects that analyze a general concept (a genre or a technique) in time and place, often in the context of specific literary traditions (in my case a training in French and Arabic literature). And this gesture of de-universalization bespeaks a practice of situated reading in which language, history, and culture inform how texts take place. Admittedly then, when I began looking at the catalogue of global Lumière films, I was tempted to tell the story of film's arrival in North Africa and the Middle East. Part of this endeavor was to attend to instances at the end of the nineteenth century when the first cinemas were founded in Alexandria and Algiers, a story eloquently explored in the work of film historians Ahmed al-Hadari, Samy Helmy, and Viola Shafik.[7] And because early cinema followed a tradition of Orientalist travel, part of the endeavor was also to situate these films in the context of colonial practices of capture and display, be it travelogues, archaeology, world's fairs, lithography, or photography in the work of scholars such as Fatimah Tobing Rony, Alison Griffiths, and Jeffrey Ruoff.[8]

And yet the Lumière Brothers films pose a conceptual cartography of a different sort. Those films shot in North Africa and the Middle East are a mere fraction of a broader collection, and the Lumière catalogue has a general grammar for its global collection, rather than for a specific part. If situated readings (in time and place) structure much of what we do in the humanities and social sciences, then the Lumière catalogue confronts us with a particular view of the world—that is, with a distinct collection that captures, organizes, and visualizes the world in a particular way. Comparative literature may have cultivated my foundations in specific languages, but the Lumière Brothers catalogue is a sort of cinematic Esperanto, a vision of the world that purports to transcend the particularities of place with the radical indexicality of motion photography.[9] In the Lumière Brothers film catalogue, then, we encounter a time capsule for a vision of the world—an archaeology of moving images alongside ever-shifting conceptions of how the world itself is understood.

At the backbone of this book is the transnational history of the Lumière Brothers' efforts to picture the world. Focusing on Promio's trip across North Africa and the Middle East, each chapter connects a general filmic principle (such as framing, tracking shots, and scale) to the sites where they are made visible (a rooftop in Algiers, a train station in Jerusalem, and the Jaffa Gate). Across the chapters, I situate North Africa and the Middle East in film history not simply as locations, but as generative of formal and aesthetic dimensions. This microhistory of Promio's journey is meant as a historical intervention (telling the story of the global Lumière Brothers) and as a methodological model for film scholarship committed to transnational analysis across various languages, territories, and media. At each site, I consider how film disrupts the politics of location—that is, film form counteracts film history by picturing the world in new ways, often in excess of the colonial clichés depicted on-screen. The book thus embraces an extended scope for film history (across national traditions and languages) and for global media (across photography, the photorama, and contemporary video art). In the end, this microhistory of world cinema illuminates the complexities of a world produced, imagined, and rendered through film. Out of Promio's ellipsis, we might say, arise the transnational origins of filmmaking and the global future of film history.

A Flashback to Cinema's Elsewhere

A short entry in *al-Ahram* from November 9, 1896, describes what is thought to be the first display of the Lumière cinematograph at the Toussoun Stock Exchange in Alexandria, and a similar entry follows in the French newspaper *La Réforme* on December 1, 1896, describing displays at the Hammam Schneider in Cairo. The Arabic account details the demonstration, the price for adults (4 piasters) and children (2 piasters), and the screening times every half hour between 5 P.M. and 11 P.M. The French account describes the curiosity and admiration that audiences had for the fifteen lively animated scenes.[10]

Similar accounts exist for demonstrations held in Algiers and Oran in Algeria, which is to say that even before Promio's arrival, the soil had been tilled for the arrival of the cinematograph.[11] Shortly following Promio's visit, additional entries appear in Algerian and Egyptian periodicals highlighting both the technology and the reactions that accompanied the demonstrations.[12] Descriptions of the cinematograph arise in local Arab newspapers as they do for audiences encountering the vision of the Lumière cinematograph across the world.[13] At this curious moment in film history, the cinematograph was as foreign in Lyon, Algiers, and Cairo as it was in Montreal, Berlin, and Jakarta. The device had yet to be known as an origin point for what would eventually be described as the rise of cinema.

Promio's travelogue is a small—some might suggest unknown—story in the foundational fictions of film history, but one with global implications. Already in 1925 when Promio reflects on his time working for the Lumière Brothers, he does so in response to those, such as Coissac, helping to establish an origin story.[14] Crucial to this account are the brothers Louis and Auguste Lumière, experimenters with motion photography in Lyon, France, who, in the most grandiose telling, are celebrated as the inventors of cinema. More empirically grounded film historians credit them in a limited manner with having projected film for the first time to paying audiences.[15] As the story goes, on February 13, 1895, the patent for their cinematograph was officially filed, and the next month, on March 22, 1895, they projected a film to an audience of two hundred at the Society for the Development of National Industry. On December 28, 1895, a date memorialized in the annals of film history, they held their first commercial screening in the Salon Indien in the basement of the Grand Café in Paris. The cinematograph was just one of many inventions explored by the Lumière Company, including color photography, the photorama, and x-rays, but it is the cinematograph that would have an ultimately transformative impact on what we now understand as film history.

The Lumière cinematograph borrowed heavily from a series of experiments and patents linked to chronophotography.[16] And yet the novelty of the Lumière device—in contrast to others of the period—was both its compact size and its capacity to record and project moving images. Weighing roughly 5kg, the cinematograph was a simple wooden box that sat atop a tripod (Figure 1).[17] With the rotation of its hand-powered crank (*la manivelle*), the device reeled a 35mm celluloid strip of roughly 17 meters in length. Each of the 800 photograms on the flexible strip (*la pellicule*) had perforations on either side to be gripped by clips as it spooled in front of the lens. Internally, the device, which was modeled on a sewing machine, employed an intermittent motion with which to freeze each photogram for exposure—a distinct contrast to the continuous motion of Thomas Edison's kinetoscope.

Accounts of this foundational moment are often rather fanciful in their telling, enough so that the film historian Laurent Mannoni remarks, "The two brothers told so many different versions in later life—mixing different accounts at different times, each promoting his own claim to attribute the merit to himself—that the truth became completely obscured, a nice irony for inventors whose very name translates as 'light.'"[18] It is widely accepted that Charles Moisson—a key technician who helped to craft the prototype of the Lumière cinematograph, which the engineer Jules Carpentier, who would eventually help to craft ten more—offered one of the more authoritative accounts, or at least one that seems to align with filed patents.[19] Where other experimenters with early cinema, including Thomas Edison, Max Skladanowsky, and William Friese-Greene, remained

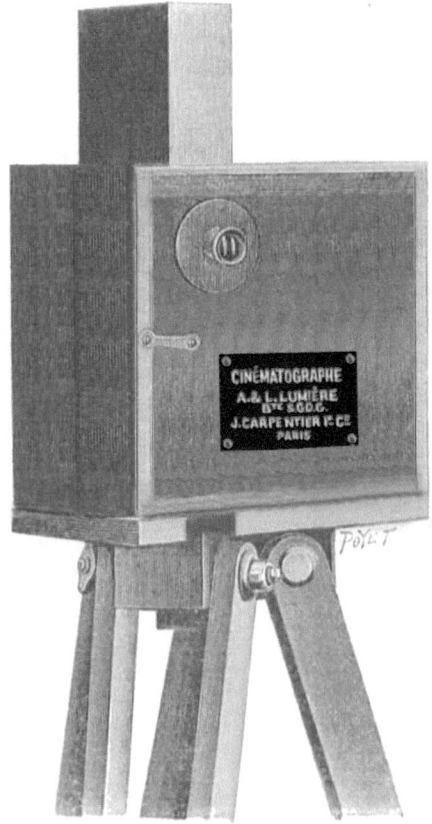

Figure 1. Lumière cinematograph.

bound to studios, the Lumière Brothers almost immediately globalized their network, capitalizing on the portability of their cinematograph to send it across the world.

As a witness to these origins, Promio positions himself in the travelogue as a key player in an emergent global network of Lumière camera operators. His story begins with his astonishment attending one of the first Lumière screenings at the Congress of Photography in the summer of 1895: "Like everyone else," he tells us, "I was amazed [*je fus émerveillé*] and, from that moment on, I made every effort to be introduced to Mr. Auguste and Mr. Louis Lumière." At the time, Promio was a photography enthusiast, but his fate would soon change: "Thanks to the intermediary of Mr. Pascal, whom I had known at

La Martinière, I had the honour of entering into the service of these gentlemen at the beginning of 1896."[20] In a sequence of events whose outcome seems almost predetermined, Promio describes his emergent role:

> First of all, I got acquainted with the new device [*nouvel appareil*], then these gentlemen entrusted me with training the staff that were to be sent to the posts set up in France and abroad. At that time, there were only a very small number of printed reels, shot by Mr. Louis Lumière himself; but this very modest stock was well seen to be insufficient, and after having had me make a few trial shots, Mr. Louis Lumière asked me to go on a trip, with the objective of collecting new views [*vues*], as quickly as possible, to supply the demands.[21]

Promio sheds light on the various trips taken, almost in order, and in a manner that corresponds to the indexing of these films in the Lumière catalogue.

> My first trip was to Spain. I was feeling a little emotional [*J'étais quelque peu ému*]. I felt very lonely, completely on my own, and I dreaded a failure. A telegram from Lyon, after my first shipments, was an important encouragement; I gained confidence and continued the journey with less concern.[22]

With this newfound confidence, Promio would go on to produce more films in the Lumière catalog than any other operator.

When Promio notes that he was "entrusted" with "training the staff to be sent to the posts set up in France and abroad," he refers to the techniques developed to assist camera operators in the skills associated with positioning the cinematograph, turning its handle at the proper rate, as well as developing and projecting images. Promio was but one among a cadre of representatives whom the Lumière Brothers sent to locations from Mexico to Palestine to Hungary to Vietnam.[23] The list of operators includes the technician Charles Moisson, as well as figures such as Gabriel Veyre, Francis Doublier, Constant Girel, Marius Sestier, and Félix Mesguich. Where Promio leaves behind the brief notes of his travelogue, Félix Mesguich and Gabriel Veyre both published lengthier reflections on their time traveling for the Lumière Company.[24] Wherever they were sent, each of these camera operators had a hand in the visualization of the world through the cinematograph. From Japan to Italy to the United States, their films constitute an uncomfortable prehistory to most national film histories because they attest to the fact that the cinematograph had been globalized prior to local infrastructure for film production.

For his part, in just the first few months of traveling, Promio was on hand as a representative of the Lumière Brothers at the Royal Palace in Madrid, the funeral of Queen Victoria in London, the opening of the Stockholm Exhibition, the Grand Canal in Venice, the National Exposition in Geneva, the Kleith theaters in New York, and the Auditorium Theatre in Chicago. He is often credited with the first tracking shot, which he captured by mounting the camera on a gondola in Venice, and his catalogue of films forges techniques at the intersection of fictional artifice (such as the reenactments of historical episodes) and documentary (such as his focus on street scenes and everyday life).[25] Not entirely shy about his role, Promio ends his travelogue by describing his celebrity status, especially in the United States, where he appeared on the front page of a newspaper in New York and was hit with a spotlight as a guest at a screening in Chicago: "You have to have lived through the first hours of these screenings," he recalls, "to grasp the effect produced [*pour se rendre compte de l'effet produit*]."[26]

For all of the cultural and historical importance of the Lumière Brothers, the cinematograph, and the camera operators, I am struck by a certain refrain in the various accounts. In Promio's flashback is a quest to imagine not only images of the world but also to grasp "the effect produced" by the animated views projected on-screen. These lines echo those at the opening of his travelogue when he recalls his first experience as a spectator seeing the cinematograph at the Congress of Photography: "Like everyone else, I was amazed [*Comme tout le monde, je fus émerveillé*]." I focus on Promio's wonder and on the effort to describe the effect of first seeing a projected film because to speak of the cinematograph is not simply to address the technology. Engaging with this early moment in world cinema is as much a matter of visions and imaginaries as it is of places and portraits. Promio's small story contains at once his travels across the world but also the disjuncture between the capture and projection of his moving images. When he suggests, "You have to have lived through the first hours of the screenings," he gestures to a moment of wonder that even he—having seen it all before—could not himself have shared with the audiences to whom he presented. In the end, the projections the device offered to audiences exceeded the bounds of comprehension and posed a challenge to understanding the experience of seeing the world as never before.

Promio's travelogue helps us envision a constructive anachronism in its flashback to a time before cinema and its effort to reconstruct the wonder of seeing a moving image for the first time. I have been influenced by the meticulous work of film historians attending to the role of camera operators, but what follows here is less a cultural history of a moment than an effort to think of the potentials that arise from Promio's ellipsis. The various films he leaves behind structure anachronism into the very mode of looking—a world fractured between now and then, between the Ottoman Empire of 1897 and Turkey of 1925, and a world before the framework through which cinema has come to be known. This story of world cinema is ultimately less one of ethnographic capture than the possibilities of projection and the afterlife of an image beyond the intentions of the camera operator. In the eyes of the spectators of these early films is a capacity to see and imagine the world as it could never quite be seen again.

Microhistory: Excess as Method

In an interview from October 2022, the Italian historian Carlo Ginzburg—one of the foremost practitioners of microhistory—reflects on his method. Where microhistory is most often understood to have been forged in the archival musings of historians, Ginzburg's interview borrows from film theory to make claims about the craft of history. True to the microhistorical method, he flashes back to his childhood to share a story: "When I was ten years old, my mother [the writer Natalia Ginzburg, 1916–1991] regularly brought me the books published by Einaudi. One day I came across *The Film Sense* by Sergei Eisenstein."[27] Ginzburg continues, "I understood very little of the book's content, but the impression it made on me was immense, even though I had not yet seen Eisenstein's films."[28] He then arrives at the impact the book had for him: "Then I read his text on the close-up, which became very important for me."[29]

Ginzburg embraces Eisenstein's discussion of the close-up for its relevance to the task of the historian. He initially sets up an analogy: "Working on a case in an analytical way is close to this," he says, before offering a caveat, "but, of course, you also have to take into account the off-screen, otherwise the close-up would not make sense."[30] Shuttling between the close-up and the off-screen leads Ginzburg to his more critical point regarding microhistory and global perspectives: "This implies that in any close-up the global perspective is implicit. Every singular case assumes the possibility of a generalization, and there is a back and forth between the one and the other."[31] At play for Ginzburg is both the singular case and the possibility of a generalization, all framed analogically alongside the close-up and its implicit global perspective. I am struck here by the possibilities that Ginzburg outlines for imagining the close-up as a case and the off-screen as an implied global perspective—here, in Ginzburg's reflections on microhistory via his encounter with Eisenstein, the detail and its system remain closely connected.

Such is the dynamic that this microhistory of world cinema is meant to chart. In the close-up on details from films left behind from Promio's voyage across North Africa and the Middle East arises an implicit global perspective—the isolation of a part bespeaks an engagement with the whole. Here, in other words, we encounter a microhistory of world cinema. At the heart of this inquiry is neither Promio as a celebrity camera operator nor the Lumière Brothers as his employer, but an ellipsis, forgetting, or gap in a travelogue that overlooks a journey across North Africa and the Middle East. If I begin with Promio's oversight, I do so to point to a model of microhistory predicated less on the textual or discursive archive than on a practice indebted to the critical afterlife of visual evidence. The story that follows could well be the story of Alexandre Promio himself—a figure buried in the archives of early cinema yet responsible for many of the films visible from the inception of the history of the cinematograph. In fact, when I began this project over a decade ago, I was keen to add to this study the travels of Félix Mesguich and Gabriel Veyre, but doing so seemed to recapitulate a human-centered focus on the camera operator. And yet there is a limit to understanding Promio as the driver of this history of world cinema—just as there would be in centering any one of the operators. The cinematograph was an apparatus that facilitated image-making in novel ways, and Promio could be understood to be an extension of the apparatus, contingent on the rotating handle through which the cinematograph recorded. The human turning the crank was a contingent part of this device, but by no means the determinate driver of how the story of world cinema would emerge.

The historical record of Promio's travel is rather vague. Promio's biographer notes that it remains unclear whether Promio undertook his voyage initially to Turkey and then to Egypt or the reverse, and the exact dates remain blurred in the catalogue in echo of the ambiguity of the itinerary. In fact, as the biographer has it, these early films constitute a section simply titled "Orientalist views," a mere fraction of Promio's extensive filmmaking practice and a seeming addendum to a global corpus consistent with images of the region.[32] There are parallels here to other engagements with the global voyages of Lumière camera operators. Daisuke Miyao, for example, provides insightful analysis of the Lumière camera operator Gabriel Veyre and the prevalence of Japonisme in early cinema, and Promio's Middle East and North African films can be seen to share in a broader Orientalist imaginary.[33] Among Promio's many films are depictions of prayers, pyramids, funeral processions, camels, and Nile boats—all motifs that have a vexed recurrence in depictions of the Middle East.[34] Indeed, these recurring thematic dimensions make places more readily recognizable, and yet, as I explore in what follows, however hackneyed the tropes, these sites take place anew cinematically. One could even say that the repetition of the thematic dimensions is precisely what allows the formal novelty to register. The repetition of the Orientalist fantasy makes the otherworldly site recognizable to the extent that film form registers as all that is foreign. In this microhistory of Promio's ellipsis, we are left not with words, but with images—and a close-up on the global perspective his films offer.

The more I engaged with the early Lumière films from North Africa and the Middle East—as opposed to their operators—I came to realize that the afterlife of these images inheres neither in the history of Promio nor the apparatus itself, but in the projection of the scenes and those captured within the frame. Whether Algiers, Alexandria, Cairo, or Jerusalem, the cinematograph took place at each of these sites both as an apparatus that captured scenes and as a tool for the projection and circulation of moving images. I have been drawn here to a certain understanding of pragmatics in aesthetic analysis that accounts not just for what we see, but the when, where, and how by which it takes place. In this quest is not a fantasy of origins, but the reckoning with the anti-foundationalism of a medium predicated less on film stock than on its projection. The material history at stake, then, lies as much in the ambivalence of the moving image (between recording and projection) as it does in the sites and situations of its imagined grounds.[35]

What might it mean to account for the global trajectories of early cinema not simply as the product of a specific operator and their travels, but as the cinematic production of the world? What are the implications of visualizing place in motion and in time, and how does the dissemination not only of the camera, but of projected images inform, inflect, and transform how to see? The answers to such questions necessarily toggle between the microhistory of films from Promio's Middle East and North African voyage and the macrohistory of what it means to visualize the world through the cinematograph. It should be noted that this is not an argument for the radical exemplarity of the Lumière catalogue, so much as its shared framework with other media forms. In world's fairs, colonial expeditions, and travel photography, plenty of accounts have been offered of journeys that could be seen to parallel that of Promio. There is clear overlap between colonial optics and the Lumière trajectory, and yet the novelty of the Lumière catalogue had less to do with what was shown than how.[36] Exotifying views of elsewhere were well known to most audiences, but the cinematograph itself was foreign to the world nearly everywhere it traveled. The terms of the estrangement it offered were formal, aesthetic, and technical, as the world came to life anew with the flicker of light. To recognize a site on-screen relied on the uncanny illusion of seeing it in motion and in time.

Illusions of Index, or the Ethnographic Mirage

The first depictions of Arabs on-screen come not from Promio's trip to Algeria, Egypt, or Ottoman Palestine, but from a trip to the 1896 Swiss National Exhibition in Geneva shortly after the invention of the cinematograph (Figure 2).[37] Film number 310 in the Lumière catalogue, *Cortège arabe*, depicts a procession of roughly twenty Arab dignitaries, shot from behind, as they proceed through a crowd at the Swiss exposition. Above the crowd, along the roofline of a building, is a prominent sign, "Thé Divan des fées," and various onlookers observe from the side of the street as others navigate around the procession on the street. In the mix of costumes and cultures—the Arab dignitaries, the pedestrians, the onlookers, and an African delegation passing in the opposite direction—is an overall indifference to the cinematograph. Those processing in line down the street are already on display, performing for an audience watching them from the sides of the street. And refracted through the triangular lens of the cinematograph, these Arab dignitaries become part of a collection of early Lumière films eventually screened across the world.

Number 311 in the catalogue is a film titled *Danse égyptienne* that was also taken at the Swiss National Exhibition (Figure 3). Even prior to Promio's voyage across North Africa and the Middle East, the film rehearses all the trappings of Orientalist fantasy by recording two belly dancers performing for a seated audience. Like magic lantern shows or the world's fairs, this Lumière film structures a colonial viewing position for observing, as Tom Gunning would describe it, "the whole world within reach."[38] The archway, traditional costumes, and instruments depict what was already understood through centuries of Orientalist representations of the region, and the dance itself transpires in the Egyptian café at the Parc de Plaisance. These two films of Arabs at the Swiss National Exhibition underscore the vexed politics of colonial representations of the Arab world, a seemingly direct echo of questions raised in Timothy Mitchell's *Colonising Egypt*, Edward Said's *Orientalism*, and Ella Shohat and Robert Stam's *Unthinking Eurocentrism*.[39]

And yet it is not that Promio's films of the Arab world somehow capture a more authentic reality (in motion and in time), but that they shift the terms of illusion. I mention these two Swiss films because they take as given the artifice they present—that is, those on display in Geneva are already performing for

Figure 2. *Cortège arabe*, a Lumière film depicting a ceremonial procession at the 1896 Swiss National Exhibition in Geneva.

an audience. The conceptual challenge is not so much the rehearsal of Orientalist viewing positions, which were well known across painting, literature, and photography, but rather, the slippages, accidents, and fault lines that the films introduce. In fact, if there is a connection to the Arab world in these films (beyond the Orientalist tropes they employ), it is curiously through the Swiss inventor François-Henri Lavanchy-Clarke, who in the 1870s worked in Egypt, helped facilitate Promio's visit to Switzerland, and who appears in the second film wearing a tarbouche.[40] Among his many entrepreneurial endeavors, Lavanchy-Clarke coordinated philanthropic work with the blind during his time in Egypt, and his signature in these films extends beyond the Orientalist valences of his costume to the circuits of empire and capital that these films embody. A history that simply focuses on the representational dimensions of the film misses the constitutive social and economic formations that converge in this moving image.[41]

We also encounter in these early Lumière films a fundamental reframing of the terms of illusion, something integral to understanding the ethnographic mirage they present. Shortly following a film screening for the Congress of Photography in June 1895, roughly a year prior to the trip to

MICROHISTORY: ENVISIONING ELLIPSIS

Figure 3. *Danse égyptienne*, a Lumière film presenting a traditional Egyptian dance performance at the 1896 Swiss National Exhibition in Geneva.

Switzerland, the local Lyon paper, *Le Progrès*, published an account of a film screening:

> We saw workers leaving the Lumière factory by foot, on bicycles, and in cars; we saw ten tableaux vivants, animated with an absolutely intense life, men walking, jumping from trams, moving in such a way as to give the absolute illusion of reality [*l'illusion absolue de la réalité*].[42]

I draw attention to this passage for what it reveals about the viewing experience. Not only does the account allude to the films shown as tableaux vivants, but it employs the language of illusion, focusing both on what was seen and the conditions of its "absolute illusion of reality."[43] Against the notion of an unreflexive spectator tricked by what was seen on-screen, the newspaper places emphasis on the images "animated with an absolutely intense life" and the illusion by which it happens. Art and technology align in the sort of wonder that the film screening offers—artifice and illusion are here inseparable.

The emphasis on illusion recurs in an essay by Dai Vaughan, who famously refutes the notion that spectators were simply deceived by what they witnessed on-screen.[44] Vaughan describes a response to Edison's kinetoscope:

"In 1894 Henri de Parville wrote of it in *Les Annales politiques et littéraires*: 'Tous les acteurs sont en mouvement. Leurs moindres actes sont si naturellement reproduits qu'on se demande s'il y a illusion.'"[45] "What he presumably meant by 'illusion,'" Vaughan tells us, "was some system by which the images of live actors might have been brought by mirrors under the eyepiece of the machine."[46] As the essay continues, Vaughan shifts from the comment about Edison to consider ripples in the water of a harbor of an early Lumière film:

> But it is clear that the relevance of this lies not in similarity but in contrast; for there was no way that the image of a French harbour could have been reflected by mirrors into the auditorium of the Regent Street Polytechnic. The gentlemen with the walking sticks were not trying to discover how the trick worked. Their concern was not that they might have been victims of an illusion, but that they had experienced something which transcended the cosy world of illusionism altogether.[47]

Almost immediately, Vaughan counters the perception that audiences of early cinema were somehow duped by illusion, and he points instead to the sort of details that eclipsed the intended actions: "We need look no further than [the French film scholar Georges] Sadoul's standard *Histoire générale* for evidence of the fact that what most impressed the early audiences was what would now be considered the incidentals of scenes: smoke from a forge, steam from a locomotive, brick-dust from a demolished wall." And then, turning from the "incidentals" to a nearly theological claim, Vaughan proclaims, "The unpredictable has not only emerged from the background to occupy the greater portion of the frame; it has also taken sway over the principals. Man, no longer the mountebank self-presenter, has become equal with the leaves and the brick-dust—and as miraculous."[48]

If I quote Vaughan's essay at length, I do so because of the richness it provides for thinking about the wonder of early cinema. What is striking about illusion is that it has less to do with the image than the social and political horizons of its reception. This framework, Jordan Schonig qualifies, is not *accidental*, as Vaughan seems to suggest, but like the water effect and wind in the trees, it is rather *unplannable*.[49] For Schonig, it is motion itself that is at stake in these early films, and his study helps illuminate an entire epistemology of motion capture. Both Vaughan's argument and Sadoul's claim address the terms of audience perception rather than the stakes of the image itself. For Vaughan, it is what audiences respond to, the inquiry with the stick at the image of the harbor, rather than something intrinsic to how an image ought to be understood. Film obviates an inquiry into the status of the world being seen, and illusion is critical not as a flawed representation of the real, but as the condition of a technological feat.

When it comes to the nature of worldly images, then, the artifice is already a given, and the Lumière cinematograph sets up a different, perhaps even more critical, inquiry into what constitutes a world picture. Against the laws of framing and epistemology is a world apprehended in motion, coming alive in novel ways to combine the tension between capture and projection, revealing in the process layers of artifice and techne, a collision between realism and illusion—that is, the absolute illusion that the cinematograph can provide. Where Orientalist realism has an extensive vocabulary for descriptive efforts, the fate of the Lumière films was never strictly one of documentation in a scientific sense, but in the capturing of images.[50] The illusion at stake was always predicated on the trick of the eye, which was already understood to be a framework for perception. The magic of these early Lumière films was not in the absolute referent (what was behind the screen), but in the trick, the device, or the machine that made the world visible in this particular way.

It is this tension between ellipsis and illusion that animates how *Cinema before the World* engages with the archives of early cinema. What is meant by absolute illusion is not the false apprehension of a world to be known better, but an intense focus less on *what* was seen than on *how* it was seen. In world cinema it is not a spectator pretending to apprehend the world through the camera, but a spectator curious, engaged, and puzzled by the terms of the illusion. In the annals of film history is a consideration not of some ignorant capturing of the world, but the framing, filming, and projecting of an absolute illusion of what the world could be. In these endless iterations, not all audiences, not all images, and not all sites are the same—hence the emphasis on what we might consider a potential history of world cinema.

Conceptual Cartography

Out of an ellipsis, then, arises an ethnographic mirage that constitutes the groundlessness of world cinema. This book does not purport to offer *the* authoritative account of the Lumière Brothers in North Africa and the Middle East. It is meant instead to stage an encounter with the limits of world cinema from this overdetermined moment in film history. Drawing together methods of microhistory with the potential afterlife of the image, each chapter constitutes unto itself a particular world—the past and the potential of the moving image. Each specific case tracks a key question in early cinema through a particular trajectory across North Africa and the Middle East. I embrace the optics of a view to the world that does not center Lyon, France, or Europe in the history of the archive. This is not an effort to point to a unique and essentialized undoing of film history so much as an affirmation of perspective, a sense that there is always a view from somewhere, even when taking into account that thing we call the globe. Each chapter takes a microscopic detail—a single Lumière film from among the countless possibilities—to weigh a critical term. Each chapter also adopts a broader question of film form as a treatise on a method of writing, embracing the close-up, for example, as a model for film analysis. The turn here is to see the world in the image and to imagine the potential worlds that images make possible.

The book traces each of the various stops in Promio's voyage. The first chapter begins at the end—that is, with the centenary celebration of the Lumière Brothers cinematograph in March 1995. On the grounds of the Lumière Estate in the Monplaisir neighborhood of Lyon, there is a photograph on a wall that captures five global directors walking arm-in-arm to commemorate and reenact the iconic film *La Sortie de l'usine* (Workers Leaving the Factory). The chapter takes this photograph as an emblem of world cinema, and it refracts various replays of the iconic film: first, in the centenary celebration of cinematic internationalism; second, in the archival history of the "original" film; and third, in a camera operator's reshooting of the scene at a brick factory in Hanoi. Moving from the logic of atlas to archive and empire, the chapter highlights crucial dynamics connecting what it means to read the world in a detail—and what it means to engage every image as a vision of what the world can be.

The story continues back in time to link an event in Lyon to the arrival of the cinematograph in North Africa. Promio was first introduced to the cinematograph when he attended the Congress of Photography in Lyon and beheld it demonstrated for an audience. Shortly after, in December 1896, he undertook a voyage with the new device to Algeria on behalf of the Lumière Brothers. I draw attention to the dynamic role of the cinematograph mirroring an audience on-screen or serving as a window to elsewhere for a type of cinematic travel. Noting the temporal disjuncture between filming and being seen, I pair looks at the camera in Neuville-sur-Saône and at a market in Algiers to reflect on the challenge of locating location—the event of the camera, the screening, and the *hors cadre* of colonialism. What does it mean to be located? To what extent is a look at the camera located in time and place? How might we weigh the significance of an archival look—when the spectator of world cinema, returning the gaze, is out of time and space with the look itself. Following Promio's journey, in the following chapter, we encounter on a rooftop in Algiers a competing frame story for early cinema. I look closely at the mis-framing of a prayer as a counterpoint to the ethnographic dimensions of world cinema. I take as my point of departure a famously mis-framed "prayer" shot on a rooftop in Algiers, which I situate alongside the story of Promio's Algerian experience. Weighing the frame story with the eventual emergence of the photorama, a device meant to surround the spectator in an immersive image, this chapter ponders the place of Algiers in the cinematic imaginary of frames, futures, and pasts.

Following the two chapters on Algeria, the next section of the book tracks Promio on a journey through Egypt in March 1897. The fourth chapter looks closely at an 1897 film of the Khedive 'Abbas Hilmi II and his later appearance in a 1907 documentary often regarded as the first Egyptian film produced by an Egyptian filmmaker. I argue that these two films stage a tension between sovereignty (the authority embodied by the khedive) and seriality (the reproducibility of the khedive's body in cinema). To explore this tension, I situate these films alongside a broader archive of cinematic representations of sovereign power and question the ever-shifting grounds of national cinema. In the next chapter, we move to consider duration by exploring the 50-second film of the pyramids at Giza. The viewing of this particular film is cast against philosophical reflections on time, many of which turn to the pyramid as a sort of figure for theories of the event. Weighing the mythological pyramid against the vernacular temporality of the filmic image, the chapter explores valences of time that cinema helps make thinkable.

In the last stop on our voyage, we follow Promio to Ottoman Palestine in April 1897. The sixth chapter focuses on a train departing from a station in Jerusalem, and it contrasts this film with the famous *Arrival of the Train at La Ciotat*. The chapter draws together Philippe Dubois's and Georges Sadoul's formal analysis of the train at La Ciotat with the sociohistorical analysis of the departing train from Jerusalem. The intersection of these two tracks provides a farewell to cinema as it was known at the time. The coming and going of the cinematograph, the tracks of arrival and departure, lead to questions of location and the dispersal of the filmic archive. Extending the stop in Jerusalem, the seventh and final chapter zooms in on a face in close-up at the Jaffa Gate. Reflecting on scale in film and world systems theory, the chapter charts a course for imagining the world close-up—that is, for addressing the place of a cinematic detail in the understanding of a broader world system. Taking the detail from the archive and casting it against the backdrop of world cinema, I then turn to the iconic image of the globe from the Apollo Mission (the Blue Marble) to question what it means to apprehend the world in visual form.

And finally, in a closing epilogue, the book moves from the world to the planet. Noting the appearance of the astronomer Jules Janssen in an early

Lumière Brothers film, this section describes Janssen's role turning the camera from the world to the stars to track the passage of Venus in front of the sun. Janssen's vision leads us to Gayatri Chakravorty Spivak's discussion of planetarity before we turn to Larissa Sansour's wave at the earth from the moon. In each of these various instances, the Lumière films and their global afterlife are taken not simply as a testament to the transnational spread of early cinema, but as competing framings, conceptualizations, and visions of the world.

All of the chapters counterpose film form with film history and embrace a perverse perspectivalism as method—a global history of film form, we could say, but one that performs the tension between detail and generality at its core. It is not so much the case that the world acts as an explanatory matrix through which particularity comes to be understood. Instead, moving from details outward, particularity comes to reveal the world anew. This is the provocation and challenge of what follows. The Lumière catalogue is less an ur-text whose various components function as a gesture to a deep historical real than it is a reservoir for the poetic potential of re-screenings, reiteration, and reimaginings. Those looking for authoritative and orthodox readings of films in time and place often seek indexicality in the fantasy of an elsewhere. The chapters that follow blur screens, windows, and mirrors toward a refractive optics of otherworldliness. A foreign, adjacent, and radically unsettled sense of what it means to see, know, and apprehend location, the book addresses the poetics of "here" as the site of a primary slippage.

A Preface to Prehistory: A Potential Future of Cinema

The first line of the preface to Coissac's *Histoire du cinématographe* states: "The cinematograph has been, for a long time, an entire world [*Le cinématographe c'est, depuis longtemps, tout un monde*]."[51] Coissac's book charts a monumental history of cinema on its pages, and it reorients an extensive history of optics as an anticipation of film. But what might we make of this preface to a book about origins? How does one account for the moment before the emergence of cinema? Time is of the essence in this preface, especially in its anticipation of a future history of film's origins. In the sentence itself, "*depuis longtemps*" is of course a temporal indicator of the long durée of film history, but there is also a shift to geographical coordinates in the seeming capaciousness of "*tout un monde.*" The resonance here is a sense of worldliness, when, in effect, the medium described is inseparably bound up with the world it claims to record. There are echoes of "*tout un monde*" as a mode of capture—terms such as *"à la conquête du monde," "autour du monde," "cinéma-monde"* that reverberate through a moment of colonial cinema, highlighted aptly in Vanessa Schwartz's exhibition *Paris: City of Cinema*.[52] And yet, here, on the opening pages of the preface to the origins of cinema, we confront a world framed temporally as much as spatially.

At the risk of sounding hyperbolic, it is the time of the world that is at stake, and this time, as we see, is already a preface to an origin—such is the anachronism when dealing with early cinema. The world, its time, is inseparably bound with the apparatus through which it comes to be seen, and here too, the moment of seeing, apprehending, and sensing is itself subject to the deferral, the preface, the time before the origin that cinema itself inaugurates. After all, to focus on the act of filming is to address the preface to what is seen. It is to consider a moment before development, and it is to anchor a history of cinema in the act of production prior to the production, to the upbeat of the visual score that the camera reveals. In the work of Tom Gunning we can find inspiration in the possibility of thinking across temporal markers organizing a kind of progressive history, and in a different key, we could even detect a sort of temporal blurring in André Bazin's famous proclamation that cinema has not yet been invented.[53] And so it is, combining times and worlds, pasts and futures, that the question posed by this prehistory is less one of origins than a consideration of a future past.

In the time of film history is the persistent question of when cinema ever was. André Gaudreault's *The End of Cinema* gestures to the tangle, which he further discusses as a translational matter drawn between the English-language cinema and the French cinema.[54] Richard Abel offers a distinction among early film historians: Nöel Burch, Kristin Thompson, and Barry Salt, who suggest a rupture between primitive and classical cinema; Tom Gunning, André Gaudreault, and Ben Brewster, who emphasize "a dialectical interplay between presentation and representation, spectacle and narrative, showing and telling"; and Charles Musser and Thomas Elsaesser for whom representation is determined by "a historically specific interplay of economic, social, and cultural forces."[55] I track these conversations, but I am concerned with a sort of microhistory of these early years of the Lumière cinematograph, torn between the historical dimension of a moment before cinema as-such and a geographical dimension of global routes.

This endeavor is invested as much in a theory of worlds as it is in attending to the image—as window, as mirror, as a site through which location itself is made visible. As we journey across the world in space and time in the chapters ahead, we will equally be zooming in and out, back and forth, recognizing that film itself is both a technology of capture and projection and that archiving is about the art of decay and future lives of images. I look forward in the pages that follow to tracing the pasts, presents, and futures that the curious Lumière archive helps make thinkable. The next step in our travel brings us back to the persistence of this past—that is, to a photograph of an event marking the centennial celebration of the Lumière Brothers cinematograph.

1
World
The Labor of Representation

On a wall adjoining the Villa Lumière in the Monplaisir neighborhood of Lyon, a photograph hangs to commemorate the centenary of the Lumière Brothers film *La Sortie de l'usine* (Workers Leaving the Factory) (Figure 4). The caption reveals that on March 19, 1995, five global directors (Carlos Diegues of Brazil, André de Toth and Jerry Schatzberg of the United States, Mrinal Sen of India, and Youssef Chahine of Egypt) restaged the procession of workers out the gates of the original Lumière factory a century prior. Five figures of modern French cinema (Bertrand Tavernier, Jean Rouch, Paul Vecchiali, Jacques Deray, and John Lvoff) follow this first row, framed by onlookers, photographers, and filmmakers. All had gathered to celebrate the centenary of the Lumière cinematograph.[1] This photographic tribute to "the first film" appears on "Le mur des cinéastes" (the filmmakers' wall) on a street aptly named "Rue du Premier Film" (street of the first film). A testament to the global spread of cinema, the wall contains numerous small copper plaques, each bearing the name and year that a world-famous actor, director, or writer visited the site: Xavier Dolan, Tilda Swinton, Wong Kar-Wai, Jane Campion, Mehdi Charif, and Guillermo del Toro, to name a few. In a local neighborhood purporting to be the birthplace of cinema, this commemorative photograph and the wall of copper plaques honor the expansive geographical coordinates of cinema. The scene invites us to celebrate the global afterlife of the Lumière cinematograph.

The photograph also frames critical questions in discussions of world cinema and accompanying echoes of empire, transnationalism, internationalism, multiculturalism, and globalization that inform its history. From the 1895 production of *La Sortie de l'usine* to its 1995 commemoration, we

Figure 4. Commemorative photograph from the centenary celebration of *La Sortie de l'usine* at the Institut Lumière in Lyon. Photo credit: Patrick Ageneau.

confront a range of worldly visions. In the century between the film and the photograph, we move from the height of French imperialism to the flourishing of a multicultural imagination. And we move from experiments with motion photography to a star system of actors, directors, and writers. In the shift from 1895 to 1995, there is another crucial transformation at stake: The labor of the Lumière factory workers is subsumed by the celebrity status of iconic directors, and each director stands in for a particular nationality. This snapshot reveals how the discourse of multiculturalism inaugurates a representational logic. Borrowing the grammar of national film production, the collective of directors linked arm in arm represents a constellation of nations bound together under the logic of world cinema—that is to say, the supposed sovereignty of national cinema (be it of Brazil, the United States, India, or Egypt) is under the command of world cinema (and its model of iconic global directors). We ultimately confront how multiculturalism transmutes alternate conceptions of the world in the story of cinema's global spread. The labor of world cinema depicted in the photograph is, we could say, a labor of juxtaposition. Only by placing directors alongside one another does the image demonstrate the global reach of the medium.

As the photograph captures a moment in time, its significance is amplified by its location on the grounds of the Lumière estate. Just behind the commemorative wall stands the reconstructed factory famously known as the location of *La Sortie de l'usine* shot on March 19, 1895. This location functions almost mythologically as the point of departure for age-old debates about what constitutes the first film, and a concrete modernist hangar honors the original site of the film with a series of staggered glass plates, each containing a photographic still from the film, leading toward the street.[2] In a reversal of the outward movement of the original film, the restaging of the site now draws tourists, researchers, and cinephiles toward the display, all part of a commemoration—and assertion—of the foundational role that the Lumière Brothers play in the history of cinema. Behind the factory towers the large building, the Villa Lumière, which initially housed the Lumière family and now serves as a museum, exhibition space, and library. Various cameras and optical devices arranged alongside signs and artifacts weave the story of the Lumière family, their factory, and their team of camera operators into the history of photography and film. Next to the museum stands the Lumière library, which contains a wealth of books devoted to the history of early cinema as well as digitized versions of 1,428 Lumière Brothers films, each roughly 40 seconds long (35mm wide, 17 meters long, with approximately 800 photograms) with scenes of daily life, urban markets, ports, railways, and iconic sites from across the world.[3]

I begin with the centenary commemoration of the cinematograph to highlight the ambivalent time and place of the moving image, torn between recording (the site at which a film is shot) and projection (the site at which a film is seen). In the move from *La Sortie de l'usine* in 1895 and the photograph of its commemoration in 1995, we confront concentric frameworks that inform labor on-screen: on the one hand, factory workers for the Lumière Company, and on the other hand, global directors celebrating the history of cinema. This chapter focuses on the iterative replay of the film across three sites to highlight an understanding of world cinema predicated on constructive displacements. The gap between being recorded and projected, between scene and screen, informs the labor of the image, whether the elaborate mise-en-scène for each reenactment or the trafficking of the film to new locations. In what follows, this iterative story will be part of framing and reframing *La Sortie de l'usine* as it travels across time and space from the hands of the camera operator to various audiences, artists, and constructive appropriations.

In its three sections, this chapter analyzes various iterations of *La Sortie de l'usine* to grapple with cinematic worlds. In the first, we look at the geography in and of the 1995 commemorative event with iconic national directors. In the second, we look at how the 1895 Lumière film captures a future camera operator riding a bicycle through the factory gates. And in the third, we look at Gabriel Veyre's 1899–1900 iteration of the factory film in Hanoi, at the edge of the French empire, a testament to globalized labor practices in film history.

Each of these three turns (geography, archive, and empire) offers a model for thinking the limits and potentials of the world in world cinema.

On Atlases and Adjacency

Like many visitors to the Monplaisir neighborhood, I arrived at the Lumière Institute to see the local history of the cinematograph, lured to a site that claimed to be the birthplace of cinema and to a street that claimed to be the location of the first film. Amid all that there was to see, I found myself not simply captivated by a single photograph, but by a particular detail within it—the Egyptian director Youssef Chahine (Figure 5). As the director of over forty films, including the iconic *Bāb al-Ḥadīd* (Cairo Station, 1958), *al-Arḍ* (The Land, 1969), and the Alexandria Trilogy (1979–1989), Chahine is known as one of the foremost auteurs in the Arab world. His films address particular moments in Egyptian history and the global dissemination of Arab cinema through transnational production and screening circuits.[4] As I stood staring at the photograph, I could not help but wonder about Chahine's presence alongside directors from Brazil, the United States, and India. Did he somehow stand in for Egypt as a site within world cinema? Or did he function as a sign of world cinema marked simply as a generalizable elsewhere? What, I wondered, was at stake in the substitution of nineteenth-century Lumière factory workers with these iconic twentieth-century directors? At the intersection of labor, art, and politics, this simple photograph lured me to rethink the grounds of world cinema. In this one photograph, the nineteenth-century discourse of empire seemed to blur into the twentieth-century discourse of multiculturalism. Just what is the world that this image makes thinkable?

These questions proliferate from the ambivalent site of the photograph, which, on the one hand, entails a recognition of the restaging of *La Sortie de l'usine*, and on the other hand, a recognition of the various directors walking arm in arm as a gesture to world cinema. What arose in my mind as questions might better be understood as a layering of possibilities: The photograph performs all of the functions outlined above, and it does so especially for those who recognize figures within the frame. The significance of the photograph exceeds its frame for those who see within it a recognizable face, and the image conjures yet another recognizable world within the generalizable idiom of world cinema. Like the world system it invokes, there is a contingency to the detail (in this case Chahine) through which to understand the broader whole (the global spread of cinema). Its potential

Figure 5. Detail of Youssef Chahine and Mrinal Sen from the commemorative photograph. Photo credit: Patrick Ageneau.

relies on the recognition of the details in the photograph, and its limits are those for whom these details carry less significance. The generality of the world system was eclipsed for me by the particularity of Chahine and my admiration for his work.

But the photograph also functions on account of the adjacency and juxtapositions it offers—in fact, adjacency might underscore its internationalist ethics. The full photograph captures world cinema as a system of interlocking parts, and in the bond between Mrinal Sen and Youssef Chahine, in the linking of their arms, arises a particular geography upon which the world system relies. The juxtaposition of these two directors conjures the possibility of a global imaginary well beyond the particularity of any national films. Spatially, these two directors index India and Egypt side-by-side, that is, adjacent to and beside one another. Their positioning recalls Eve Kosofsky Sedgwick's investment in the term "beside":

> *Beside* is an interesting preposition also because there's nothing very dualistic about it; a number of elements may lie alongside one another, though not an infinity of them. *Beside* permits a spacious agnosticism about several of the linear logics that enforce dualistic thinking: noncontradiction or the law of the excluded middle, cause versus effect, subject versus object.[5]

We might go so far as to say that world cinema is always beside itself, contingent on the spatial, geographical, and national arrangements that make adjacency its defining feature. In this understanding, world cinema is not simply circulation beyond national borders, but the interconnections of those nations that make the conception of the world thinkable—in this instance, as an image of one director, one country, one filmic tradition, beside another, arm in arm, rehearsing the mythological origins of cinema.

Those viewing the centenary photograph might be celebrating their recognition of Carlos Diegues, Jerry Schatzberg, Mrinal Sen, or any of the numerous names represented by a plaque on this small street as a portal onto a set of films. From these specific names, films, and national cinemas, we encounter the generality of world cinema and its vision of a story to be traced back to the Lumière factory. This myth of world cinema functions insofar as the particularity of each of these global directors is in effect substitutable as a sign of the global: Egypt, India, Brazil, the United States, and France matter as parts of a global collage upon which can be projected the fantasy of a sort of cinematic internationalism. When positioned alongside one another, every director, film, national cinematic tradition is a nodal point of a broader system that the Lumière cinematograph is seen to have rendered possible. I mention this framework, in part, to provincialize its terms. The world of global directors, the cinematic internationalism that the photograph celebrates, would have been unthinkable at the time of Alexandre Promio's travels with the cinematograph—and so too would the understanding of the world that the photograph celebrates.

In her essay "On Becoming Less of the World," Samera Esmeir insightfully traces the appearance of the word "international" in 1789 to designate a new branch of law. She notes how soon after its coinage, "the scope of 'international law' extended backward and forward in historical time, and the concept began to be used to describe any set of relations that exceeded a single body politic."[6] The term "international" begins to be used interchangeably with the term "world," to the extent that world's fairs come to be referred to as international exhibitions. Esmeir goes on to specify:

> An adjective with specific juridical beginnings, signifying the relationship between states, international has become over time intimately related to the concept of the world in its multiple dimensions, overlapping with or even occasionally supplanting it, while never fully replacing it. The occasional interchangeability of the two concepts marks not their correspondence, but an unevenly realized kinship.[7]

Reckoning with the intertwined Benthamite, Marxist, and Ottoman dynamics in this "unevenly realized kinship," Esmeir arrives at a set of critical questions. One, in particular, resonates strongly with the challenges posed in thinking of world cinema: "What layers of the world are lost," she asks, "when it is framed through the grid of the international?"[8] Where Esmeir focuses on the juridical and cultural formations that define the connections among the world and the international, we might be led to wonder what world cinema would look like if not framed through the assembly of national cinemas. Is there an alternative to this vision?

It is telling that neither the centenary photograph nor the Lumière Brothers films use the language of the world or the international; instead, they invoke it visually. In the context of film studies, Masha Salazkina is among few scholars who have endeavored to think about the critical purchase of the term "world" in discussions of world cinema:

> Can we imagine the "world" in World Cinema as a space that could be inhabited and laid claim to by all of us, and not as that "other" place of dwelling, the space on the margins (of race, citizenship, gender, sexuality, "civilization," "Europe," or any other normative hegemony). Performing this shift would therefore mean that, in the first place, the term world would need to be hijacked, disassociated from its persistent commercial-industrial (as in "world music") or academic usage meaning cultural output from outside the West.[9]

Salazkina pushes us in a different direction—and importantly away from the use of world cinema as a celebratory elsewhere. She considers:

> If, instead, the term could usefully point towards an exploration of the uneven and heterogeneous processes that constitute the relations across, between, and within cinematic cultures globally, cinema as an object would also need to be further interrogated.[10]

Like Esmeir, who takes the postulate of the international to consider the worlds foreclosed, here Salazkina questions world cinema to reimagine how to define cinema as an object. Her inquiry draws her to film festivals and the circuitry of dissemination, but her work, like that of Esmeir, is open, speculative, and generative. In both of these essays, the world is not a geographically mappable elsewhere, so much as a demand to question the parameters of knowing itself—for Esmeir, the connections among law, history, and culture, and for Salazkina, expanding how cinema is defined.

It is no surprise that scholars of world cinema often turn to debates in world literature to help orient their inquiry of world cinema.[11] What Dudley Andrew describes as "An Atlas of World Cinema" gestures to questions raised in Franco Moretti's *Atlas of the European Novel*.[12] Michael Gott and Thibault Schilt borrow their title *Cinéma-monde* from Bill Marshall, who himself transforms the expression from debates around *littérature-monde* in the fields of francophone studies and world literature.[13] And in *World Cinema: A Critical Introduction*, Shekhar Deshpande and Meta Mazaj embrace what they call a polycentric world cinema, a term that draws from Borges and Goethe as well as scholars such as Vilashini Cooppan, Kristen Ross, Emily Apter, and David Damrosch.[14] Robert Stam is even more explicit as he tracks the parallel trajectories of world literature and transnational cinema in what he calls the "transartistic commons."[15] The geography of cultural production as well as considerations of publication, circulation, and reception subtend the inquiry that these scholars help to make possible. United in the quest to conceptualize a world beyond frameworks of national cinema and to reckon with the dynamic networks in which films are produced and distributed, scholars of world cinema seem to be reckoning with a vision that the photograph outside the Lumière factory renders so abundantly visible.[16]

What these various conversations share in common is an understanding of world cinema and world literature at the intersection of geography and world systems. Andrew's "Atlas" proliferates the types of mapping that world cinema offers (political, demographic, linguistic, orientation, and topographical), and he makes a passing allusion to the Lumière Brothers films: "Films from the outset," he tells us, "were primed to invade foreign screens." He adds, "The Lumière brothers dispatched camera crews around the world before their invention was two years old, showing films shot in one place to audiences in another." The story he tells proceeds quickly, leaping from the Lumière Brothers to the rise of Pathé and an emergent competition among national cinemas.[17] In the geographical spread he offers, however, there is a curious anachronism—at the time of the Lumière cinematograph, all screens were foreign, even those in Lyon and Paris. In "Jet Lag and Time Zones," Andrew constructively engages this disjuncture in the time of world cinema. He outlines chronologically what his atlas offers thematically, distinguishing cosmopolitan, national, federated, world, and global phases.[18] Andrew is careful to note how these phases overlap: "Cinema in my view is constitutionally out-of-phase with itself." And here again, the Lumière Brothers figure as a key motif for Andrew: "Many parts of the globe were touched by the *cinématographe*, each responding to this international phenomenon at its own speed, each stamping it with its own image and its own temporality."

In the atlas that Andrews describes, world cinema, like world literature, comes to be conceptualized spatially and geographically as a map, a system, and a network, uniting locations across the world. The labor here is one of juxtaposition—Youssef Chahine and Mrinal Sen, global directors and a remake of an iconic first film, national cinemas and world cinema. Seen in this manner, even though the photograph presents a single image, there is an evocation of montage with each director a metonym for a national culture. In the atlas model, world cinema expands outwardly, accumulating and conjoining film traditions, celebrating the movement of a discourse of world cinema from the present to the past and from Lyon to the world.

An Archive of Potential Worlds

And now a second scene in world cinema: On March 19, 1895, workers pass through the gates of a factory wall of the Lumière Company at 21–23 rue Saint-Victor in the 8th arrondissement of Lyon (Figure 6). The roughly 40-second film depicts women dressed in hats and full-length dresses, men dressed in dark suits and straw hats, a dog, bicycles, and eventually a carriage drawn by two horses. The various figures proceed through the gates before scattering as they pass the cinematograph positioned in front of the exit. From our angle on the street, we have a glimpse of scaffolding visible through the gate. The angled curve of the sidewalk provides a contrast to the various right angles that frame the scene: the rectangular opening through which the workers pass, the triangular shape of the interior roof, and the smaller rectangle of the door on the left. But most of all, the film captures not only the routine departure of workers, but their passage through a threshold delimiting work and leisure. This film captures this scene in 800 photograms at a rate of 16 frames per second to yield the illusion of continuous motion. Such is the miracle of this "first" film.

I draw attention to this origin story to highlight that this representation of labor on-screen turns on a particular labor of representation. To begin with, the recognizability of the film stems from its mythologized status as a first

Figure 6. *La Sortie de l'usine*, the seminal 1895 Lumière film portraying workers departing the factory in Lyon.

film. Even though *La Sortie de l'usine* is now understood more accurately as among the first publicly projected films, it remains an iconic origin story within film history.[19] As has been well documented, the film was initially screened on March 22, 1895, to an audience of roughly two hundred spectators at the Society for the Development of National Industry in Paris. And like any origin story, its beginnings are fraught and multiple. *La Sortie de l'usine* itself was shot in various iterations. At least three known versions exist in the Lumière catalogue, numbered as 91.1, 91.2, and 91.3, or alternatively, as the two horses, one horse, and no horse versions. In each, over the course of roughly 40 seconds, workers stream out the factory gates. The various films have similar framing, but different clothing, different movements, different days, and different seasons differentiate one from the others. The origin of cinema is itself already a remake, serialized and multiple.

In addition to its iterative form, *La Sortie de l'usine* is often understood for its significance in visualizing a threshold.[20] On one level, there is the physical threshold that the gate offers to differentiate the inside and the outside of the workspace. We witness workers as they pass from the routinized labor of the factory to life outside the gates. On another level, there is the film itself as a particular threshold in which the timing of the workday encounters the timing of the film. Here the calculated hours of labor confront an order of time contingent on the flicker of the image at 16 frames per second. The labor seen in the image turns on the labor of the image, a threshold between film and photography, the image in motion. At the cusp of a fundamental transition in visual culture, *La Sortie de l'usine* serves as a transition from one moment to another, photography to film, contingent on the capturing of motion in time.[21]

There is, however, an additional dimension to this oft-cited film that is crucial to the consideration of world cinema. Of everything the film renders visible, a seemingly accidental detail anticipates a future of the global dissemination of the cinematograph. Riding on a bicycle that afternoon in 1895 was a young factory worker, Francis Doublier. Unknown to anyone at the time, Doublier would go from being a courier for the company to serving as a camera operator for the Lumière Brothers.[22] He recalled in an interview years later that he was present that day in 1895, amazed both to be part of the workers leaving the factory and amazed to see his own image on-screen days later. "I remember well," he recounted, "because I was there as a bicycle errand boy, and I pedaled past the camera, behind the workers dressed in the long dresses that were the style at that time."[23] His recollection of the specific dates in the interview conflict with the current dating of the film, but regardless, this film captures him on a bicycle as a specter of the future global dissemination of the medium. His appearance embodies a labor of the image that would follow in the months after capturing the film.

Along with the technician Charles Moisson, Doublier was on hand for the preliminary screenings of the cinematograph in Paris on December 28, 1895. He was also among those camera operators who, like Alexandre Promio, whose journey we trace in the following chapters, helped to market the device across the world and to capture films wherever he visited.[24] Doublier traveled to Russia, Germany, Spain, the Netherlands, and Hungary for the Lumière Brothers, before eventually moving in 1902 to Fort Lee in New Jersey, where he worked as a technician. With his extensive travels, Doublier was an early force in the global dissemination of the cinematograph.

In addition to his work as a camera operator, Doublier was also a key figure in helping to memorialize the place of the Lumière Brothers in the history of cinema.[25] When he eventually moved from the Lumière Company offices in Burlington, Vermont, to the Éclair studio in Fort Lee, New Jersey, he sat for interviews, shared his experiences working with the Lumière Brothers, and assisted with the memorialization of the history of early cinema.[26] He was part of a shift in attention from the cinematograph as a technical device to the history of cinema as a collection of texts. As the film industry developed, he was a key figure in helping to gather and preserve Lumière films, recognizing that the various shots taken were not merely demonstrations of the device, but artifacts of film history, destined to be preserved and shared as part of the emergence of film culture more broadly. Doublier thus helped to facilitate the Lumière films and the global routes of the various camera operators as part of a canon of world cinema.

Of all potential details, I focus our attention on Francis Doublier's appearance in *La Sortie de l'usine* for how it anticipates the conditions through which the cinematograph would eventually travel. Little was it known when the film was shot that Doublier would have a hand in the dissemination of the cinematograph, and yet the film captures this potential future of world cinema. *La Sortie de l'usine* offers a temporal ricochet between the moment it preserves and the world in which it is eventually projected. There are thus competing conceptions of worldliness that this film makes available—not simply the world indexed through location (the factory in the Monplaisir neighborhood of Lyon), but the world understood as the future history that Doublier embodies. He appears on-screen at a moment of leisure, swerving in front of the cinematograph while riding a bicycle, and he becomes a key force in the labor of disseminating the cinematograph, archiving its early films, and memorializing the place of the Lumière Brothers in the history of cinema. In the representation of labor on-screen, we encounter the labor of representation of an image projected across the world.

Allow me to add a brief remark on the implications of Doublier's archival future. I admire and learn from the rich reflection on worlds in the work of Debjani Ganguly and Pheng Cheah.[27] Textual traditions traffic in a world of symbols to be deciphered and decoded, and literacy cultivates behaviors and disciplines essential to the reading of texts. World literature offers a world of scripts, letters, alphabets, and languages shared among communities of speakers and readers. World cinema, in contrast, offers a lure of a different sort—a seeming indexicality freed from the constraints of reading and therefore aligned with the possibilities of the alternate modalities of being seen. In different ways, both Tom Conley and Edgar Garcia illuminate the nature of scripts, but Doublier's appearance in *La Sorte de l'usine* shifts us from the aesthetics of representation (as a matter of mimesis) to the fantasy of indexical capture. His appearance on-screen testifies to the potential, the accident, the haphazard, and the chance appearance.[28] In the archival print, we encounter a specter of world cinema.

From the commemorative photograph to *La Sortie de l'usine* is a move from world cinema as an amalgam of national directors to the representation of labor on-screen. It is a move that suggests an archaeology of the sort of world to be imagined, be it the multicultural logic of the twentieth century or the circuitry of a world tour at the end of the nineteenth. What we now celebrate as transnational, international, or global has a historical dimension, and what might it mean to reckon with these sedimented pasts not simply as sites for critique, but as a refraction on the limits of the present? Such is the challenge that this critical genealogy of world cinema offers.

Iteration and Empire, or the Labor of World Cinema

And now, a third iteration of this iconic first film, this time only years after the initial version. Sometime between April 28, 1899, and March 2, 1900, as part of his travels across what was then known as Indochina, the camera operator Gabriel Veyre shot a film of child workers leaving their worksite at Meffre and Bourgoin's brick factory. Numbered 1275 in the Lumière catalogue, *Sortie de la briqueterie Meffre et Bourgoin à Hanoi* appears as a nod to the film shot in Lyon. Much like *La Sortie de l'usine*, the camera in Hanoi visualizes a threshold, and it mirrors the shot structure of the Lumière factory with a large door on the right of the screen and a smaller opening—in this case a window—to the left (Figure 7). As the gates open, two men in white hats oversee the exit, and the young workers proceed roughly in single file as they pass through the gate. In this instance, the cinematograph visualizes a threshold between labor and leisure: spatially, a large door on the right of the screen delimits inside from outside the factory, and temporally, workers are shown at the end of their working day. Here a gesture to the iconic Lumière film finds its apparent colonial repetition.[29]

In this film, another unmistakable detail: a white helmet. The location of the shoot is no longer Lyon, but Hanoi at the time of French occupation. Whereas the first Lumière film positions the spectators as those surveying the scene, here there is a double surveillance, marked by the white helmet standing beside the door, watching the workers as they file out. The sedimented history that the film captures here is quite different. The film is a reminder that empire and colonialism are part of an emergent globalized grammar of labor practices. As each of the workers files out, they pass their timecard to the attendant at the gate, and they walk outward toward the camera. An initial few workers cross almost immediately to the left while others file out and pass in front of the filming camera. Where the 1895 version involves a scattered rush out of the gates, here in a near single file, the workers proceed in an orderly fashion across the screen, with most making eye contact with the cinematograph as they pass. This film is listed in the Lumière catalogue alongside other

Figure 7. *Sortie de la briqueterie Meffre et Bourgoin à Hanoi*, a Lumière film by camera operator Gabriel Veyre documenting workers at a brick factory in colonial Indochina.

films shot during Veyre's monthlong stay in Southeast Asia. At the time, he had already traveled to the United States, Mexico, Cuba, Venezuela, Martinique, Canada, Japan, and China before arriving at what was then French-occupied Indochina. Veyre was among the cadre of camera operators (including Alexandre Promio, François-Constant Girel, Félix Mesguich, and Francis Doublier) hired by the Lumière company to capture views from various locales and display the cinematograph to audiences across the globe.

What is the discipline on display in this particular film? On one level, there is the discipline of the white-clad colonial official overseeing the attendant, who in turn is overseeing the gathering of the timecards. But here, beyond the colonial optics performed on-screen, the cinematograph surveys the scene in what could be understood as a metacolonial gesture. In line with the optical regime that Nicholas Mirzoeff helps to highlight, colonial order is on display not only thematically but also in the placement and arrangement of the cinematograph and the command it holds over the space.[30] If we move from the various iterations of world cinema understood as a pantheon of national cinemas to world cinema as the world within the frame, then here we reckon with a cinematic empire captured on-screen. A wealth of scholarship helps cast the racial dynamics of such scenes against the backdrop of early cinema and ethnographic display, all part of the violence of colonial display from the world's fairs to documentary photography.[31]

For all of the emphasis on iterative difference in the move from Lyon to Hanoi, part of the effectiveness of this film derives from the echo it offers of the Lumière factory and the standardization of global labor practices. Harun Farocki remarks that *La Sortie de l'usine* plays upon the significance of visualizing labor, noting that the horizon between work and play underscores a key axis in the history of cinema. The voice-over in his film describes workers leaving factories as if "impelled by an invisible force," juxtaposing the 1895 Lumière factory with footage from the 1975 Volkswagen factory in Emden, as well as workers running away from work sites in 1957 in Lyon and 1926 in Detroit.[32] "In the Lumière film of 1895," Farocki writes in an essay version of the film, "It is possible to discover that the workers were assembled behind the gates and surged out at the camera operator's command. Before the film direction stepped in to condense the subject, it was the industrial order which synchronized the lives of the many individuals. They were released from this regulation at a particular point in time, contained in the process by the factory gates as in a frame."[33] He attends to the dynamics of the collective workforce and the individualized worker: "The work structure synchronizes the workers, the factory gates group them, and this process of compression produces the image of a work force. As may be realized or brought to mind by the portrayal, the people passing through the gates evidently have something fundamental in common."[34]

Veyre's film already bespeaks the sort of standardization that Farocki describes. As a colonial document, in its repetition, it is a testament to globalized labor practices in the early twentieth century. Years later, in 1936, Charlie Chaplin's *Modern Times* would mock the routinization of labor, and crosscutting would enable workers filing along to appear suddenly as sheep—a splice that makes thinkable a sort of cinematic connection, analogy, transposition that became characteristic of filmmaking.[35] Drawing attention to global labor, Jean-Marie Straub and Danièle Huillet's film *Too Early, Too Late* itself contains a scene restaging *La Sortie de l'usine* as part of an inquiry into the conditions of a global proletariat.[36] Mahmoud Hussein's voice-over accompanies reflections on peasant uprisings in Egypt, counterposed with characteristic long takes and slow pans of the landscape.[37] As we stare at a factory in upper Egypt, the voice-over lends the image its particular resonance in an act of tethering, something that the Lumière film does not necessarily have. But insofar as the Lumière film is untethered, it is malleable to reiteration, appropriation, and reuse. It is this iterability that Farocki's film and Straub and Huillet's reflections draw to our attention.

Looking at Veyre's film from Hanoi, then, it is not necessarily that the image has inherent within it any particular reading. What the film captures is a sort of scattering—on the one hand, a scattering of the Lyon film into its iterative re-staging and, on the other hand, its scattering of workers as they clear the factory gates. In both the film histories oblivious to colonial dynamics and those attentive to it, there is a tendency to center the filmmaker. We could understand Veyre as the cinematographer or the Lumière Brothers as the overseeing company, and the condemnation of the colonial gaze would remain fixated on this practice of centering, keeping the Lumiere company the site of filmmaking no matter where in the world the films were shot. Part of a decolonial optics involves observing observation—resisting the fetish of imperial optics and embracing the possibilities of looking in detail. What stares back at the spectator is a type of knowledge predicated on a game of recognition and reconciliation, a method for thinking differently about the relation of cameras and worlds. The goal is not to survey the optics of world cinema, each film filing out in an orderly fashion, but instead to consider the possibilities of the swerve, the slant, and the askew as sites from which to reorder the world. Such a method takes details to matter, adjacency to be crucial, and foreignization to be critical to the reading practice that world cinema offers.

What, then, might it mean to meet the gaze of the worker in Hanoi leaving the factory? While relatively much is known in the historiography of the Lumière collection about who held the camera and cranked the handle (*la manivelle*), much less is known about the world beyond the frame. This is not to say that "the Orient" is some unknowable elsewhere, or that the knowledge of labor somehow escapes the frame—on the contrary, it looks us, as spectators, squarely in the eyes. It is to ask instead for an alternative speculation, one that embraces the power of the detail to break the system and structure of an organization predicated on a world system, on the very order embodied in the surveillance of the white helmet. Reading for the swerve, in other words, is itself a tactic of embracing a de-centered world, of watching films not for an orthodox assertion of what they ought to mean, but for the potential of the various viewing positions they offer. At times this entails a mode of surface reading and at other moments reading against the grain, but in either is a belief, or rather a hope, that there is a productive and disruptive possibility to be had in looking otherwise at the past.[38]

In the optics of early cinema is a model for a yet-be-formed spectatorship and for the capturing of images that are resolutely undisciplined in the trajectory and movement they offer. From Chahine as the site from which to think global cinema to Doublier as the site to read *La Sortie de l'usine* to the workers in Hanoi are three methods of apprehending worlds, each scattered in different ways across time and space and across the past and future of what we might call world cinema. At the very foundation of early cinema, that iconic early film is itself repetition and iteration—the various iterations of the supposedly first film and its subsequent reiterations in Hanoi and at the centennial. What follows from this non-origin of an image designed to be reproduced and screened for audiences is part of the goal of thinking this global scatter of early cinema. From each layer emerges not the bedrock of national cinema, but the tension between capture, circulation, and projection, each a dynamic of how cinema functions—and a dynamic that allows it a curious place in the history of archives.

Afterimages of Future Pasts: Glass and Bricks

I see in these three versions of workers leaving the factory a lesson for those of us engaging the dynamics of world cinema. On the one hand, we have the standardization narrative: Do the workers in Lyon share "something fundamental in common" with those in Hanoi? Is Veyre's iteration of the factory scene a critical commentary on the global worker struggle that Farocki describes? If so, we might see in Veyre's film a repetition based on the success of the original, a nod to a brand that had been produced, and that—like the product that mechanized labor produces—is subsequently churned out again and again. In the classic typology of the stereotype, we could see Veyre quite literally replicating a known scene of global labor practices from the Lumière factory in Lyon to the brick factory in Hanoi. Workers as a genre film in the history of world cinema.

On the other hand, we have the narrative of colonial difference: Veyre's gesture to the iconic Lumière film contains an unmistakable detail: the white helmet, an index of colonial difference. Where the first Lumière film positions the spectators as those surveying the scene, here there is a double surveillance, marked by the figures in white helmets standing beside the door, watching the workers as they file out, and standing in for the sort of observation that the cinematograph undertakes. This less than subtle detail is a reminder that empire and colonialism are part of an emergent globalized grammar of labor practices. If there is repetition here, there is repetition with colonial difference on full display. Formal affinities are eclipsed by the white helmet. World cinema functions here as the index of cultural difference.

Allow me to end here on a more polemical note. In this ricochet between locations (from Hanoi to Lyon) and moments in time (from 1895 to 1995), we confront critical questions about world cinema. There is—as we see in the image—a multicultural model that celebrates a montage of icons representing particular national cinemas, assembled together—brick by brick—to generate an image of world cinema. There is also—as we see in Veyre's film—a model of world cinema that considers indices of cultural difference on-screen (the persistence of the white helmet). Far from a celebration of cinema's global spread, Veyre's film makes visible the dynamics of colonialism and empire as they subtend the work of cinema—that is, in the double surveillance at the brick factory in Hanoi.

In Lyon, the development of glass plates for photography, and in Hanoi, the making of bricks—and here a sort of collision. Recall that when Sergei Eisenstein critiques Kuleshov's theory of montage, he does so with attention to bricks. He draws attention to "what is taught by the old, old school of film-making, that sang: 'Screw by screw, Brick by brick . . .'"[39] And he takes aim at Kuleshov for espousing this framework:

> Kuleshov, for example, even writes with a brick:
>
> If you have an idea-phrase, a particle of the story, a link in the whole dramatic chain, then that idea is to be expressed and accumulated from shot-cephers, just like bricks.[40]

Eisenstein glosses this approach, noting, "The shot is an element of montage. Montage is an assembly of these elements." And he goes on to add, "This is a most pernicious make-shift analysis," offering us instead an understanding of montage not as accumulation, but as conflict.[41]

> By what, then, is montage characterized and, consequently, its cell—the shot?
> By collision. By the conflict of two pieces in opposition to each other.
> By conflict. By collision.[42]

In numerous films highlighting the labor world cinema, I derive inspiration from Eisenstein's observation. It is the conflict staged between the first Lumière film and Veyre's remake in Hanoi that is at stake, and it is a conflict that does not merely articulate the second as one in a series—but one that unsettles the foundations of early cinema. In Veyre, we are held to confront the colonial optics and the standardization of labor. This critical consciousness is not the brick-by-brick multicultural celebration of world cinema, so much as the possibility of a critical confrontation: from glass plates in Lyon to bricks in Hanoi. In the eyes of the worker, a potential future past for world cinema. We move from the atlas model of world cinema to the sorts of constructive unsettling that Esmeir's etymology and Salazkina's unsettling world offer us. World cinema as conflict.

In the move from the three images of world cinema, we transition between the sorts of worlds that projection itself makes possible. We began with the recognition of Youssef Chahine in a photograph that bespeaks adjacency as a defining feature of the geographical imaginary of a cinematic world, and we moved to consider the appearance of Francis Doublier mounted on a bicycle in the archival print of *La Sortie de l'usine* as a figure who would go on to help the cinematograph reach audiences across the world. We turned then to Gabriel Veyre's re-creation of *La Sortie de l'usine* in Hanoi to engage the afterlife of global capital within circuits of exchange, and the reverberations of this motif in the work of Harun Farocki as well as Jean-Marie Straub and Danièle Huillet. From geography to archive to empire, we delimited various conceptual fields through to see *La Sortie de l'usine*, but also a broader framework from which to understand the valences of world cinema and the conditions of being in the world.

As we will see in the following chapters, the network of global Lumière films poses an awkward origin for national film histories. At the outset of her foundational study of Arab cinema, the film historian Viola Shafik remarks, "The film medium was invented in the West at the end of the nineteenth century, by which time significant parts of the Middle East and Maghreb were already considered as British and French protectorates." Echoing scholars Georges Sadoul, Roy Armes, and Guy Hennebelle, Shafik includes the Lumière Brothers under the framework of colonial cinema. In these accounts, national cinemas arise out of the ashes of colonial cinema. The model of national filmmakers celebrated in the 1995 commemoration persists as the organizational rubric through which the world of cinema comes to be understood.

I suggest here neither a celebration of the Lumière catalogue nor an effort to embrace its colonialist past as a global present, but an effort instead to reckon with its ambivalent temporalities. I would align this story with various afterimages of world cinema that frame ways of seeing and enfold questions of time. When Alfred Kahn sets out his "Archive de la planète," he aims to document the diversity of the world's populations under threat from the standardization of an emergent global economy.[43] Paula Amad's remarkable study on counterarchives and Katherine Groo's *Bad Film Histories* inform how I have come to see, relate to, and understand the Lumière films.[44] In 1926, when Dziga Vertov shoots *A Sixth Part of the World*, he endeavored to visualize cinematically the simultaneity of the Soviet Union, using camera operators to gather and record material from disparate lands.[45] Lisa Park's discussion of the *One World* broadcast can be seen as a similar echo, the novelty of watching babies born in Tokyo and Mexico City in the simultaneity that satellite broadcasting can offer.[46] Or perhaps as famously, the world emerges as the Blue Marble from the Apollo mission in 1972. In each of these instances, visual culture makes visible a particular understanding of what it means to live in the world, and it makes thinkable a broader sense of adjacency, simultaneity, and belonging.

Much like the iconic image of global directors with which this chapter began, the Lumière catalogue offers a worldly text of a particular sort—and an invitation to consider the limits of national, linguistic, and historical frameworks for the global vision that the Lumière Brothers' potential history of world cinema offers us. In these various films, we encounter a media archaeology, one reckoning with the various dynamics of technology, culture, and transformative conceptions of art. In the next chapter of our story, we return to Alexandre Promio and the Lumière Brothers in 1895. Our journey begins with the encounter between photography and cinema in a voyage from Lyon to Neuville-sur-Saône and extends onward to a market in Algeria.

2
Location
Locating Looks in World Cinema

On the morning of June 11, 1895, the French industrialist and engineer Louis Lumière turned his newly invented cinematograph upon those attending the annual Congress of Photography (Figure 8). The conference itself took place in Lyon, France, but on this particular morning, the participants traveled up the river to Neuville-sur-Saône, where they were filmed by Lumière's cinematograph as they disembarked from their boat. Labeled *Le Débarquement du congrès de photographie à Lyon* (The Photographical Congress Arrives in Lyon) in the archive, the film enjoys a rather celebrated place in the history of early cinema. It was initially shown to the participants at the culminating event of their conference, where it was meant to demonstrate the magic of the cinematograph. Six months later, it was among the ten films that were famously shown on December 28, 1895, in the commercial screening at the Grand Café in Paris. As with many of these early Lumière films, the composition of this 50-second animated view is remarkable in its spatial arrangement: the bridge in the background, the gangplank in the middle of the frame, and the participants approaching the cinematograph in the foreground. Many of those streaming off the boat acknowledge the Lumière device directly—a woman arranging her dress, a man pausing with his camera, another few exhaling smoke, and still others tipping their hats as they pass by. Fully aware of the power of photography, the participants break any imaginary fourth wall with their looks at the camera, a feature that has led Tom Gunning to characterize this moment in film history as a cinema of attractions: "This is a cinema that displays its visibility, willing to rupture a self-enclosed fictional world for a chance to solicit the attention of the spectator."[1]

Figure 8. *Le Débarquement du congrès de photographie à Lyon*, an 1895 Lumière film depicting the arrival of delegates at the photography congress.

Where many of the first Lumière films were shot at the Lumière family estate in the Monplaisir neighborhood (*La Sortie de l'usine*, *Repas de bébé*, etc.), the move from Lyon to Neuville-sur-Saône in *Le Débarquement du congrès de photographie à Lyon* is a demonstration of how location comes to matter. As film scholars have often noted, the understanding of location is torn between the aesthetics of capture (the artifactualization of the site of filming), the semiological command to decipher place (through analysis of the mise-en-scène), and the pragmatics of projection (where the film plays for audiences).[2] John David Rhodes and Elena Gorfinkel cogently summarize a common understanding: "Films take actual places—take images of places, record impressions of the world's surfaces—and archive them on celluloid."[3] Neuville-sur-Saône appears in the film as it did the morning of June 11, 1895, and its recognizability hinges on various details visible within the scene, be it the bridge in the background or the style of clothing, types of cameras held by the participants, or architectural details on the opposite shore. And yet Rhodes and Gorfinkel also emphasize a relation between the local and the global that films make possible: "The ability of an image of a place to be circulated globally suggests that such an image may be one of the most powerful means at our disposal to pose challenges to the unimaginable, unrepresentable totality of our globalized contemporary condition."[4] When listed in the catalogue of Lumière films, *Le Débarquement du congrès de photographie à Lyon* becomes one local place among numerous others, and the specificity of its location becomes one site in a broader mapping of the global reach of the cinematograph. Priya Jaikumar insightfully extends the politics of location to the colonial dynamics of visualizing place: "The history of filming a location, in India or indeed any place in the world, is necessarily a history of the competing assumptions, knowledges, experiences, and practices that underwrite the production of a territory as a visual environment."[5] From the positioning of the camera to the very the possibility of filming, every film distills a complex layering of the geopolitical stakes of place alongside the construction of cinematic space, all bound within the pragmatics of location.

Torn between an aesthetics of capturing, deciphering, and projecting, *Le Débarquement du congrès de photographie à Lyon* is a site in early film history that invites not only the thematization of motion and transit (bodies and boats), but also a broader poetics of taking place. We might go so far as to say that location in world cinema is always already dislocated. Jaikumar astutely questions "why knowledge appears placeless in some forms and situated in others; theoretical when produced in relation to some geographical locations and empirical in relation to others."[6] She notes the role that colonization and slavery play as material histories, and her spatial film historiography helps unsettle distinctions between local and foreign films. We see echoes of these questions in the work of Nicholas Mirzoeff and Ariella Azoulay. In the restaging of travel in early cinema, especially in those films shot by Alexandre Promio, we encounter the shifting coordinates of what it means to take place.[7] Entangled in the seductive logic of here and elsewhere, the cinematograph at this moment in film history is foreign to audiences across the world, and the defamiliarization the screenings offered were often a matter of the *how* rather than the *what* of display. Each of these films harbors an invitation into the dynamic world of an image that exceeds the conditions of capture. The looks at the camera and the acknowledgment of the scene of being filmed keep alive the conditions through which the foreign device becomes part of the scene. Every nod, wave, or wink at the camera underscores a mode of address to the foreign device that places the conditions of filming in the social world the device captures.

If I begin here with *Le Débarquement du congrès de photographie à Lyon*, I do so to draw attention to how transit, motion, and location are animated at this nascent moment in the global history of the cinematograph. Given these dislocations between filming and projecting, no particular reading is hardwired into the composition of the film. It is a film in transit that, dislocated unto itself, takes place in different conditions, whether shown to audiences shortly after having been shot or projected well outside of the local context. And yet how this film takes place exceeds the conditions that the aesthetics of capture offers, and it has a critical afterlife when sequenced alongside other films, when included in the Lumière catalogue, or when juxtaposed alongside other films in an argument about travel. With this in mind, when *Le Débarquement du congrès de photographie à Lyon* screened for the participants of the conference, it functioned as a device meant to dazzle the audience. Part of the awe it was to inspire turned on its function as a mirror, reflecting back on the spectator moving images of a recognizable scene. Months later, when the same film screened in Paris, it functioned more as a window, providing a view of elsewhere, 48 seconds in time from the morning of June 11, 1895. I gesture to these distinctions because how the film takes place underscores the contingency of location, the dynamics of recognition, and the critical role the image plays in serving as both a mirror and a window.

What follows in this chapter tracks and troubles an epistemology of the screen either as a mirror of the local or as a window to the foreign. In the screening to the participants at the conference, we encounter cinema's power to mirror back the practices of everyday life. Here apprehending oneself on-screen, in motion and in time, is part of the magic of cinema. And in the screenings months later in Paris, we encounter cinema's power to open a window onto the world—the screen does not reflect so much as it shows. The ground of this recognition is less a matter of seeing oneself than imagining an elsewhere, known through an archive of trafficked symbols. In its thematization of the relationships among geography, history, and form, on the one hand, and the screen as a mirror or as a window, on the other, *Le Débarquement du congrès de photographie à Lyon* thus stages critical axes of world cinema. As this exploration proceeds, I walk through the afterlife of locations within the film. At the start of the chapter, I look at the formal dynamics the film animates and then consider the implications of Alexandre Promio's own attendance at its screening for the culminating event at the Congress of Photography. It was this event that inspired him to travel the world with the cinematograph. The chapter pairs *Le Débarquement du congrès de photographie à Lyon* with a film Promio shot during his 1896 voyage to Algeria: *Marché arabe*. Looking at the various looks, I draw together film history (the matter of where a film takes place) and film form (how this place is seen on camera) to understand the shifting locations of production and reception.

Mirror: A Local History of World Cinema

On the evening of June 11, 1895, as part of the culmination of the Congress of Photography, the participants were shown the film that had been taken of them disembarking the boat that same morning. They had seen *Workers Leaving the Factory* (*Sortie d'usine I*, 91.1) at the conference just the day before, but on this last day of the gathering, they beheld themselves mirrored on-screen—that is, they looked at themselves looking at the camera. In this twist, the audience became spectators of themselves earlier that day. As Bridget Alsdorf notes in *Gawkers*, many spectators were drawn to early cinema by the chance that they too might appear on-screen: "People caught on camera—or who simply *believed* they were caught on camera—were understandably eager to see themselves on screen."[8] With cameras frequently positioned on public streets, audiences were drawn to the cinema in hopes of seeing themselves. From the outset, the cinematograph functioned as a mirror for the narcissism of the spectator (above and beyond structures of identification predicated on the filmic hero).[9] And so too on this night, those who had earlier in the day been enchanted with the cinematograph were in turn enchanted by their own appearance projected on-screen.

I highlight the location of looking (at the camera and at the screen) in order to draw attention to crucial regulatory dynamics at play in this early film. Livio Belloï notes how the positioning of the cinematograph makes possible the capturing of faces, and he highlights a common spatial arrangement shared between *La Sortie de l'usine* and *Le Débarquement du congrès de photographie à Lyon*. In each film, crowds are concentrated to pass through a threshold (a door in the first and a gangplank in the second) before dispersing centrifugally in front of the camera.[10] The positioning has implications for the sort of looking relations that result:

> At a respectable distance from the profilmic event, the observer and his machine invest the precise point where a centered, orientated action dissipates into a multitude of centrifugal movements, directed to the lateral segments of the frame, opening onto an off-screen space in which all subjects disappear one by one, to the left or right, leaving behind them a space devoid of human figures.[11]

In Belloï's reading, the gradual emptying of the space of human figures is part of an interactive scene presented. Because of the constraints imposed by the gangplank, the camera maintains a steady distance from the crowd passing off the ship, which in turn ensures that the faces are legible when captured by the cinematograph.

In his analysis, Belloï helpfully illuminates the social constraints of the formal dimensions in the film. He highlights three different ways that these passengers engage the camera: the first is "an indirect recognition of the camera"; the second, quite a bit less frequent, is a negative response to the camera; and the third is an outright positive reaction to the camera. He writes, "Such is the principle which establishes the program of the view in a way that leaves no doubt as to the attempted control and regulation that it seeks." He continues by suggesting that the limited duration of the glances helps to de-individuate each particular reaction: "It is a question of betting on a social circumstance where interpersonal constraints take priority over individual curiosity." True to the privileging of "interpersonal constraints" over "individual curiosity," he underscores his point regarding the careful regulation that the scene entails: "Though a filmed subject might be intrigued by the activity of the observer, his look can last only for several seconds, or even a fraction of a second."[12]

Implicit in the location, we could say, are the terms in which the crowd—and the individual faces—are themselves part of a scene that conditions how properly to face the camera. But if we move from the looks at the camera to the looks at the screen later that same day, we confront the ambiguity of location. Looks might be captured on-screen, but the projection of the film highlights another location at which the film is seen—in this instance, by eyes that come to recognize themselves in motion and in time on-screen. In this move from being filmed to being screened, the various participants transform from actors to spectators, from those moving on-screen to those immobilized watching. The third chapter of Christian Metz's *Imaginary Signifier* describes the mirroring potential of the screen quite explicitly: "Thus film is like the mirror."[13] The declaration follows a lucid description of the psychoanalytic contours of the medium and draws from a moment when the parameters of film spectatorship differed from what they were at the time of the Lumière Brothers. That said, Metz is careful to attenuate the mirror as a framework for cinema and to place emphasis, as noted in his initial phrasing, on film being "like" the mirror. The claim is that film parallels the operations of mirroring intrinsic to establishing the consciousness of oneself. In this psychoanalytic scene, the child comes to perceive not only "the familiar household objects, and also its object par excellence, its mother, who holds it [the child] up in her arms to the glass." "But above all," he writes, "it [the child] perceives its own image."[14]

The contrast with film, for Metz, is important, and he notes that in film "there is one thing and one thing only that is never reflected in it: the spectator's own body." In a web of metaphors, shifting between the psychoanalytic register and the medium itself, Metz dramatizes a sudden transformation: "In a certain emplacement, the mirror suddenly becomes clear glass."[15] The transformation of the mirror to clear glass revolves, for Metz, around the fact that the spectator's body is never reflected on-screen, which is to say, it is not mirrored back for the spectator. But on the evening of the screening in 1895, recognition is a key attribute of looking—and specifically the recognition of the site, the location, and the self. One could highlight the psychoanalytic dynamics of the screen as mirror, but the screening of Le Débarquement du congrès de photographie à Lyon to local audiences almost literalizes structures of identification. For those seeing themselves on-screen, there is no passage from the mirror to clear glass. Apprehending oneself as an image, one takes part in the imagined doubling of the world that cinema seems to offer.[16] In this film, we could say, arises the legibility of the self in cinema.

At the same time, what is staged in Le Débarquement du congrès de photographie à Lyon has complexities that exceed the mirror framework, or rather, refract it through coordinates of location understood both historically and culturally. When Metz describes the mirror function of cinema, he characterizes a sense of cinema as a social space quite distinct from the world of the Lumière screening. There is a wealth of scholarship that draws attention to the historical and cross-cultural histories of spectatorship, and each helps to provincialize the conditions through which looking at a screen occurs. Hamid Naficy, for example, helps localize theories of spectatorship by addressing its "undertheorized" social and collective dimensions of the cinema. In modern Iran, he notes,

> The intervention of interpreters and student translators in the reception of the movies was, in a sense, subversive of the apparent intention of the filmmakers. Since these intermediaries had to translate the intertitles, the subtitles, or the foreign language dialog in real time, they often resorted to colorful Persian phrases and expressions, thereby indigenizing and enriching the film experience.[17]

By no means determined by its formal characteristics, the meaning of the film comes alive at the site of reception. In Fatimah Tobing Rony's reflections on watching Tarzan, for instance, the dynamics of looking are caught in a network of recognition and displacement: "What does one become," she asks, "when one sees that one is not fully recognized as Self by the wider society but cannot fully identify as Other?"[18] And in Scott Curtis, Vance Kepley, and Haidee Wasson's work, we confront the historical conditions that help inform the rise of spectatorship.[19] In each of these instances, the psychoanalytic terminology of the spectator finds itself situated both geographically and historically—location matters for each of these scholars, but it is not determined by the film so much as the social situation of its reception.

On the evening of the June 11 screening, there was an allure to the novelty of what was being seen (one's own face) and also the manner of its display (in motion and in time). There was, as I have tried to demonstrate here, something radically local about the display: an audience shown to itself.[20] And yet, in the annals of film history, we also confront here a film that places photography squarely within its frame—that is, the mirror made possible in this film is not only the recognition that each spectator has of themselves, but a reflection of film as a medium through the looks at the cinematograph. Whether through the appearance of photographic cameras on-screen or the depiction of photographers themselves, the film is remarkable for how it captures a media archaeology, the layering of one medium upon another. It functions, quite literally, as a film of photography in motion. How, might we understand the mirroring of photography through cinema? When most of the participants greet the camera, they do so with familiarity with the conventions of having their photograph taken, but each is foreign to the conditions of what it means to be filmed. If there is a recognition at stake, it might be more aptly described as a misrecognition greeting the cinematograph as though it were simply a type of camera.

One particular detail stands out: A man, passing off the gangplank, turns his camera to the cinematograph before dispersing out of frame (Figure 9). His face is captured staring at the cinematograph, but so too does his camera look back at the cinematograph. There is a mirroring here, but it is one of a photographic camera staring back at the cinematograph. In the eyes of each onlooker is a confrontation with the conditions of being seen, and in this recognition is an understanding of world cinema as part of a broader optical regime engaged at looking through a lens to the great beyond. All of this to say that for the duration of the film, we not only look upon those coming ashore, but also confront the fascinated stares of those investigating the cinematograph. The photographers observe a strange boxlike camera modeled on a sewing machine and operated with a hand-rotated crank. Film culture as it would come to be known is not yet part of the world we see here. Instead, photographers behold the cinematograph *before* the emergence of cinema, and the various greetings on-screen salute a camera most likely misrecognized as a strange type of photography. The novelty of a streaming crowd entering and exiting the frame or a puff of smoke appearing and disappearing marks a mode of capture that does not simply freeze an instant in time so much as it embalms its duration. What we witness, encounter, and confront in this film is not only *our* enchantment beholding this scene from 1895, but the enchant-

Figure 9. Detail of a photographer recording the filming of delegates at the 1895 Congress of Photography in Lyon.

ment of those disembarking the boat beholding the camera. What the film captures are stares at a camera before the rise of cinema. The mirror, if we can call it such, is itself a kaleidoscope of mis-recognition: the camera torn between cinema and photography, and an audience out of time and place with itself. In the passage from Lyon to Neuville-sur-Saône lies the poetic interplay of location, the shift from capturing to projecting, and the transformation of the human figure into a spectator.

Window: A World History of Local Cinema

Let us move for a moment from the reflection of the film in Lyon to its projection outward across the world. In this move, from local spectators to a global audience, arises a shift beyond what Metz described as clear glass. No longer a mirror, the cinematic screen functions as a window onto an elsewhere.[21] In the archive of travel films more generally, it might well appear that location matters less as a recognition of oneself than as the view of elsewhere— the mirror, in other words, becomes a window onto a world not one's own, surprising less for familiarity than for its difference.

Recall that during the June 11 screening at the Congress of Photography, Alexandre Promio was among those photography enthusiasts in the audience to behold the presentation of the cinematograph. Promio's memories of this occasion appear memorialized in his travelogue, where he alludes to the screening as a key moment: "In June 1895, I had the good fortune to attend the first screening of animated projections set up in Lyon by Mr. Louis Lumière, at the end of the Congrès de photographie." He adds, "Like everyone else, I was amazed and, from that moment on, I made every effort to be introduced to Mr. Auguste and Mr. Louis Lumière."[22] The conversation eventually led to his work with the Lumière company: "Thanks to the intermediary of Mr. Pascal, whom I had known at La Martinière, I had the honour of entering into the service of these gentlemen at the beginning of 1896."[23] Promio would be one of the first camera operators and a key figure in training a legion of camera operators to traverse the globe with the cinematograph. At each site, the operators would capture films for the Lumière company and display the device to local audiences, enacting a vision of bringing the cinematograph to every corner of the globe.

Out of this early film from the Congress of Photography, then, was not only a moving image of photography, but a spectator (in this case, Promio) so moved as to help organize the dissemination of the technology across the world. What would follow is a catalogue of over a thousand films attesting to the global dissemination of early cinema through the cadre of camera operators. From a factory in the Monplaisir neighborhood of Lyon to the riverbank at Neuville-sur-Saône emerges a local history of a particularly global vision for cinematic enchantment. To understand how the global dimension to a local history takes shape, we catch up with Promio as he embarks on his travels for the Lumière Brothers. This is where our story continues.

In mid-December 1896, nearly six months after the film from the Congress of Photography, Alexandre Promio—now working as a representative of the Lumière Brothers Film Company—traveled to Algeria, where he turned the cinematograph on the streets of Algiers. Among the films he took is a scene from an Arab market with vendors selling goods, pedestrians walking, and children playing (Figure 10). Indexed as 199 in the Lumière catalog, this film testifies to both the global spread of the cinematograph and the colonial dynamics of a foreign camera operator capturing views of the Algerian street. And like *Le Débarquement du congrès de photographie à Lyon*, *Marché arabe* not only looks at those passing by the cinematograph, but it also captures them looking back.

This film is but one in a series taken by Promio on his trip through Algeria in 1896, which included a prayer on a rooftop, donkeys descending a ramp,

Figure 10. *Marché arabe*, an 1896 Lumière film illustrating a North African marketplace.

and various urban scenes in and around Algiers.[24] Where the very first films recorded domestic life in Lyon, often adjacent to the Lumière household or their summer retreat at La Ciotat, the global travels of the camera operators extended these animated views across the world—of trains, boats, public streets, state pageantry, military parades, animals, dances, and iconic monuments. Promio's biographer notes that the films of the Algeria period, following from his films in the United States, make use of space in intriguing ways. His film *Ânes*, for example, plays with the on- and off-screen spaces, while others, following what would be true of his films in Egypt and Turkey, "explore the streets ... with a sort of detailed ethnography."[25] It is quite common for these films from Algeria to be understood as modeling what would become ethnographic films, and as a result, they have a rather uncomfortable place in the rise of national cinema.

I focus on this particular film to consider one of the forms of cinematic enchantment it stages, namely the fantasy of virtually traveling to an Arab market in Algiers. The film seems to provide a sort of window through which to apprehend the street in motion and in time. And on January 10, 1897, shortly after the film was shot, it was screened in Lyon, France, as part of a routine program of various animated views. Programmed as *Alger:*

Marché arabe, the title helped index the location that the film displayed. Not only could the audiences behold this site from Algiers, they could behold it in motion, in time, in a mode of capture that seemingly approximated the experience of being there. Common as a street scene was, the camera operator functioning as a flâneur, as Belloï's reading of *Le Débarquement du congrès de photographie à Lyon* suggests, positioning the camera on the street and harnessing the movement of the market. Unlike those leaving the boat funneled onto the gangplank or those departing the factory through a door, here the camera is a participant in the scene with vectors of action transpiring all around it. The viewing distance is not established in the same manner as it is in the other films, and the unpredictability of movements correspondingly becomes part of the film's appeal.

One would be remiss not to note the echoes that this film has with a broader colonial context. The nineteenth century saw a rise of tourism, transportation industries, colonialism, and the expansion of empires. Against this backdrop, Cooks Travel or Baedeker Guides cemented routes for curious travelers. Alongside the emergence of the postcard and the stereoscope, travel lectures also increased in popularity, and figures such as John L. Stoddard and Burton Holmes often accompanied their lectures with images, which, as Charlie Musser notes, forge a sort of proto-cinematic display.[26] Gunning astutely frames travel alongside the role of image-making: "In the modern era the very concept of travel becomes intricately bound up with the production of images. The image becomes our way of structuring a journey and even provides a substitute for it. Travel becomes a means of appropriating the world through images."[27] Gunning addresses how audiences apprehended travel, and he equally points us to the dangers of such enchantment: "These expositions [the 1901 Pan-American Exhibition, the Paris 1900 Exhibition, the 1893 Chicago World's Fair] were explicit hymns to the colonial expansions of the industrialized nations. They provide searing illustrations of spectacle as appropriation, as the traditions and inhabitants of the unindustrialized world were posed for the contemplation of citizens of the modern world."[28]

Seen in these terms, *Marché arabe* could be seen to follow the logic of the nineteenth-century travelogue as a window onto another world. Another world being crucial insofar as this "other" world is inseparable from an epistemology of travel—an epistemology of cultural otherness, ethnographic capture, and Oriental enchantment. Seen in this way, the Lumière film is inseparable from extensive Orientalist traditions from Eugène Delacroix to Gustave Guillaumet and Eugène Fromentin, the shortcomings of which Malek Alloula and Assia Djebar help to critically illuminate.[29] Out of Lyon, then, is a vision of the world imposed on the world, reproducing a script forged for how to understand the world, the mass reproduction of stereotype and cliché from the hand of the artist to the crank of the cinematograph . . . or so it might seem.

Film scholars help open our eyes to connect these early Lumière films to the critical intersections among colonialism, ethnography, and cultures of travel and display.[30] Rony describes the ethnographic origins of cinema, pairing the proto-cinema of Félix-Louis Regnault, who sought to capture gesture as an index of race, with feature films such as *Tarzan* and *King Kong*. Rony draws our attention to how "the movie screen is another veil" and "how these films explode the seemingly mutually exclusive boundaries of science, art, and entertainment."[31] With reference to Frantz Fanon and W. E. B. Du Bois, Rony ultimately helps elucidate the dynamics through which cinema animates and forecloses structures of identification, something she performs in her use of the first person to describe the viewing of *King Kong*.

A caveat, or amplification, of these questions emerges in the work of Alison Griffiths, whose *Wondrous Difference* speculates about the use of Lumière films. Like Rony, who herself highlights an ambiguous legacy of ethnographic films, so too does Griffiths allude to the historiographic challenges posed by this archive:

> While historians might wish to speculate on the ways in which indigenous peoples are rendered as "spectacles-to-be-watched" in commercially produced films, in most cases there is little if any reliable information on the arrangements made between camera operator and native peoples (such as compensation for appearing in a film). In almost all cases, the only surviving evidence we have of this encounter is the film itself.[32]

Griffiths helps to conjure a scene in which the camera itself is a participant, vividly describing a metamorphosis: "With its metallic glass eye fixed on a crowd or group of individuals," she writes, "the camera undergoes another metamorphosis as it is transformed into an attraction that pulls people's wandering gaze over to its boxy head and three-legged frame."[33] Just as Ariella Azoulay and Nicholas Mirzoeff will help us to see, the camera is by no means a neutral observer on the scene, but a participant integral to an emergent optical regime.[34]

When Promio stands in the Algerian market, he is himself an appendage of the camera, and the eyes that stare at him fit within a longer legacy of observer and observed relations. There is a novelty to the apparatus viewing the market (with its "boxy head and three-legged frame"), but there is equally a well-known dimension to the presence of a colonial observer at the scene. In the epistemology of the window, the Lumière film is less a mirror for local audiences than an agent in exotification, embedded in a colonial regime through which Algeria was to be apprehended out of time and out of place as a distant, timeless elsewhere. The routes that Promio traveled, the sites he viewed, and the basis of his voyage, we could argue, are continuous with imperial regimes through which the world would come to be known. In the words of his fellow camera operator, Félix Mesguich, he would become "a hunter of images" with all of the elements of conquest aligned in the motif of the camera as a sort of gun.[35] Promio might be an appendage of a camera, but he is an appendage to a camera commissioned by a company based out of Lyon whose coordinated circuit of travel involved gathering scenes from around the world meant to leverage the sales of films around the world. Such is the logic of the window as it pervades the move from mirroring audiences on-site to serving as a window to audiences abroad.

(The Postcolonial) Pivot: Unlearning Imperial Enchantment

Much as I am drawn to the framework of imperialism and travel, I am equally overcome by some assumptions that this approach must necessarily make—namely, that the film shown is one beheld by audiences abroad. It was, however, often the case that these supposedly global films were displayed for local audiences. The travel of the camera operators was not only a matter of collecting footage, but also about marketing the technology, and the films captured were often incorporated into public displays shown on-site. That it is to say, there were indeed audiences for whom this film was less a window onto a world than a mirror of the sort we witnessed with the Congress of Photography. Jennifer Lynn Peterson points out the complexity: "Different kinds of spectators all over the world watched different kinds of travel views of locations all over the world."[36] She notes the diverse contexts in which these films were viewed, something pronounced in the shift from the dockside in Lyon and the market in Algiers. Where it is possible (and important) to recognize the nature of the film within the context of colonial expeditions, this film (and the archive of which it is part) richly complicates the conventional narratives of here and elsewhere.

During Promio's brief visit to Algeria from Tuesday, December 15, to Friday, December 18, 1896, he not only gathered footage from various sites, he also took part in a demonstration of the cinematograph for local audiences. The cinematograph had been shown earlier in November, but Promio's visit helped emphasize the importance of the device. In both instances, the presentation of the cinematograph occurred alongside theater and music, nestled into a program that was meant to entertain audiences.[37] "Between two plays," the newspaper announced, there were "projections from the remarkable Lumière Cinematograph, made by the operator M. Promio on behalf of the Lumière company." As though to underscore that this was an evening of entertainment, the announcement continues, "During the evening, the admirable Spanish orchestra will be heard."[38] It was in this context that early Lumière films in Algeria initially were shown to audiences.

If we look closely at *Marché arabe*, we can see various indices of location: the site of the market itself, the architectural details in the background, the clothing of those in the frame, and the visible script "Au bonheur des dames" on the building. There are also various layers of action: the onlookers in the foreground, the goods parading across the field of vision, and the pedestrians in deep space against the backdrop of the arches. And yet what is especially enchanting has less to do with the overall setting, which is already well known in maps, paintings, and photographs, than with the stare of the children at the camera. They appear initially in shadows and then in light, and they crisscross among objects and adults on-screen, disappearing behind the passing goods only to reappear moments later. In their various appearances on-screen, they help make visible the act of filming. Here, it would seem, we are forced to confront the location of looking itself: those enchanted by the technology on the street in Algiers and those of us enchanted by what we see on-screen, all of us entangled in the dynamic worldly vision of the global dissemination of the cinema. These archival looks take place anew with each iteration of the film, contingent on the situational framing and reframing that projection itself offers—whether in Lyon, Algiers, or Paris.

It is telling that even those scholars committed to framing the imperial nature of these early films often resort to a postcolonial pivot, especially prominent when they engage a particular film rather than assess the overall genre. Gunning, for example, provides a reading of a short 1903 Edison film from Nassau at the end of his essay. The action seems fairly straightforward: A woman washes a baby, the baby gets soap in its eyes, and cries. As Gunning has it, "It [this film] is typical of a large number of travel films in which the inhabitants of other lands, particularly of less industrialized nations, are treated as curious sights not unlike the landscape."[39]

And yet brackets upon brackets, Gunning eventually performs a postcolonial pivot—a turn both as trope and a turn of the camera. "Suddenly the camera pivots," he tells us, "making a swift panoramic turn. In a sort of reverse angle we discover that the process of turning the daily life of native people into a spectacle has itself become a spectacle as the camera reveals a group of native children and adults watching the filming."[40] From this remarkable turn, he arrives at his own utopian conclusion:

> The spectacle makers themselves have become a spectacle, the tables turned with the camera's pivot. And, finally, a sublime moment as this witnessing audience refuses to become a spectacle in turn and takes off, escaping the frame and the camera, running off into unimaged space. The film captures and contains, mocks and reduces, but then it responds to its own capacity for motion and also reveals. It shows what possibly no other form of travel representation could represent, the escape of its subject, its pure transito and flight.[41]

If I dwell on this minor detail at the conclusion of the essay, it is on account of how it seemingly enchants Gunning as a critic. His focus on escape seems to provide a break from the aesthetics of capture, and it provides a classic move whereby those represented seemingly resist the terms of representation itself. But what escapes in this framing of escape as a mode of utopianism? In the straitjacket of enchantment as ideology, we are left with descriptions that not only read films as symptomatic of the cultural world in which they supposedly stem, but that reproduce the terms of reception in the process. When, at the moment of engaging a specific film, Gunning does so to address escape, he is himself escaping the mode of enchantment to be had in capture—and instead turning to the enchantment of critique. His essay, focused largely on imperialism and travel, concludes rather than opens with this utopian gesture as he embraces a hopeful pivot toward something different.

Gunning's reading offers a particular instance of the postcolonial pivot, and this gesture is common across many engagements with early cinema, each of which aims against the reductive logic of objectification. We see even in Belloï's reading of Lumière films a pivot away from reductive understandings of how looks operate. Much as the Lumière films involve the capture of a scene, they involve layers of looks with an emphasis on interaction over and above objectification:

> The Lumiere view therefore cannot be reduced to a simple matter of looking, which would require only a thought of frame and duration: in a more or less explicit manner, it also involves a thought of the space of interaction, of its places, practices and uses.[42]

The push against the logic of the objectifying look has formal implications, and Belloï highlights how the view itself frames a "double observation":

From this perspective, the view emerges indeed as a double observation: the observer openly bets on subjects observing microsocial conventions, with the sole intention of directing and regulating their movements. Insofar as moment, duration and space are the objects of a careful calculation, the direction de badauds then can operate in a latent form, not a la baguette any more [the coordination of those passing by can occur without overt control].[43]

We can see similar gestures in Katherine Groo's rich reading of the Ashanti films, which trouble a model that presumes the passive nature of those observed by the camera. "In the Ashanti films," she writes, "a fault line emerges. It marks the insecurity of an encounter between bodies and gazes joined in tension," before noting that this fault line moves across the whole of the Lumière archive. From the particular detail in a particular film arises a law of genre. In the art of the pivot, scholars attend to the layering of looks that the films make possible, the refractions of ethnography contingent in part on the location not simply of shooting, but of looking. In the work of Gunning, Belloï, and Groo, the Lumière films involve a weaving of vantage points in and of the film.

Returning to *Marché arabe*, in the fixed frame of the Arab market, we have less a pivot or an escape than we do an encounter, a visual inquiry, an enchanted stare at the act of filming. The children do not run from the camera so much as they observe it observing them, enchanted by the process by which they are seen. Here in the fixed frame, we have a collision between the representation on-screen and the act of representation, an anachronistic pedagogy in facing the camera. As with the Congress of Photography so too on the streets of Algiers, there are layers of looks—those looks at the camera captured on-screen and those looks of audiences at the screen.

I have framed an opposition between mirrors and windows. And yet if we assume that the domestic film offers a form of mirroring and the global, worldly, or foreign film derives from the logic of the window, then we overlook the complexity by which film complicates location in the very iterability of the image: the capturing of a shot on location and the deferred locations of being screened. Is there a distinction between the enchantment of seeing oneself as against seeing an elsewhere through the camera? Like Gunning in the closing lines of the essay, my temptation is to embrace a postcolonial pivot and to see in the film of the Arab market a resistance to the imperial look. Here, after all, is less an objectifying gaze than a collision of looks as two children cross in and out of view, shielding their eyes, at once illuminated and overexposed, and integrally connected to making visible the conditions of being seen.[44] The enchantment is not only that of the audience apprehending what occurs on-screen, but those on-screen apprehending the camera itself. The film highlights an entire poetics of what it means to see, read, and critique.

Portal: Beyond the World Picture

As we weigh the role of location, allow me to extrapolate the lesson that the early Lumière films offer us for a sort of inquiry into the practices we share as comparatists, as readers, as those enchanted by the poetics of reading, looking, critiquing. Whether a film or a book, representation is a seductive lure: on the one hand, the investment we have in the politics of who or what is thematized (made recognizable), and on the other hand, the text itself as a pedagogy in how to read, apprehend, and make sense of worlds. Much cultural criticism is lured by the enchantment of depiction (what we see), but in doing so, often forecloses the enchantment with the techniques, procedures, and disciplines through which this figure becomes visible (how).

The film of the Arab market stages an encounter between the lure of an elsewhere and the politics of the here—that is, the enchantment with a critical otherness as a ready-made vocabulary (Orientalism, ethnography) and the enchantment with the critical techniques of visualization (photography, film). To thematize the film is to address the scene it makes recognizable to us as an audience: Algiers, market, street scene in 1896. And yet the film exceeds the parameters of thematization for how it takes place in its various iterations: screened in Lyon or in Algiers, whether seen as a travel film or as a critical example in a lecture on cinema. What the film ultimately makes visible, though, are stares at the camera—that is, a moment of technical enchantment when eyes apprehend an unfamiliar apparatus, as alien to those disembarking from the boat as to those passing through the market. For those of us habituated to the camera's ubiquity within visual culture, this originary estrangement is a sort of unknowable limit. We cannot perceive the device as though for the first time, nor inhabit the phenomenological rupture that structures the encounter with the camera. Whether in France or in Algeria, the cinematic apparatus had yet to be understood as it would be a few years later—its future remained unknown, even for the operator behind the lens.

In the two films, one from Neuville-sur-Saône and the other from Algiers, is a kernel of the future of cinema. Whether the greeting of the camera by photographers or the stares on the streets of Algiers, we learn to look anew at a past staring out at us. This lesson is a fold in the dynamic enchantment of looking, reading, and seeing—we see not only the dynamics of an elsewhere framed geographically, but also framed historically, in a sort of cinematic beyond.

From Algiers to Lyon to Neuville-sur-Saône is a portal onto the prehistory of world cinema.[45] Beyond the enchantment of travel, or the aesthetic wonder of an elsewhere, the films usher in the immediacy of seeing and being seen, a manner of looking beyond the frame of the present, the location, and the film itself—a gesture to the critical elsewhere that this portal to a time before cinema offers.

In this local story of world cinema—that is, the screening at the Congress of Photography as a kernel of the global travels of the cinematograph—is a particular lesson about the unstability of location when it comes to early cinema. These films not only show the world to the world, as the Lumière Company would suggest, they also capture and project looks at the cinematograph. They thus fold a medium upon itself wherever in the world it ends up taking place. This worldly horizon might be embedded in early cinema, but so too are broader questions on the techniques through which the world comes to be seen. As part of this continued journey, we move in the chapter that follows from the question of location to the frames through which the world comes to be known. We follow Promio on his journey through Algiers to a rooftop above the city—and to the generative mis-framing of the muezzin's prayer.

3
Frames
De-Centering Orientalist Optics

Listed as 197 in the Lumière catalogue, *Prière du muezzin* is one in a series of films that Alexandre Promio shot on his voyage to Algeria in December 1896. Alongside various street scenes from Algiers and Tlemcen, the prayer stands out for being notably off-center, enough so that the figure praying comes in and out of the frame. When included in the compilation *The Lumière Brothers' First Films*, Bertrand Tavernier's voice-over draws attention to what is likely obvious: "When we said that Louis Lumière always put the camera at the right place," he tells us, "this is an exception. The film is not well framed."[1] Tavernier shares an anecdote about a conversation with a friend at the Lumière Institute to suggest that the prayer the film claims to depict is not only off-center, it is made up: "It is not a real prayer."[2] What we have before our eyes in *Prière du muezzin*, then, is both misframed (off-center) and fabricated (not a real prayer). In the context of Promio's films in the Lumière catalogue, we could say that this particular film is remembered as much for *how* it depicts its subject matter (off-center and fabricated) as for *where* it was shot (colonial Algiers). Allow me, for now, to place it at the center of the chapter.

In formal terms, what is immediately striking is the austerity of the film's composition, especially when cast alongside the polycentrism of Promio's street scenes, including *Marché arabe*. On the rooftop in Algiers, we have a minimalist setting with a plain floor, a line of ceramic tiles, and a clear sky. The dress of the praying man (wearing a black caftan and a white head covering) helps distinguish him against the prominent horizontal axis of the shot. And most notably, as he performs his fabricated prayer, he moves in and out of the left side of the frame, drawing attention to the limits of the screen (Figures 11a, 11b, and 11c). That the film is shot in Algiers is almost inconsequential given the abstract flatness of the image. Not only is the image bisected by the roofline, dividing the upper and lower portions into a contrasting black and white, but there is almost nothing visible in the background. The coordinates indicating East, West, North, and South, important as they are to the prayer itself, are illegible. There is no particular dimension to the figure rising and falling, no flow of crowds from deep space, no approach of an oncoming train, and no interplay between the foreground and background characteristic of the street scenes. Instead, this long shot of a slightly off-center figure in an otherwise symmetrical composition introduces a visual dissonance between subject and frame.

When listed in the Lumière catalogue, *Prière du muezzin* is not only framed by its title and the number 197, but by explanatory notes indicating what is visible in the film. A short description describes the film's contents: "A Muslim man prostrates himself, gets up immediately, and repeats this gesture several times."[3] Unlike the title, which alludes to a prayer, here the description focuses quite strictly on the movements of the figure on-screen. An additional note clarifies that the original title (*Prière du muezzin*) is misleading (*trompeur*): "Misleading title: it is not a muezzin calling to prayer, nor a real prayer." We learn, in other words, that we have neither a muezzin, who might offer a call to prayer, nor do we have an actual prayer. Instead, functioning like the caption to René Magritte's famous pipe, the catalogue description negates what the film purportedly shows—as though to say, "ceci n'est pas une prière."[4] What is written about the film draws attention less to the formal mis-framing (the placement of the figure) than to the inaccurate titling, which mis-frames what we supposedly see on-screen. Overcoming the artifice of the film—its deceptive status as neither a muezzin nor a prayer—means reckoning with the importance of the explanatory note.

From the voice-over to the catalogue notes to the edge of the screen, I begin with these various frameworks for how they direct our eye to this curiously off-center and fabricated film. How might we frame the questions that this off-center film poses? Ought it be read as a colonial artifact on account of its subject matter? Is this staged performance symptomatic of a pernicious colonial gaze set to objectify otherness through religious practice? Or might it be that this performance is eclipsed by its form: refracted, flipped, distorted, and out-of-frame? In line with Tavernier's voice-over, there is a temptation to read this film as a mistake—that is, as a failure to center the subject and to imitate an actual prayer. But if it is a mistake, then it registers as such and

Figures 11a–c. *Prière du muezzin*, stills from the 1896 Lumière film depicting postures of what is assumed to be prayer: standing, crouching, and hands raised.

thereby deviates from the classical composition of the Orientalist traditions of painting. That it is off-center and mis-framed, in other words, means that the film disrupts the central viewing position. The omniscience that would be so integral to classical framing and the command of the observer over a scene is here thrown asunder.

Far from a mistake, then, the film almost appears to defamiliarize, destabilize, and ultimately unsettle conventions of Orientalism, all in the process of quoting them so deliberately. If *Prière du muezzin* is a colonial artifact, then it is one that curiously points to the edge of Orientalist intelligibility. What follows in this chapter is a sort of frame story for the significance of centers and framing in the history of early cinema. At the limits of the physical frame and the engagement with theater is a critical illumination of the contours of viewing positions and Orientalist artifice in this off-center film. The chapter is, on the one hand, the story of a cinematic frame (as revealed in an 1896 shot of a prayer in Algiers), and on the other hand, the framing of how we tell the story of cinema (as revealed in the technology set to render cinema itself obsolete). These two dimensions ultimately intersect in Algeria in a story that draws together what and how the world is made visible.

A Frame Story

In December 1896, Alexandre Promio's visit to Algeria lasted merely four days, and it included a trip from Algiers to Tlemcen, over 500 kilometers to the west. Of the ten catalogued films Promio shot, six capture views of streets and plazas, two take place at the port in Algiers, and two additional films remain: the fabricated prayer (*Prière du muezzin*) and another, listed as 198 in the Lumière catalogue, of donkeys descending a ramp (*Ânes*) (Figures 12a and 12b). Of all the films in this series, both the prayer and the donkeys stand out for their unique experimentation with off-screen space. Where *Prière du muezzin* appears off-center, *Ânes* has the donkeys appear at the top of a ramp to the right and descend across the center of the image before proceeding off-screen to the left. The symmetry of the shot—and the progression of the donkeys across the screen—does not register as a mistake in quite the same way as the prayer. And yet in these two films, the frame gestures to a world beyond what we see on-screen. Insofar as both films accentuate a horizontal axis (with the ramp in *Ânes* and the roofline in *Prière du muezzin*), they stand in contrast to those films that accentuate the depth of field. All of this to say, these two exceptional films from Promio's journey to Algeria not only frame Orientalist clichés, they also introduce a challenge to how framing has been understood in early cinema.

Accounts of framing tend to deduce their rules from practices observable across a range of films, and when it comes to the Lumière catalogue—whether films from Algeria or from elsewhere in the world—certain general principles are derived. In the frame story here, I place *Prière du muezzin* at the center to help demonstrate the limits of the frame, the role of off-screen space, and the broader implications for the stories we tell of film form. Were we to reframe our story, taking a wider scope both historically and geographically, we might even say that the story of cinema could be told as a story of framing.[5] In *The Virtual Window*, the visual theorist Anne Friedberg tracks the development of perspective and editing across a range of debates in visual culture.[6] She highlights the function of the frame in painting, photography, and cinema, noting similarities and differences across these media. She cites film theorists like Stephen Heath and Jean-Louis Baudry, who focus attention on the standard aspect ratio and who help contrast the use of space and perspective in cinema to what we see in painting.[7] Her argument is that "the cinematic frame [functions] as a container for the fractured multiplicity of spatial and temporal perspectives inherent in the cinematic moving image."[8] Where Renaissance perspective in painting negotiates spatial and temporal coordinates within a fixed frame, practices in filmmaking, which cut between various shots, help to shift the role of framing and by implication, the world enframed. Friedberg ultimately engages classic debates in film theory, especially in regard to invisible cutting and the continuity of space, to position cinema as a crucial chapter in a broader story about framing in visual culture.

As this story is told, the Lumière Brothers films, which transpire within a single take and a fixed frame, tend to be seen as distinct from later conventions in filmmaking that employ editing to help construct narrative space.[9] The exceptionalism of early cinema is pronounced enough that the French film historian Noël Burch distinguishes a "primitive mode of representation," which he observes in films from 1895 to 1903, from a later "institutional mode of representation," which begins most prominently around 1914. The institutional mode of representation naturalizes many of the editing techniques to which contemporary spectators have grown accustomed, including the sort of spatial and temporal coordinates that Friedberg so insightfully addresses.[10] By contrast, Burch notes that the "primitive mode of representation" tends to frame all narrative action within a stable shot, leaving movement and activity to transpire within deep space.

Whether *La Sortie de l'usine*, *Le Débarquement du congrès de photographie à Lyon*, or *Marché arabe*, each of these films could be seen to correspond in its own way to the characteristics that Burch attributes to early cinema. Among the primary formal traits is the following:

Figure 12a. *Ânes*, an 1896 Lumière film showing donkeys descending a ramp.

Figure 12b. *Prière du muezzin*, still of a man standing.

> Any given tableau will remain unchanged in its framing throughout its passage on the screen, and from one appearance to the next (in the event of a recurring set or location); it is complete unto itself and never "communicates" with any other. In other words, the successive spaces depicted are presumed to occupy a common diegetic framework, but that is all: their spatio-temporal connections remain fundamentally unspecified.[11]

This first trait is readily observable in the collection of Lumière films, each of which captures a scene in a single take without splicing together images. As we see across a range of examples, each of Promio's films captures a particular moment in time within the frame as though a photograph in motion.

An additional trait in Burch's typology entails the importance of the frame as a "possible playing area," capturing all of the action occurring within it without shifting the camera.

> The second primary trait which I distinguish may be called the *"non-centred quality"* of the image, and it must be considered under two separate heads: first, the entire frame is a possible playing area. The areas close to the edges of the frame are as likely to be the site of vital action as those more centrally located.[12]

In this second trait, the non-centered quality, Burch already anticipates a contrast with conventions that would emerge in continuity editing that place action at the center of the frame. In the street scenes, there are multiple centers, and even in films that seem to center action (such as the doors in *La Sortie de l'usine* or the gangplank in *Le Débarquement du congrès de photographie à Lyon*), there are multiple trajectories for the action captured. As Burch continues, he stipulates:

> It is often difficult for the eye—at least for our eye—to locate the narratively significant centre of the diegetic action—and there are times when none actually exists at all, when the entire image is being offered simultaneously to our gaze. The most famous films of Louis Lumière come to mind here, of course (*Workers Leaving the Lumière Factory, The Arrival of a Train at La Ciotat*), but also countless tableaux of narrative films as well.[13]

Note here that Burch employs the language of the tableau, borrowing from painting to think about the role of the frame at this moment in early cinema. The examples he cites (two iconic Lumière films) describe "an entire image ... being offered simultaneously to our gaze." In telling the story in this way,

Burch centers the question of framing, and he helps elucidate the worlds that these Lumière films make visible. The power of his account hinges on its description of formal principles seemingly evident across many of the films known from the Lumière catalogue.

A story as prominent as the one Burch tells is bound to have its detractors, and a number of scholars have drawn attention to the limits of the argument. Livio Belloï, for example, offers the following gloss:

> Trying to define the pragmatic principles of the Lumiere view, Burch maintains that it consists of "choosing a frame as suitable as possible to allow for a 'trapping' of an instant of the real, than to film this frame without any concern for controlling or centering the action."[14]

And he follows with the important caveat,

> Burch seems to overestimate the effects of non-centering—which allows him, in turn, to contrast radically the supposedly decentered space of early cinema with the centering that would later come to specify the "institutional mode of representation."[15]

For scholars like Belloï, Burch places too great of an emphasis on the distinction between the primitive and institutional modes of representation, and in turn, mis-frames the centers of early cinema. Certainly a film like *Prière du muezzin* gestures to the limit, or the edge, of the claim about the role of the frame. In Promio's off-center film, there is a compositional element that stands in contrast to the elements that make up Burch's story.

Within the annals of debates in early cinema, Tom Gunning's critique of Burch centers, importantly, on the question of framing—and in turn, on the role of artifice. Where Burch emphasizes the idea of the frame over and above the shot, Gunning turns attention to the concealed substitution splice in the work of Georges Méliès. He does so, in part, to complicate the generalized claims that Burch offers. For Gunning,

> the frame presents the action displayed to the spectator. It is the unity of this framed viewpoint that addresses the spectator specifically and directly, and this is the continuity the filmmakers wished to preserve. However, such framing is far from a passive act, and not at all due to either a primitive lack of expertise or a purist's desire to avoid manipulation.[16]

With attention to the active role of framing, Gunning distinguishes between "enframing" and "emplotting":

> Early films are enframed rather than emplotted, and what is contained by their framing is often a result of a complex and detailed labor, one

which, in the tradition of nineteenth-century illusionism, labors to efface its traces just as surely as did the later classical style.[17]

There is a blurring of the strict line that Burch draws between periods here, and for Gunning, the attention to details in what is enframed ("a result of a complex and detailed labor") is all part of the power of these early films. It is telling that Gunning shifts from the formal question of the frame to the question of theatricality, and the two terms come together:

> However, as we have seen, this unity of framing should not be identified with theatricality. Rather, a more primal fascination with the act of display grounds the theatrical tableau, the medium shot of such facial expression films as Edison's *May Irwin Kiss*, the mobile vantage point of the "phantom railway rides," and the magical transformations contained within a single framing but created by substitution splices.[18]

Gunning pushes against the notion that these tableau-like shots function akin to theatrical illusion, and he highlights details (facial expressions, mobile vantage point, and substitution splices) that enable what he describes as "a more primal fascination."

From Friedberg to Burch to Belloï to Gunning, how the story of framing is told turns on the specific example enframed by the storyteller. And here, placing *Prière du muezzin* back at the center of our discussion, we might wonder how it refracts through the various claims about centers. What is striking about this particular film is that its exceptionality derives both from its being mis-framed and from its deceptive performance—the trick of the eye is as much a deception on the basis of performance as it is the technical placement of the camera. In fact, the question of framing seems to outweigh the verisimilitude of the prayer itself, or so it might seem. I draw our attention to framing in part for the indelible connection it has to theatricality in discussions of film theory—which is to say, the relation of the two aspects of the prayer's exceptionality might not be so unrelated.

Enframing the Unpredictable

Toward the end of his life, Louis Lumière spoke with the film historian Georges Sadoul and reflected on his role as a technician: "I have never done what is called 'staging' [*la mise-en-scène*]," Lumière remarks, "And I can't see myself very well in a modern film studio."[19] As he continues, he notes the waning of the cinema of technicians and the current epoch of theater: "In cinema, the time of technicians has passed, it is the era of theater."[20] By drawing a distinction between the technical and the theatrical, Lumière makes possible a common understanding that his films capture everyday life and are therefore void of the artifice that would come to dominate cinema in the years shortly following. Where scholars of this period of film history—Vincent Pinel, Noël Burch, and Georges Sadoul, for example—might echo Lumière's claims, there remain crucial questions about the aesthetic implications of a certain number of films in the Lumière catalogue.[21]

What is striking in Lumière's remarks is his outright disavowal of theatricality. As Dai Vaughan would have it, the various Lumière films astound audiences less for what they intend to show (workers leaving a factory, a train arriving at a station, or a baby being fed) than for the unpredictable details that the camera happens to capture. In his reading of *Barque sortant du port*, for example, he derives an entire theory of the unpredictable:

> What is different about *A Boat Leaving Harbour* is that, when the boat is threatened by the waves, the men must apply their efforts to controlling it; and, by responding to the challenge of the spontaneous moment, they become integrated into its spontaneity.[22]

The implication borders on cosmological: "The unpredictable has not only emerged from the background to occupy the greater portion of the frame; it has also taken sway over the principals. Man, no longer the mountebank self-presenter, has become equal with the leaves and the brick-dust—and as miraculous."[23] Vaughan draws a broader lesson from this scene to demonstrate what the unpredictable poses for communication systems more generally:

> But such an invasion of the spontaneous into the human arts, being unprecedented, must have assumed the character of a threat not only to the "performers" but to the whole idea of controlled, willed, obedient communication. And conversely, since the idea of communication had in the past been inseparable from the assumption of willed control, this invasion must have seemed a veritable doubling-back of the world into its own imagery, a denial of the order of a coded system: an escape of the represented from the representational act.[24]

Beyond the "willed control" of communication, Vaughan makes possible a manner of thinking "an invasion of the spontaneous" as part of "an escape of the represented from the representational act."

The contrast that Louis Lumière and Vaughan both seem to address is between the theatrical nature of the trick film (and its enframing of action for the camera) and the spontaneous unscripted dimension of Lumière films (in the capturing of the everyday). And yet *Prière du muezzin* offers something quite different. In the flatness of the image is a rehearsal for the camera, but also a moment of theater—in multiple senses of the term. The rooftop functions as a sort of stage, and even though the décor is limited, the clothing of the performer suggests location. And the performance, the rising and falling of the performer in a semblance of prayer, is itself theatrical, appearing as anything but unpredictable. As one of many films in the catalogue, is *Prière du muezzin* somehow one that exceeds the explanatory frame of film historians? On what level is the mistake it offers to be registered: as a formal conflict of framing the theatrical performance or as a theatrical performance that misses its referent?

I highlight Vaughan's reading of the unpredictable to draw attention to Promio's film of the fabricated prayer. In contrast to other Lumière films, in *Prière du muezzin* seemingly all elements of the composition have been placed intentionally before our eyes: no particular objects, only lines, bodies, clothing, and gestures. These elements make all the more surprising the fact that the film—composed, contrived, and controlled as it appears—is actually off-center. The body that rises and falls in its action drops in and out of the frame in such a way as to draw attention to the limits that the screen imposes. There is a gesture to the persistence of off-screen space, but the unpredictable is here predicated less on the rustle of leaves than the positioning of the apparatus. Less the "doubling-back of the world in its own imagery," here we have the conditions of the apparatus laying bare the artifice of the nature we perceive. Despite all that the film may say about centered viewing positions, it ends up breaking the frame in novel ways. The on-screen elements of the mise-en-scene appear strictly regulated and choreographed. And as such, unpredictability is not to be found in this carefully orchestrated scene, but rather, in how it is framed. The formal surprise, in other words, is only heightened by the staged nature of the scene depicted.

Beyond Icon and Index, or a Prayer for Mimesis

I have argued thus far that the unpredictable in *Prière du muezzin* is less a matter of *what* it enframes than *how* it enframes, and yet this claim is not to detach the film from the Orientalist clichés enacted on-screen. There might be a temptation to read *Prière du muezzin* formally—that is, to detach Promio's film from the world in which it was produced and the various institutional, procedural, and colonial frameworks that facilitated both his travel and the image repertoire he produced. Ali Behdad notes a tendency "among historians of photography studying European images of the Orient to reduce the politics of photographic iconography to mere exploitation while valorizing formal concerns as a pure and noble form of aestheticism."[25] The problem with this approach, he argues, is that it "dichotomizes the iconic and the indexical, the form and content, and thus overlooks the complex ways in which aesthetics and politics coincide and coalesce in the image."[26] When it comes to *Prière du muezzin*, such a separation (between the iconic and the indexical) is nearly impossible—the formal surprise turns on the cliché that is depicted. The collision is not between the viewer and an image of Otherness so much as a formal disconnect in how this image is framed.

In this account of framing, Linda Williams's remarkable essay on Eadweard Muybridge's motion studies troubles the notion that there is somehow a world outside the staging of the image. As Williams investigates Muybridge's carefully staged photographs, she notes "a gratuitous fantasization and iconization of the bodies of women that have no parallel in the representation of the male."[27] She acknowledges, "Some of the movements and gestures in the women's section—walking, running, jumping—parallel those of the men," and continues, "Yet even here there is a tendency to add a superfluous detail to the women's movements—details which tend to mark her as more embedded within a socially prescribed system of objects and gestures than her male counterparts."[28] Whether "the inexplicable, and rather coy, detail of having her walk with her hand to her mouth" or "the gesture of grasping her left breast with her right hand," these various movements and gestures constitute "an extra mark of difference which far exceeds the obvious anatomical difference between the male and female."[29] Here, then, "a supposedly scientific study of the human body elicits the surplus aesthetic qualities of incipient diegesis and mise-en-scène in the treatment of his women subjects alone."[30]

Where Williams addresses the mark of sexual difference in Muybridge's image repertoire, Promio's film turns on the mark of Orientalist difference. The adornment of the body and the performance of a supposed prayer embed what would be an otherwise abstract figure in a "socially prescribed system of objects." The prayer is not only a fantasy of elsewhere marked through clothing, but through motion, even if the motion itself is predicated on a fantasy of what a prayer ought to be. Important to *Prière du muezzin* is not simply its theatrical staging, but that the performance is meant to be cast as an index of what happened—that is, that the movements on-screen are meant to resemble those of a prayer. We have in the elaborate staging what we might call a prayer for mimesis. There is ultimately no foundation to the performance offered so much as the semblance of a projection of a prayer within the broader frame of Orientalism.

In *Orientalism*, Edward Said is careful to highlight the importance of the text's surface rather than the presumption of "some great original." Countering the quest for an innate authenticity, Said outlines a method of reading: "The things to look at are style, figures of speech, setting, narrative devices, historical and social circumstances, *not* the correctness of the representation nor its fidelity to some great original."[31] As Said has it, "Orientalism is premised upon exteriority, that is, on the fact that the Orientalist, poet or scholar, makes the Orient speak, describes the Orient, renders its mysteries plain for and to the West."[32] And so too, it would seem, with *Prière du muezzin*. The allusion in the prayer and in the overall mise-en-scène connects to an image repertoire that bears more in common with Orientalist texts than with practices in Algeria. The film makes possible its verisimilitude not as an observation of daily life in Algiers, but in its affirmation of clichés and in how Orientalist discourse always already frames what comes to be seen.

The example Said offers in his reflection on method is a work of theater, Aeschylus's *The Persians*. In Said's reading of it, Aeschylus's play is remarkable on account of how "the Orient is transformed from a very distant and often threatening Otherness into figures that are relatively familiar (in Aeschylus's case, grieving Asiatic women)."[33] Concerned as Said is with textual evidence, he turns to a claim about the audience response: "The dramatic immediacy of representation in *The Persians* obscures the fact that the audience is watching a highly artificial enactment of what the non-Oriental has made into a symbol for the whole Orient."[34] With attention to "a highly artificial enactment," Said helps direct attention to the dynamics through which Oriental and non-Oriental are distinguished one from the other. Likewise in the prayer, an enactment (in this instance, entirely fabricated) stands in for the location, and comes to function as a symbol, a synecdoche freighted with the logic of the Orient itself.

Much like Williams, who draws our attention to fanciful social codes for gender, so too does Said help direct attention to the "style, figures of speech, setting, narrative devices, historical and social circumstances" constitutive of Orientalism. As he has it, "That Orientalism makes sense at all depends more on the West than on the Orient, and this sense is directly indebted to various Western techniques of representation that make the Orient visible, clear, 'there' in discourse about it. And these representations rely upon institutions, traditions, conventions, agreed-upon codes of understanding for their effects, not upon a distant and amorphous Orient."[35] Indeed, these codes of understanding extend both to the mise-en-scène and to the formal constraints through which this world becomes visible.

In the story of Promio's film of the prayer, then, is both a question of framing and a matter of theater. The realism of the world depicted cinematically is itself the belief that beyond the frame is a space not represented—that is, the assumption that film has a relationship to the time and space coordinates of the act of recording and that what we cannot see as an audience might have still happened beyond the confines of the frame. Beyond the Orientalist artifice, then, is still an underlying belief that there is a diegetic space beyond what the camera captures and that the head of the body rising and falling does not simply disappear. This illusion of an illusion—to return us to an earlier moment—is part of a broader and fundamental fantasy that the film frames.

An Expanded Field

Let us turn now to another rooftop in Algiers nearly one hundred years following Promio's film. In the opening scene of the Algerian director Merzak Allouache's 1994 film *Bab El Oued City*, we encounter the sound of a morning sermon broadcast from a loudspeaker on the roof of a building overlooking the sea.[36] As the sermon plays on the soundtrack, the camera slowly pans to the right along the electrical cord and upward to a shot of the loudspeaker. The sermon continues, and the camera pans left across the roof, revealing a panoramic view of Algiers before arriving back to the loudspeaker. We then see a shot of a young man emerging from around the corner while putting on his shirt. He walks briskly, passes between two sheets hanging out to dry, and makes his way across the roof. In a medium shot, he clutches the loudspeaker and starts to detach its wires. As he does so, the sound of feedback can be heard from the speaker, and the sermon—even when cut off from this one loudspeaker—is all the while audible in the distance. Amid it all, a shot reveals an older women peering out of her window before we cut back to a close-up on the young man's hand still working to detach the wires. The camera pans from his hands up his arms to his sweating face, and he looks to the left off-frame as the sequence cuts to reveal, yet again, the face of the woman peering out of her window. The soundtrack shifts to nondiegetic sound and the title track begins to roll.

Beyond the symmetry by which Allouache's film stages a rooftop prayer in the Bab El Oued neighborhood of Algiers are a number of crucial details. First, where Promio's film mis-frames the fabricated prayer, in Allouache's film, the rooftop is presented in a panoramic sweep, initially up the cord toward the loudspeaker and then across the skyline. Second, in this scene, the loudspeaker is itself the focal point, and the two characters connect through their interaction with the device. And third, we have staged in the film a parallel set of interruptions: on the one hand, the technical interruption of the loudspeaker, and on the other hand, the dramatic witnessing of the action with the crosscutting of the woman peering out her window

(Figures 13a and 13b). Here, then, framing plays out in multiple senses to escalate the dramatic tension. The crosscutting interrupts both the panoramic sweep of the rooftop and the activity of the young man cutting the sound to the speaker (Figures 14a and 14b).

I am drawn to this scene as a counterpoint to Promio's film, but also as it exemplifies the coherence of a filmic world through sound—the ambient sounds from a rooftop in Algiers and the resonance of the sermon across the various loudspeakers in the neighborhood. If Promio's film mistakenly titles itself *Prière du muezzin*, then Allouache's film provides an instance where the sermon echoes across film history, offering the sound of the voice but not the physical body of the speaker. The technical interruption occurs less through mis-framing than through the tension between the two tracks, heightened by the feedback from the loudspeaker and the crosscutting of its observation. The woman's gaze is a judgment that frames the activity of the young man in an anticipation of the drama that the film's narrative tracks.

The suggestion here is not that Allouache intentionally replays Promio's film, but rather, in this constellation of religion and rooftops is a tension about the legibility of frames. There is in Allouache's work a critique and a figuration of so-called fundamentalism. It is not that his work is somehow a less vexed representation, but in both Allouache's and Promio's films there are fundamental questions about religion on-screen, projected, refracted, and framed. In the figure in the window, we might suggest, is a sort of embodied optics made possible. Her distance from the scene hinges on an Orientalist cliché. She is structured into the narrative as alterity, the classically gendered and racialized figure who aligns here as the site of judgment.

As a paradigm of the institutional mode of representation, the space depicted on this rooftop is held together through the soundtrack, which bridges the cuts between the panoramic view of the city, the close-up on the boy's hands, and the cuts to the woman's face. This particular introduction to the film stands in contrast to other films that begin in Algiers from on high. Julien Duvivier begins *Pépé le Moko* with a reflection on seeing as the eye is guided from a map of the city, replete with a commanding voice-over to connect the collage of shots that follow.

The opening scene draws the eye to the geography of the Casbah, and an image of a map offers a false sense of command over a space that the various alleyways render less legible (Figure 15a).[37] As the film toggles between the colonial fantasy of the map and the lived reality on the streets, it makes possible a question of framing, something it performs through the classical techniques of cinematic storytelling (Figure 15b). It rehearses every colonial cliché, including a montage of various communities in the city, and its

Figures 13a–b. Stills from *Bab El Oued City*: a man tinkering with a loudspeaker and a woman looking out a window on a rooftop in Algiers.

camera movements pan across the city from on high, looking down into the streets, up staircases, and cutting to a collage of wall signs. With these movements, cuts, and use of sound, both Allouache and earlier Duvivier reveal the important role of off-screen space, making the rooftop in Algiers a site from which theories of observation and oversight become thinkable.

Figures 14a–b. Additional stills from the rooftop sequence in the opening of *Bab El Oued City*: an urban panorama and a close-up of a loudspeaker.

Landscape here is less a horizon than a quest to enframe a labyrinth of activity below.

When it comes to *Prière du muezzin*, the optics of its horizontal axis gesture to off-screen space as the head falls in and out of frame, but the performance leads us less to a visual command over the scene—as a witness, a map, or a

FRAMES: DE-CENTERING ORIENTALIST OPTICS 79

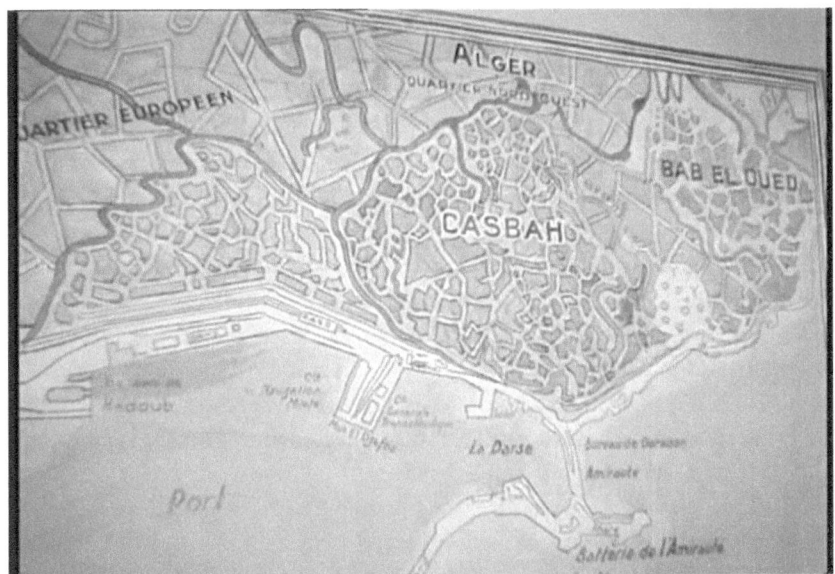

Figures 15a–b. Stills from *Pépé le Moko*: a cartographic representation of Algiers and a view of the Casbah from Julien Duvivier's 1937 film.

landscape might offer—than to the Orientalist artifice it formally unsettles with its off-center performance of a fake prayer. In the future history of cinema, the frame is less a hard limit than a horizon onto a world beyond. Here in the strictly staged film of the prayer, the frame enacts an error of camera placement and a reflection on the conditions through which we come to see.

The Photorama, or a World without Frames

And now, another turn and an expanded frame. When first introduced to the world, the cinematograph was thought by its inventors to have a life of six months, and the various camera operators hired were expected to be out of a job in a short time. That this machine was to have been without commercial success was taken as a given, and even the early shows were seen to derive more from scientific curiosity than from a specific aesthetic investment in the medium.[38] And so it was that Auguste and Louis Lumière continued their inventions well beyond the discovery of the cinematograph. Auguste would explore the world of x-ray photography, and in 1900, at the Exposition Universelle in Paris, Louis unveiled his photorama—a device that employed twelve different lenses to capture a full scene that was projected around the spectator on a circular screen measuring six meters in height.[39] Gone was the perspective of painting, and in turn, the world was made visible with the viewer surrounded, enveloped by the scene the camera captured.

For his part, sensing the end of cinema, Promio eventually retired to the very place where he shot his early films: to Algeria. And believing that cinema had run its course, he too turned his attention to the photorama and the promise of a world without frames. In 1903, Promio shot the port of Algiers in a sweeping photorama, employing the new technology to bring the scene to life. Where William Henry Jackson had in 1895 published images of this same location for *Harper's Magazine*, Promio's photorama placed the viewer in the midst of a world as part of the image itself (Figure 16).[40] Almost in direct contrast to the highly abstracted shot of the prayer, Promio's photorama unfurled an elaborate scene with water, boats, and modern buildings lining the street. Its duration was seemingly indefinite. The glimmer of the water, the shadows flickering on the street or the movements of the people all looped around the screen, giving the impression of a continuously bustling scene.

Allow me for a moment to reframe the film previously at the center of the chapter. By 1903, at precisely the moment film was emerging in narrative form with cuts and storyboarding, Promio was imagining a future of a different sort, and he was, in this process, investing in an alternate mode of visual representation. Where the early Lumière films echoed in form and subject matter the formal attributes of painting, binding a scene in four frames and playing with deep space, the photorama made possible a viewing experience of a different sort—a world without a center. It did away with the frame as it had been known in painting and as it would come to be known in cinema.

That said, the panorama was not unknown in nineteenth-century visual culture. The painter Robert Barker had at the end of the eighteenth century experimented with the panorama to present scenes of battles and military conquest. As Denise Oleksijczuk remarks: "Barker's innovation lay in improving on a painting's form by translating the rules of perspective to a curved and continuous surface, and by making it possible for a painting to do what late-eighteenth-century theorists felt was beyond the limits of the medium, namely, to represent a total view, open on all sides."[41] His son Henry Aston Barker would go on to extend his father's fantasy to sites long known in an Orientalist imaginary. In 1801, he presented his Panorama of Constantinople, and shortly afterward he offered a Panoramic View of Grand Cairo, which he painted on over 10,000 feet of canvas for display in Leicester Square. Each of these panoramas involved multiple viewing positions, not only displacing the centered viewing position long considered the staple of Renaissance perspective, but making possible a sort of embodied viewing experience surrounding the viewer in the image.[42] Women and men were seen to respond differently to this aesthetic experience, and even animals were to have been tricked by the realism involved. A journal of the period reports a Newfoundland dog leaping over a handrail at a panorama to rescue men in the painting seemingly drowning at sea; and an entry years later describes a cat being chased from a panorama attempting to find refuge by climbing a tree only to find, in the end, the tree merely painted on the canvas.[43]

Scholars rightfully note the embeddedness of this visual form within Orientalist optics. Ali Behdad, for example, describes how panoramic views "engendered a sense of mastery over the landscape, positioning the viewer to have a total view of the cityscape below, representing the 'right of (over)sight' that the European tourist assumed in Istanbul."[44] Roger Benjamin helps highlight how these sorts of displays "offered novel physical sensations, a less earnest didacticism aligned with the pleasures of modern tourism," and Angela Miller's work connects the panorama with the cinema.[45] And yet I bring us to Promio's photorama, the supposed afterlife of cinema, for what it offers us as a way of understanding not only the limitations of the frame, but an imagination for what cinema might have otherwise been. The film that was read as a mistake in framing was later corrected by centering the camera on what was observed, but it is especially telling that the camera operator went on not simply to correct this perceived error, but to reimagine an aesthetic world without frames—to reframe the medium itself rather than tinker within the tableau. What might the history of cinema and Orientalist depictions of the world have looked like if the path of the panorama—as opposed to the tableau—were taken? How different might the world look if presented without a center?

Here it is interesting to note how the panorama undoes the logic of a viewing position.[46] There were, as I mentioned, lecturers to help coordinate what

Figure 16. William Henry Jackson, *Algiers—The Embankment and Boulevard de la République*, gelatin silver print, published in *Harper's Weekly* (1895). (Library of Congress, World's Transportation Commission Collection)

was seen and to draw attention to certain locations in the viewing area; and there were later printed guides, initially presented circularly and later linearly, to orient viewers on their own. In either case, though, how the world was to be seen was given over to multiple viewing positions, uncut and expansive, drowning the spectator in the scene itself. How small, how provincial, how bounded the cinematic image comes to appear in relation to these monumental panoramas. Promio's cinematic afterlife preserves him not so much as failure or an operator who pursued an unrealizable dream, but a seeming instantiation of André Bazin's famous proclamation that "the cinema has not yet been invented."[47]

De-Orientalizing Optics

In the end, the future of cinema was seen by the Lumière Brothers to lie not with the moving picture bound by the four corners of the screen, but by the infinite expanse of light projected around the viewer surrounded by images that exceeded the possibility of being framed. Reality, in this scheme, knew no bounds—the world, the image, was not a thing harnessed through a frame, but an experience of being immersed in place. Through the photorama, seeing this or that image receded into the phenomenology of seeing in general. When, years later, Bazin famously contrasted the centripetal frames of painting with the outer edges of the screen, he, like many of us, ignored the vision of those who, in the fantasy of defeating frames, sought to surpass the medium they themselves labored so intently to develop.[48] The photorama would unveil a reality of a different sort—a world without frames, a scene without borders, and an experience for seeing the world anew. Such was the case with Promio's photorama of the port in Algiers.

As the story of cinema developed, it is quite easy to note that the utopianism embraced by these pioneers of the photorama was eclipsed by the staying power of the framed world of moving images. Panoramas were complicated to disseminate and costly to reproduce in mass form. But films continued to live on as the foundations of a now globalized medium. The cinematic cut would make possible the emergence of narrative space in cinema, and films ranging from Julien Duvivier's *Pépé le Moko* to Gilles Pontecorvo's *Battle of Algiers* to Merzak Allouache's *Bab El Oued City* would splice the tableau, breaking apart the streets of Algiers into shots arranged in narrative form.[49] The casbah, in this regard, would transform from the panoptic overhead map to images corresponding to the travels of the camera through the streets. The cut would make possible the dissolution of the frame into the spatial logic of narrative, and a world would be slowly revealed by storytellers' scripts, the camera's movements, and the editor's scissors.

I return in the end to the question of film form and film history with which I began—that is, the instance of mis-framing on a rooftop in Algeria. My chapter has linked the question of framing to the history of Promio and the global travels of the Lumière Brothers. I have emphasized not only how formally this film undoes the logic of Orientalism, disrupting the conventions of perspective and the centering of the camera, but also how Promio eventually thought past the frame. He did *not* simply follow the path of narrative cinema—something that the Edison company, but also Edwin Porter and Cecil Hepworth, would help to forge—but he rethought the very basis of the medium.

If I seem to emphasize film form, it is because of what it offers us by way of unsettling the foundations for understanding sites. As scholars of Middle East cinema, what is the optical regime through which a region is intelligible? What do early experiments in cinematic seeing do to disrupt or reinforce this regime? What might it mean to see the world otherwise—not as a framed vision but as an immersive panorama? Lina Khatib and Derek Gregory among others note that Orientalism translates visually as a distinction between the observer who sees and the observed who is mapped, displayed, and rendered according to mathematical rules of perspective.[50] Part of my goal has been to investigate an alternate story for thinking about seeing—one that acknowledges different relations to film, to the history of the medium, and to the world it makes visible.

I would emphasize in closing the importance of linking the site of film form and film theory—not solely a thematic treatment of place, but the inscription of Algeria into the signifying practice of the medium. Thinking of the place of form and the form of place allows us to reframe not only what it means to see Algeria on film, but how film transforms the manner with which Algeria is understood and known. And it is here—both at the edge of the frame and in the photoramic world without frames—that the transnational history of film form comes to matter.

As Promio proceeds onward from Algeria to Egypt, he turns his cinematograph both to the ceremonial procession of the Ottoman Khedive in Cairo and to the seemingly timeless pyramids in Giza. In each of these locations, his films help connect both what and how these iconic scenes are made visible, enframing and illuminating the dynamic tension between capture and projection in this potential history of world cinema. Allow us to expand our frame and turn our attention to the serialization of sovereignty.

4
Sovereignty
Iterations of Cinematic Statecraft

In March 1897, Alexandre Promio arrived in Egypt and turned his camera to some of the most memorialized sites in world history. His Egyptian films depict a number of well-known scenes and monuments—Alexandria, the pyramids, the Sphinx, Cairo—and translate what had long been the subject of paintings, lithographs, and photography into the supposedly universal language of cinema.[1] Egypt was but one stop on his voyage across North Africa and the Middle East, and took part in an effort, in the words of the Lumière Brothers, to bring the world to the world. Following centuries of travelers, Promio began his Egyptian journey in Alexandria with shots of the port, al-Manshiya Square, and a train arriving at Ramleh Station. From there, he continued his voyage by heading to Cairo, then onward to Giza, where he filmed the pyramids and the Sphinx, before venturing up the Nile. His various Egyptian films were completed in a span of two months, and already in a few short years, representatives from the Edison, Pathé, and Kalem Film Companies had set out in his footsteps.[2] Each of these companies sent representatives to Egypt and incorporated footage, including images of the pyramids, markets, and city streets, into story lines centering Egypt in the global imaginary.[3]

Newspapers of the period tended to cover Promio's travels as an imperial adventure and marveled at how "the entire world" (*le monde entier*) might soon be "the conquest of the Cinématographe Lumière" (*la conquête du Cinématographe Lumière*).[4] But if the cinematograph was a tool of conquest, its arrival was not simply one-directional. At various local screenings and demonstrations, its introduction indirectly set the stage for an emergent Egyptian film culture, spawning interest in the possibilities of motion photography among a range of audiences. Even prior to Promio's arrival, the first film projection occurred in Alexandria on November 5, 1896. The demonstration catered to an audience of expatriates and elites at the Stock Market of Toussoun-Pasha. Subsequent screenings took place on November 28, 1896, in Cairo at the Hammam Schneider and December 22, 1896, at the Khedival Palace.[5] Similar accounts can be given for each of the sites that the Lumière camera operators visited. Egypt remains but one site among a number of these international locations, including Paris, London, Belfast, Berlin, Istanbul, Moscow and Tokyo. The footage collected at each of these sites was circulated worldwide, and audiences could marvel at locales from disparate parts of the globe. From Mexico City to Venice to Hanoi, these demonstrations and recordings often constitute the preliminary moment in a narrative that extends from experiments in motion photography to the eventual rise of national film histories.

Promio's films are generally recognized as the first films shot in Egypt, but they are rarely cited as the first "Egyptian" films. Instead, given the precedent for the route traveled, Promio's voyage tends to be understood within the framework of colonialism, and his various films highlight motifs (such as camels and Bedouins) that had long been the domain of Orientalist painting. Most of the sites that Promio visited already circulated as postcards, such as those famously produced by Lehnert and Landrock, and like postcards, they were meant to extend well beyond their point of origin.[6] When eventually gathered as a collection in Lyon, Promio's Egyptian films were catalogued according to date and location, appearing as two separate clusters (359–393, 414–415). Other films with what might be described as Egyptian content—such as an 1896 Egyptian dance (311) or an 1897 restaging of the assassination of General Kléber in Egypt (746)—appear according to where they were shot (the National Exhibition in Geneva and a studio in Lyon, France). Already in the organization of the catalogue, then, is an implicit grounding of world cinema according to location, even if Promio's films highlight the complex dynamics of what it means to take place.

The Lumière Company appears to play its part in this cartographic logic, gathering films from around the world as part of its collection, mirroring what would seem to be the atlas model for world cinema. No matter where the various Lumière films were shot, they end up functioning as colonial effects, property of the company rather than of those captured and collected in the frame. And yet as I hope to demonstrate in this chapter, collecting moving images is by no means so straightforward on the ever-shifting grounds of world cinema. The Lumière films exist not simply as artifacts with determined meanings, but as animated views contingent on projection, circulation, and serialization. The Egyptian papers *al-Ahram* and *La Réforme* listed program schedules of screenings for audiences in Cairo and Alexandria. Similar to the famous screening at the Salon Indien of the Grand Café in Paris in December 1895, the Egyptian screenings were not organized around the geographical locations of the films shown. In each instance, the serialized projection of a sequence of short films necessarily affects how they take place, but neither a chronological nor geographical logic prevails. This is to say that the meaning of these films is not fixed within the frame but relies in large part on the iterative conditions of screening and re-screening. In the complex dynamics of recording, dissemination, and projection, the global Lumière films both affirm and unsettle the very framework of national cinema and allow us to question what it means to situate films in the world.

In what follows, I trace the tension between Promio's Egyptian films and the framework of sovereignty in national cinema. Who or what dictates what constitutes an Egyptian film? What does it mean for a film to take place? This chapter suggests that the dynamic interplay between sovereignty and seriality, performed in the iterative logic of programming and screening, not only challenges the grounds of world cinema but also informs the potentials and possibilities that iteration has for the future of film history. Moving from our discussion of location and framing in Promio's Algerian films (in the preceding two chapters), this chapter proceeds as a picture show in two parts. The first focuses on two distinct films, shot a decade apart, of the Khedive 'Abbas al-Hilmi II in Egypt. The first of these films was shot by Promio in Cairo in 1897, and the second was shot by Alexandria-based filmmakers in Alexandria in 1907. In differing ways, each of these two films subtends contrasting narratives for national cinema anchored in the distinction between "a film shot in Egypt" and "an Egyptian film." To highlight the poetics of taking place, the second half of the chapter turns to a film shot by the Lumière Company in a French studio depicting the assassination of General Kléber in Egypt a century prior, and then its critical rereading in the last few years by the Syrian Abounaddara collective. In each instance, the chapter highlights the slippages and appropriations in the manifold locations at which the scenes take place—by no means controlled by the conditions under which these films were initially produced. Tracing the cinematic afterlives of 'Abbas Hilmi II and General Kléber, these various films visualizing sovereignty all serve as a framework for thinking the iterative future of world cinema.

Serial Sovereigns

Among numerous films shot on Promio's Egyptian voyage was a scene of the Khedive 'Abbas Hilmi II passing in a convoy as part of the procession of the sacred carpet (Kiswah/al-Maḥmal) (Figure 17). The khedive in the Ottoman period was the name given to the ultimate authority over Egypt, an honorific applied initially to Mehmat 'Ali and then formalized by official decree in 1867 as the title for Isma'il, his son Tawifq, and then his grandson 'Abbas Hilmi II.[7] The film is numbered 362 in the Lumière catalogue (*Le Khédive et son escorte*) and follows in sequence from other films that Promio gathered on his travels to sites in Alexandria, Cairo, Giza, and along the Nile River. Film 363 (*Procession du tapis sacré*), the next in this sequence, shows musicians surrounding the Kiswah, an elaborately decorated cover for the Holy Ka'aba, which was historically crafted in Egypt and presented as a gift to the Saudi Kingdom. Accompanied by the Egyptian army, the annual procession—known as the Maḥmal—would begin in Cairo, cross the Eastern desert, the Suez Canal, Palestine, and the Hijaz, before finally arriving for a ceremony in Mecca.[8] The khedive was likely already on public display as part of this celebration of gifting and diplomacy that Promio captured with the cinematograph.

Like a long history of sovereigns before him, the khedive had been depicted through various woodcuts, photographs, and official portraits. Portrait photography of government officials was well known across the Ottoman and Persian empires, but the khedive's cinematic incarnation had the novelty of presenting him in motion through the lens of a foreign camera operator.[9] Promio's film presents the khedive in a horse-drawn carriage as he proceeds in a ceremonial procession, flanked by soldiers and their horses. Carefully framed to present the Citadel and the Sultan Hasan Mosque in the background, the khedive's carriage passes in front of the cinematograph, which is positioned on the side of the street among crowds gathered to cheer the procession. Compositionally, the film follows other Lumière films that tend to align with what David Bordwell describes as staging in depth—that is, the carriage approaches from deep space before passing in front of the camera.[10] The iconic Citadel helps to situate the procession in a scene that had been depicted in Orientalist paintings and photographs for years prior to Promio's arrival.[11] The film does not simply capture the khedive on camera, it draws this sovereign into the duration of cinematic time. In the orchestrated procession, the cinematograph apprehends his movement and those of the horses, soldiers, and crowd surrounding him, animating a figure most frequently understood through formal portraiture. In Promio's film, 'Abbas

SOVEREIGNTY: ITERATIONS OF CINEMATIC STATECRAFT 89

Figure 17. *Le Khédive et son escorte*, an 1897 Lumière film depicting the Ottoman ruler accompanied by his ceremonial guard.

Hilmi II emerges as one of many sovereigns eventually included in the Lumière catalogue.

'Abbas Hilmi II was the last khedive of Egypt, and his presence in the 1897 procession marks a key moment in the history of Egyptian cinema, serving as one of the first films to be shot on Egyptian soil. Film historians such as Ifdal ElSaket, Karim Elhaies, Ilhami Hassan, Samir Farid, Viola Shafik, Georges Sadoul, and Ahmed al-Hadari nearly all reckon with the impact that the Lumière Brothers films have (and do not have) on the eventual emergence of national film industries across the Middle East.[12] They often frame these first films, including this film of the khedive, as part of a colonial moment in the history of modern Egypt, prior to the rise of a national cinema. Yet even though a wealth of research on national cinemas exists, these early Lumière films tend to complicate the conventional historiography.[13] The film of the khedive, for example, not only predates the rise of film culture (including cinemas and networks of film distribution) but also the emergence of the modern Egyptian state. This early film depicts Egypt under the authority of the Ottoman Sultan Abdul Hamid II at the intersection of the Ottoman, British, and French empires, at a moment before both national film culture and the sovereign nation-state arise. What is captured on-screen is a glimpse of a world in which the sovereignty of the modern state was thought differently than it would be only a decade or two later.

I was initially drawn to Promio's sequence of early Egyptian films both as a challenge to the rival nationalist frameworks in film history (between the United States Edison Company and the French Lumière Brothers Company) and as a testament to the global spread of the cinematograph. What, I wondered, were the implications of this cinematic internationalism for the frameworks we use in film studies? How does Promio's voyage unsettle national models of film scholarship? Given that his travels included both capturing and projecting films, how were these early instances of film received across the various sites that he visited? Such were the primary questions animating my inquiry. Against the backdrop of national film histories, it might well seem that the issue of sovereignty—reflected as we will see in the film of Khedive 'Abbas al-Hilmi II—is parenthetical to the trajectories of the global camera operators. And yet, confronted with the broader collection of films, we come face to face with a certain paradox. Even though the Lumière camera operators traversed the globe, they quite frequently did so at the service of royal courts. Promio's first trip to Spain, for example, aligned with the Spanish royal family's fascination with the cinematograph and its interest in its potentials.[14] Reckoning with the role of sovereigns in early cinema, the question thus shifts: What is it to visualize the sovereign cinematically? For all the attention to depictions of sovereign power in painting and literature, what does it mean to see the sovereign in the vernacular temporality of cinema?

Far from parenthetical to this archive of world cinema, royal sovereigns began to appear everywhere I looked. In addition to this one film of 'Abbas Hilmi II, there was a film of Czar Nicholas II in Paris (163), another of Bey Ali ibn Husayn of Tunisia and his convoy (206), the film of a parade celebrating the marriage of princess Maud of Wales (248), two of Queen Victoria returning from Windsor back to London (488/490), and another of the Norwegian King Oscar II arriving in Stockholm (537), to name only a few.[15] The list of examples reveals not only similar thematic content (heads of state), but parallels in formal execution (a steady longshot of carriages approaching from deep space along crowd-lined streets).

There is something perhaps obvious about addressing sovereignty so literally—that is to say, finding sovereignty in depictions of the sovereign. And yet this list traces a certain deep grammar of statecraft in early cinema. Whether in parades, carriages, crowds, streets, or on staircases, the pageantry of the sovereign is itself a sort of diplomatic performance, one whose codes of etiquette are the result of a long history of such interactions. Whether in

London, Tunis, Paris, or Stockholm, the various sovereigns appear nearly to the extent that one can point to a general visual presentation regardless of the particular national leader. I could not help but marvel at the serialized sovereign in the history of early cinema, one whose codes and frames of viewing are shared no matter which sovereign leader appears on-screen.

The appearance of 'Abbas Hilmi II in this sequence of Lumière films is itself not entirely surprising, especially given the long history of representing the procession of the sacred kiswah in Orientalist visual culture. What is surprising—and why I highlight the presence of the visualization of the sovereign in this way—is how the serialized images of the film and the positioning of the film within a catalogue ambiguate the grounds on which it comes to be seen. Unlike Henry Jones Thaddeus's portrait of the young khedive, which had been presented to Queen Victoria in 1893, Promio's film serves as an artifact of a different sort.[16] The cinematograph was not recording the khedive as part of any official documentation, but as part of a technological dissemination of a medium. The sovereign, if recognized in the image, takes place in the iterative logic of world cinema. As an artifact and a projection of Egypt, the sovereign performs a particular role, functioning as much to index a site as to embody state power. In the cinematic capture of 'Abbas Hilmi II we find both cinema before film culture and the sovereign before the rise of the modern Egyptian state.

To think of national cinemas, then, is to be drawn into the curious grammar of statecraft and the conditions of film production. Here in the film of 'Abbas Hilmi II is the paradox of sovereignty. This cinematic capture of the khedive presents him formally as other sovereigns in the archive—that is to say, he is but one sovereign of a series of sovereigns captured by the camera. Whether a czar, a bey, a queen, or a king, they each figure in a similar manner on public streets in processions, in carriages or cars passing through crowds. In this serialized presentation, the specificity of the sovereign fades into the background (quite literally as we see with the Citadel), giving way to a formal parallel instead. In tracking national film cultures, the very question of what constitutes a national film is itself refracted through the terms and expectations delimited by a globalized film culture, in this case through a transnational grammar of embodied sovereignty.

The Khedive's Two Bodies

A full decade following Promio's visit to Egypt, 'Abbas Hilmi II returned to the screen in a 1907 documentary film that has become another origin story for Egyptian national cinema. This second film—"The Khedive's Visit to the

Mursi Abu al-Abbas Mosque in Alexandria" (Ziyārat al-Khidīwī li-Masjid al-Mursī Abū al-ʿAbbās bi-l-Iskandariyya)—was shot by two Alexandria-based photographers, Aziz Bandarli and Umberto Dorès.[17] The duo operated a photography studio in Alexandria, and in November 1906, opened a cinema near Ramleh Station (Maḥaṭṭat al-Raml). In 1907, they famously recorded the ʿAbbas Hilmi II arriving at Abu al-Abbas al-Mursi Mosque. And most important, for scholars concerned with the origins of national cinema, it is this particular visualization of the khedive that often ranks as the first Egyptian film—with Promio's films considered a foreign importation.[18] With their photography studio and theater in Alexandria, Bandarli and Dorès were foundational figures who helped forge a cinematic infrastructure to nourish a nascent industry—both an indigenous filmmaking practice and a network of theaters for screening films throughout Alexandria and Cairo. In this version of events, Egyptian cinema was untethered from colonial imagery on the day in 1907 when the khedive visited the mosque in Alexandria. For what might arguably have been the first time, two Alexandria-based camera operators produced an Egyptian film on Egyptian soil. In this particular version of the story, images of the sovereign (the khedive captured on film) foretell the eventual sovereignty of the image (with the rise of an Egyptian national film industry).

Yet the 1907 film from Bandarli and Dorès has been lost and so circulates not as a film, but as an account of the first "local" Egyptian film.[19] One can imagine that, similar to newsreels of this period, this film showed the khedive's arrival on a particular afternoon, perhaps amid a large crowd gathered to witness the event. That said, the film's significance derives much less from what it depicts (ʿAbbas Hilmi II) than the fact of its having been shot by residents of Alexandria. In the annals of Egyptian film history, in other words, the film takes place less as a geographical site than as an inaugural moment within the sovereign tale of national cinema.

When I speak of sovereignty, I highlight an implicit tension in film history seemingly literalized in the instantiation of what we might see as the khedive's two bodies: the first captured in 1897 in Promio's film *Le Khédive et son escorte*, and the second captured in 1907 by Bandarli and Dorès. The first of these two films offers the visualization of the sovereign *in* cinema (depicted on-screen and represented in motion over time); and the second offers the sovereignty *of* cinema, which is to say, a national infrastructure for film production. Much like auteur theory, which has come to dominate how we describe films, films also tend to be catalogued according to their national sites of production. And yet when it comes to Promio's film of the khedive, the circulation of this image of the sovereign is hardly sovereign in its meaning. Framed and reframed, circulated, projected, and received across place and time, it comes to have different meanings for different audiences. Records show that Promio's film was screened on April 18, 1897, in Lyon, France, as part of a sequence of other films from the voyage to Egypt. Its iterative significance relies less on the image it contains than the situation in which it comes to be screened—either as an example of early cinema in Egypt, one of a series of sovereigns, or a film from the Lumière Brothers global archive.

Among the various debates in national cinema are scholars who question the utility of national frameworks for the analysis of early cinema. In a study of early cinema, Frank Kessler, for example, highlights distinctions between nation-as-belonging and nation-as-origin, something he traces in a discussion of a Lumière film of a Tyrolese dance shot in Cologne. He notes the curiosity whereby, "a French cameraman, working for a French company, shoots one of the earliest cinematographic views made in Germany in Cologne, a city located in the Western part of the country, filming a traditional dance from the alpine regions of Southern Germany and Austria."[20] He adds that there is an exception to this sort of travelogue, which is the moment that the national symbols appear in cinema, be it "the flag, the army, or heads of state."[21] His argument pivots to describe a scene in the writings of Stefan Zweig. Zweig describes the angry reaction of French audiences in Tours, France, when Kaiser Wilhelm II appears on-screen: "Everybody yelled and whistled, men, women, and children, as if they had been personally insulted. The good-natured people of Tours, who knew no more about the world and politics than what they had read in their newspapers, had gone mad for an instant."[22] The example Kessler offers is especially rich because it reveals the open ways that even the symbol of a nation circulates in excess of the logic of production and reception. In this particular projection, Zweig positions himself as distinct from the French audience and implicitly conjures how films of the sovereign circulate beyond borders, beyond audiences, and beyond determined meanings. An image of the sovereign cannot contain the sovereignty of the image.

A different line of analysis can be found in the work of Stephen Bottomore, who meticulously explores images of sovereign rulers in Lumière films and attends to the risks that various monarchs played in being filmed.[23] He notes that they necessarily had to restyle their image for the new medium: "Some royal families managed to attune their image to the new medium. But for other monarchies the adjustment was seen as a threat, and in some cases may even have played some part in the decline of royalty."[24] The issue was that these films risked "levelling down" the elites in a broader process of media democratization as the various sovereigns—in this case Queen Victoria—would appear to audiences "like any other old lady."[25] He adds that "once moving pictures of royal personages reached the *public* there was likely to be some confusion between the traditional image of remoteness, and the informal reception in an amusement venue."[26] Despite this tension, already by the end of 1896, soon after films were first projected, "around a dozen of the world's ruling/royal families had seen moving pictures, usually at specially arranged screenings, and many more heads of state saw films in the years immediately following."[27] Yet beginning in roughly 1899 and extending well beyond 1911, Queen Victoria and the Russian czar began crafting rules for public recordings and circulation of their cinematic incarnation.

The issue is not simply to question national cinema with the counterpoint of a global archive, nor to suggest that early cinema solves the perennial riddle of national film production. Rather, looking at the prevalence of images of sovereign monarchs on-screen reveals all sorts of serialized doublings. When we think of the khedive's two bodies in the 1897 and 1907 films, we might recall Hobbes's famous frontispiece to the Leviathan and Ernst Kantorowicz's *The Kings Two Bodies*.[28] The difference, however, with the filmic incarnation of the sovereign has to do with the animated nature of the image—which is to say, both the dynamic of capturing time and movement, but also the dynamic of projection on screens well outside the national frame. In each instance of sovereigns in early cinema, the image is not owned by the royal court so much as it becomes the domain of the Lumière company. The image, then, circulates well beyond the parameters of its being shot and is projected across the world as part of the display of the cinematograph as an emergent technological form. In each iteration, little control is offered for how audiences respond, and so, as is the case in Zweig's account of the German kaiser, different audiences react differently to the same film.

If I put pressure on the depiction of the khedive, it is because it raises crucial questions. In the doubling of the khedive is the paradox of cinematic sovereignty—on the one hand, a sovereign image captured and contained, disseminated, and screened, out of time and out of place in films already bound for projection and circulation, and on the other hand, an image that indexes the sovereignty of a medium taking root in Egypt. Part of reckoning with national film history is not only the visualization of the sovereign, but the recognition that circulation and projection complicate the historiography of rootedness. Films do not stem from the soil, they take place—and in taking place, they travel, imagine, and refigure the terms through which rootedness itself comes to be understood. The khedive and his double haunt the history of Egyptian cinema, but so too does the serialized sovereignty of this moment of world cinema (Queen Victoria, Kaiser Wilhelm II, et al.) produce an entire genre out of the seeming exemplarity of state power.[29]

I share this seemingly minute detail from an archive of world cinema to gesture to a limit. From Cairo to Lyon and onward to the annals of early cinema, the curious cinematic doubling of the khedive offers not only a historical fold in national film history but also a haunting specter, circulation, and proliferation of the khedive's body above and beyond any fantasy of the sovereign image. Repeated, replayed, and recirculated, the khedive continues to haunt how we might understand sovereignty itself.

Sovereign Cuts

And now I turn to a different sort of projection and a different model of sovereignty. Returning to 1897, another sovereign emerges in an alternate incarnation—this time staged, framed, and reenacted for the camera (Figure 18). If thus far I have traced the contours of sovereignty in regard to the double filmic incarnation of the Egyptian khedive, allow me here to reveal another vision of sovereignty. Film 746 in the Lumière catalogue is titled *Assassinat de Kléber* (The Assassination of Kléber). It was shot by Promio in November 1897, not too long after his return from Egypt, and depicts the French General Jean-Baptiste Kléber, who was appointed by Napoleon to oversee the occupation of Egypt from 1799 until he was assassinated in 1800. Kléber is shown as he strolls through the gardens of the Muhammad Bey al-Alfi palace. Surrounded by an entourage, Kléber—whose identity is marked by an iconic hat—is eventually approached by Suleiman al-Halabi, a twenty-three-year-old student from Aleppo studying at al-Azhar who is disguised as a beggar wearing striped pants and sporting a long beard. As the film proceeds, the Syrian student emerges from the elaborately painted background and approaches the French general with a letter. Then, in a sensational turn of events, with a few cuts of a dagger, Suleiman al-Halabi stabs Kléber to death. The short film concludes with Kléber collapsing on the ground surrounded by soldiers as Suleiman al-Halabi is apprehended by two soldiers on the right side of the frame.

To the French forces occupying Egypt, the assassination of Kléber was seen to be the result of a fanatical student. The trial of Suleiman al-Halabi is well known in the colonial history of Egypt and was included in the famous chronicles of al-Jabarti, who, in his record, took the side of the French.[30] For his role in the assassination of Kléber, Suleiman al-Halabi was condemned to death, tortured in public, and left on a stake as a sort of lesson both of French justice and of the severity of the transgression. His head was removed and eventually sent back to France, where his skull was displayed as part of phrenological studies of fanaticism in the Musée de l'homme in Paris. In the now

Figure 18. *Assassinat de Kléber*, an 1897 Lumière film re-creating the assassination of General Kléber in Cairo.

mythologized version of the event, Suleiman al-Halabi remains through the discourses of law (which condemned him to die) and science (which displays his skull) an enfant terrible of the colonial Enlightenment. His story remains woven into the history of modern Arabic literature, and writers from Alfred Farag to Sonallah Ibrahim have adapted and referenced his legacy.[31]

Of all possible restagings, it is worth noting what part of this story Promio decided to display. The film visualizes the assassination itself, replaying theatrically the moment at which Kléber is killed, rather than the gruesome fate that befalls Suleiman al-Halabi. Compositionally, the film rehearses the classic tension between showing and telling insofar as the scene frames a protonarrative—and it does so with strict rules of blocking and framing that allow the action on-screen to transpire within the frame.[32] The elaborate painted background was designed by Marcel Jambon and the mise-en-scène was coordinated by Georges Hatot, who was famous for his work at the intersection of film and theater. Beyond the set and the blocking of the scene, there is no film editing in the classic sense of montage, but cutting is literalized in the foreground in the elaborately orchestrated blocking that makes possible this 40-second toppling of the sovereign. That is to say, there is a cut in the film, and it is a cut that topples Kléber. Not simply the flow of a crowd toward the camera, nor the procession of the sovereign across the frame, here in Promio's film the cut provides the turning point in a short scene that frames the assassination itself.

Valentine Robert has described these sorts of early films as paradigmatic of the tableau style in early cinema. She quotes André Gaudreault in noting that these works tend to be "founded on the unity of action, space, and time, [and on] the centripetal frame of the camera's field of vision," and she draws attention to the importance of framing, staging, and style.[33] She focuses on the 1900 Pathé film *Le Duel après le bal*, which stages the famous painting by Jean-Léon Gérôme, *Suite d'un bal masqué* (Figure 19a). Gérôme's painting, she remarks, is notable for its careful negotiation of temporality: "It is as if we can see the duel in the empty space created in the center of the frame, which is something like the spatial materialization of the temporal ellipsis." This effect, she tells us, allows Gérôme to fashion what she describes as "the fruitful moment just afterward" and seems "to call out for recreation in cinema."[34] As with the Pathé film, which actualizes the before and after of the killing, so too with the Promio vision of Kléber's assassination, temporality is at stake (Figure 19b).

A key attribute of Gérôme's painting, for Robert, is how temporality "was precisely one of the main features." She notes that the painting captures what Gotthold Ephraim Lessing describes as the fruitful moment, "an ideal artistic moment that condensed the action by suggesting to the viewer's imagination what came before and after it." There is, then, already a certain cinematic quality to the painting itself: the specific moment, the various objects on the ground, and the arrangement of the two parties. As though acknowledging the painting, when the Pathé film pauses its action for a few seconds, it gestures to the intermedial nature of its allusion to the painting. With its distinct interplay between on-screen and off-screen space, the early tableau film complicates what it means to see a painting in motion and highlights what Charles Musser and Leah Lehmbeck both suggest is a certain competence engaging various representational registers.[35]

I gesture to the tradition of the tableau film for its formal resonance with Promio's 1897 film replaying Kléber's assassination. That Suleiman al-Halabi emerges from deep space is not inconsequential—it allows for the imagination of a world beyond the frame of the image, and it assists in the temporal sequencing of the event resulting in the assassination of Kléber, not dissimilar to the sort of sequencing Robert identifies in the Pathé film years later. It is worth noting the parallels of the composition overall with Kléber, clad in white pants, collapsing on the left side of the frame into the arms of two

Figure 19a. Jean-Léon Gérôme, *Suite d'un bal masqué*, 1857, oil on canvas, Musée Condé, Chantilly.

Figure 19b. Still from the Pathé film *Le duel après le bal* (1900).

soldiers, while Suleiman al-Halabi, in muted colors, is apprehended on the right side. The echo in the two scenes is not simply thematic, though both involve filming death, but formal insofar as they arrange the figures within the frame in a similar manner. As for backgrounds, just as the Gérôme painting provides a clearing deep at the center of the frame so too does the Promio film figure taller trees on either side of the frame, keeping the depth of space clearer in the center of its action. In these various ways, the film fits almost all too perfectly the genre of the tableau style of early cinema.

At the same time, the film, as a reflection on sovereignty, bespeaks the fall of a colonial power in the iterative play of coordinates not only cinematically beyond space and time, but also geographically and historically: a century late and in a studio. Given that so many of the early Lumière films are seen as part of a travelogue and documentary tradition, how might we understand this performed reenactment of history? What is restaged in this reimagining of the world in this way? We might wonder whether this film should be understood as an Egyptian film, based on its thematic treatment of Egypt, or simply as a French production filmed in a filmic laboratory in France. Torn between the figures of Kléber and Suleiman al-Halabi is the ambiguity of cinematic sovereignty faced with the multiple trajectories and dynamics that the circulation and projection of this scene make thinkable. In the cinematic reconstruction and reenactment, the sovereign power is threatened and killed by a figure who emerges out of the deep space of the set to kill the general in the foreground, all restaged for the camera as a sort of late imperial fantasy.

Sovereign Afterlives

In this detour from Promio's film of the khedive to the restaging of Kléber's assassination, I now add one last iteration among the serialization of sovereigns. In recent years, the Syrian collective Abounaddara has reanimated Promio's film to draw attention to the representation of Suleiman al-Halabi.[36] Their work on Suleiman al-Halabi highlights the intersections of colonialism and representation, and at venues ranging from La Musée de l'homme to Documenta, challenges various institutions to rethink their use of colonial artifacts. In each of these various venues, Abounaddara demonstrates how Suleiman al-Halabi embodies the fanatical caricature and racist stereotypes that persist in cinema around Arab characters. The striped pants and the beard become part of a visual excavation that the collective offers as they unsettle the film from within, turning the sovereignty of the image back upon itself. That is to say, Abounaddara resurrects Suleiman al-Halabi from the archive, turns the colonial fantasy back upon itself, and confronts the nexus of politics, law, and science by reimagining his place in the history of cinema.[37]

Speaking in an interview with the art historian Anneka Lenssen, Abounaddara highlights the importance of the Lumière Brothers, drawing parallels between the work of the collective and the Lumière Brothers' practice as "amateur" filmmakers:

> If we must be called amateurs, then we also think it necessary to revive the amateur model of our Syrian and foreign predecessors—along the lines of the Lumière Brothers who screened their shorts in cafés and cabarets—so as to produce images that correspond to the needs and desires of our society today. But we know that this model isn't economically viable anymore. We can't show our films in Syrian cafés and cabarets.[38]

It is a seemingly passing reference, but one that acknowledges the Lumière Brothers for a particular framework of public presentation. Abounaddara's critical practice, however, pushes against the sort of commercialization for which the Lumière Brothers were known, and they make "images in the framework of an anti-representative art—cinema—to propose an alternative to this regime." "Fundamentally," they tell Lenssen, "it's about finding ways to resist state and global industry with the power to conflate humans with images for the purposes of social control or commercial exploitation."[39] One might see in Abounaddara a resistance to the commercial logic of world cinema and a stark contrast even to the driving force behind the Lumière Brothers' endeavor, but they share in the short, public format of their films.

A different tone emerges at the conclusion of an interview with Moustafa Bayoumi. Here again the collective's spokesperson Charif Kiwan alludes to the Lumière Brothers, but he does so more critically focused on the contents of the specific film of Suleiman al-Halabi.[40] Kiwan notes the troubling way that the film caricatures colonial resistance under the guise of fanaticism as it inscribes the first "Syrian" in the history of cinema clad in Orientalist stereotypes: "The Lumière Brothers completely misrepresented al-Halabi, giving him a beard when he had none." The frustration with such caricatures fuels the work of Abounaddara, but they push further than a mere corrective. "We must be done with such representations," Kiwan implores, while noting that the collective's filmmaking is "our way of saying goodbye to such representations." "What we want," he states, "is nothing less than to change perception."[41] Implicit in the engagement with the Lumière film, in other words, is not simply an artifact from the history of cinema, but an effort to rethink what it means to see Syria in film. In the slippage from the discourse of misrepresentation to questions of perception is a fundamental understanding of the role cinema plays in shaping social frameworks—a task that Abounaddara enacts in its own work.

Crucial to reanimating Suleiman al-Halabi is the task of pushing him well beyond the frame in which the Lumière film—or the colonial archive more generally—presents him. One of Abounaddara's short films, *In Search of the Syrian Fanatic*, highlights the vexed dynamics connecting Suleiman al-Halabi's artifactual afterlife in France.[42] An opening shot shows the Eiffel Tower out of a Parisian window with a voice-over proclaiming, "This is the story of Kléber's assassin because his skull was brought to a museum." The film cuts to papers from the French archives as "La Marseillaise" plays as a soundtrack, before cutting to newscasters who allude to a "terrorist group" threatening to attack unless the skull is returned. The skull, the newscaster informs us, is of a "young religious fanatic" and is "mysteriously unfindable." As the film continues, we follow a man walking into the museum and inquiring about the skull. A woman states that the skeleton is "absolutely not in the collection" as "La Marseillaise" continues to play on the soundtrack. Of all the images and sounds woven together, it is telling that footage from the Lumière film appears intercut during the newscast, as though weaving together the skull, as a trace of the historical figure, and the film, as a projection and restaging of the episode. Fiction and fantasy are woven together in the dynamics uniting the museum and the film archive.

If this film highlights the quest to repatriate a skull, then it also draws attention to the impact Abounaddara has had beyond their attention to the Lumière film. In either case, the concern is not so much with the film as such, but with the framework it offers for a character whose importance crosses history, media, and politics. That is to say, the collective manages to excavate a historical character from the film and to push its limits from the shadow of the Lumière studio to the skull of the museum, all as part of a broader inquiry into the collection and dissemination of colonial tropes around Syria. The approach here is not specific to film or curating, but extends to a multimedia approach to draw attention to the implications of this character well beyond a singular frame. In an open letter to *Le Monde*, for example, the collective notes that an article in the newspaper draws from their work without citing it properly. Their action is less a quest for property rights over a historical past than an act of unsettling and de-appropriation, an inquiry into the stability that the character has as a signifier within the French imperial archive. The demand itself, in other words, constitutes an act of reanimation by bringing the character out of the frame within which he had been understood.

In the reenactment of a scene from the historical archive is a delicate interplay between the artifactual skull of Suleiman al-Halabi held by the museum, which functions almost indexically as a relic from the past, and Promio's film, which functions as a projection of various latent assumptions about Syria within the collection of Lumière films. The Abounadarra collective grants the concession in their work that Promio's film constitutes a "first" for the appearance of a Syrian in cinema, but they equally reframe and reanimate how the film can be seen by drawing attention to the parallels between the skull and the image, each one a different mode of capture. What Abounaddara helps us see is the fundamental question of repatriating images, something they pursue in demands for the restitution of skulls and in the calls for an ethics of image making. This act of unsettling the Lumière Brothers from their French origin in turn allows their films to find their place both within and in excess of colonial frames.

If I draw attention to Abounaddara, it is on account of the potential their work offers for a sort of counterarchival practice. With each edit in their film, the image breaks from the framework, and the voice-over elucidates connections and associations that help return Suleiman al-Halabi to a different sort of history. No longer is Kléber the subject of the film, nor is Suleiman al-Halabi trapped as a stereotype; instead, Abounaddara reanimates Suleiman al-Halabi, along with the image within which he had been archivally rendered. In the projection and restaging of Kléber's assassination is a curious historical replay. On the one hand, there is a tendency to treat the Lumière film as an artifact that crystallizes a certain colonial imaginary around the fanatic Syrian student replete with the adornment of striped pants and a lengthy beard. On the other hand, though, there is a way that the film breaks the frame in spite of its mise-en-scene. That is to say, it indexes a world that exceeds the intentions of its production, and it lends itself to iterative readings and rereadings contingent on the situations in which it comes to take place. Here, then, the Lumière catalogue serves not to fix images of the past with a predetermined meaning; instead, the counter-archival practice of Abounaddara embraces the perverse empiricism of rereading the Middle East in this global archive. In doing so, the sovereignty of these images is unsettled, reanimated, reenacted, and replayed as they come to resonate with the contemporary moment.

To embrace a view of national cinema anchored in the conditions of the production of the image itself—which is to say, the sort of scene in which Promio and the Lumière Brothers somehow own the material that they capture on the camera—is to overlook the complex ways that these moving images unsettle the notion of visual property. There is a plasticity and mutability of the animated image that the Lumière archive makes possible, and torn between the orthodox reading of the visual image and the situated replaying of its projections, the film reveals a world anew, refracted differently in each iteration. In the hands of Abounaddara, the archive serves the function of an illumination of the past anew—the excavation of a stereotype in the service of a revisioning of the future. This gesture, which we see both here and in the counter-archival turn of a scholar such as Paula Amad, makes of the film both a model and a method for a certain artistic practice.[43] This is less an orthodox exercise in tethering the image to its meaning than a practice of untethering the image from its framework, expanding the horizon of cinema, and pushing sovereignty itself beyond the frame. The ricochet between frame and reframings makes possible the persistence of the past in the Lumière film and speaks to the potentials of a cinema that not only captures the world, but also serves as the groundwork to rethink the terms in which the world is seen. Such is the promise of the counter-archival practice.

The Sovereign Image?

I want to return us, in closing, to the potential of reenactment—to the generative role of an archival afterlife and to the possibilities born of reanimating the past. We have considered the public filmings of the Egyptian khedive (and the doubling of his body in two films between world and national cinema) and the general of the French occupation (whose assassination plays out as both justice and a potential anticolonial future). Part of what is captured by the Lumière camera are different frameworks of sovereignty (the khedive as a sovereign among sovereigns and the assassinated general), each of which is too easily subsumed under the rubric of globality, world cinema, or transnational cinema. The question is not simply one of pointing out the myopia of these global frameworks, but of proliferating imagined networks and possible futures from and for this material. The sovereignty of the image is challenged, we could say, by the seriality of the archive (positioning the khedive in a grammar of other sovereigns in film) and the sequencing that cinema itself entails (the frame-by-frame persistence of vision intrinsic to the medium).

When Jacques-Alain Miller reflects on what he deems the sovereign image, he does so to postulate a corollary to Lacan's master signifier in the realm of the imaginary.[44] When Roland Barthes writes of sovereign contingency in photography, he describes the absolute particularity of the moment captured by the camera, noting "what the Photograph reproduces to infinity, has only occurred once: the Photograph repeats mechanically what could never be repeated existentially."[45] Whether in psychoanalysis or phenomenology, the dream image or photography, in both instances, sovereignty functionally describes the image relationally—it delimits a relation of apprehension. The image of the sovereign, which is captured by the cinematograph, remains in motion over time. In this way, it unsettles the conventional iconic image of the sovereign by articulating his or her existence within the vernacular temporality of motion photography.

A rather different conception of sovereignty emerges in Ariella Azoulay's notion of potential history. "Sovereignty," she writes, "is not a centralized power whose commands from the top—to impose borders, control the interior of a territory, rule its population, set the law, and enforce laws—are unilaterally carried out." Instead, she suggests, "The sovereign is always one among many actors in the theater of sovereignty and does not have full control over the outcome of its many scenes."[46] Each of these writers, reflecting on sovereignty in markedly different ways, harnesses the ephemeral, fleeting, transient moment at stake.

The tyranny of national cinema is exercised in its appropriation of the Lumière films as historical documents with fixed meanings, rather than as fodder for unintended dimensions that exceed the frame. If there is an argument to be had about sovereignty, it is to put pressure on the element of chance, iteration, and reframing that can challenge even those films that seem most explicitly addressed to sovereigns in the visualization of royal courts. In the case of *Le Khédive et son escorte*, we confront an unsettling of national film histories. The figuration of Ottoman sovereignty challenges the frameworks for cultural production, circulation, and reception that would predominate just a few decades following Promio's visit. In this microhistory, we encounter a kernel of the seemingly unrealized future of world cinema.

I see in these various films a lesson for those of us engaged in comparative and historical work—the necessity of frames and reframings and the fact that in the empirical slips of archival details exist alternate imaginings of potential futures. In what I have traced here, we shift from the sovereignty of the image (in which we assume the text has its own authority) to the sovereignty of its reenactments (the hermeneutic possibilities of focusing on Egypt). Sovereignty here has been both figured in the image (films depicting sovereignty) and ultimately unsettled by an interpretative regime that comes to read, resurrect, and reanimate the image in a new light. This counter-archival practice, it strikes me, is a lesson in reanimating sovereignty against itself to imagine and envision future histories of world cinema.

5
History
The Duration of Myth

Among the thirty films from Promio's journey to Egypt, the film of the pyramids and the Sphinx, initially titled *Egypte: Les pyramides et le sphinx* and later, *Les Pyramides (vue générale)*, is both a stunning monument within early film history and a testament to the international spread of cinema from its very beginnings (Figure 20).[1] It consists of a single, almost 50-second shot that displays a visual archaeology divided into three planes: in the first, a row of travelers moving across the frame; in the second, the face of the Sphinx; and in the third, the towering pyramid. In the shot's careful composition, the four sides of the screen frame the face of the Sphinx, which looks off to the right, while behind it the pyramid towers above, truncated at the top by the limits of the frame. As each of the travelers passes by, rocking back and forth with the steps of the camels, the monuments come in and out of sight, eclipsed time and again by the frequently out-of-focus bodies. In a recent re-release of these Lumière films, the French director and former director of the Lumière Institute Bertrand Tavernier notes that "the confrontation between the people on the camels and the Sphinx and the pyramids impressed a lot of directors; an Egyptian director like Youssef Chahine . . . saw that it was very, very modern."[2] The camera's low angle and the depth of field lend the film characteristics of modern composition, but for audiences at the time, whether in Lyon, Cairo, or Jakarta, the seemingly incredible feat had much to do with *how* these sites were seen—in motion and in time.

Like many travelers before him, Promio journeyed to Alexandria, Cairo, Saqqara, Giza, Banha, Tukh, and along the Nile River, and in each of these locations, his films tend to focus on everyday scenes. Some depict iconic sites in Cairo (Qaṣr al-Nīl, Opéra, 'Aṭaba, Sayyida Zaynab), and others highlight

Figure 20. *Les Pyramides (vue générale)*, an 1897 Lumière film showing the pyramids at Giza.

ports, a funeral procession, and displays of artillery. His films include a series of eight panoramas from the banks of the Nile River—barges and feluccas traveling upstream, as well as workers along the shore (386–393). His travels to Saqqara include a scene under date trees (379) as well as a film of tourists visiting the sites (380). True to the framework that many of the global camera operators adopted, Promio's films tend to focus on people, labor, and city streets, and his journey to Toukh, like his film from Alexandria (361), includes a shot of a train (385). Only two films in the Lumière catalogue are listed from his visit to the pyramids: *Les Pyramides (vue générale)* (381) and *Descente de la grande pyramide* (382), and both entail shots of Egyptians cast against the backdrop of these iconic monuments. Far from serving as models of the Lumière catalogue, these two films of the mythical monuments stand out as exceptions, seemingly expected views from the trip through Egypt and unique in their mode of presentation.

In 1897, the same year as Promio's visit, Charles Piazzi Smyth delivered a magic lantern show of the Great Pyramid. Speaking alongside the projected images, he rehearsed a classic colonial trope that sought to distinguish the time of the monuments from contemporary Egyptians.[3] His racist comments bespeak a quest often shared among Orientalist artists to purge landscapes of humans, and in this instance, to purge the monuments from any connection to modern Arabs. "The Orientalist photograph often depopulates the Orient of its inhabitants," Ali Behdad tells us, "for their presence robs the image of its quest for a romantic monumentalism and circumvent the possibility of visual appropriation."[4] This "quest for a romantic monumentalism" meant that painters and photographers notoriously evacuated any indices that might situate the monuments within the contemporary moment. A perennial challenge for photographers was the technical blurring of humans in the print—something that famously occurs in the 1859 and 1860 six-volume album compiled by Louis de Clercq. Even seated figures in these photographs appear blurred, an occurrence that scholars such as Kathleen Stewart Howe have come to read as a meditation on time inscribed in the image.[5] In the debate between intentional smudging and photographic errors arises a common understanding that the Orientalist photograph, taken in the present, was meant to capture a distant past. In the work of photographers such as Piazzi Smyth (and Francis Frith among others), any humans, if present at all, were merely to provide a sense of scale. The Orientalist photograph was otherwise meant to gesture to the imagining of a distant past—a landscape out of time and out of place.

Turning to Promio's 1897 film, we might wonder what it is to see the monuments not as a photograph or a magic lantern show but captured by the cinematograph. What are the stakes, in other words, of capturing the supposed timelessness of the Great Pyramid in the vernacular temporality of the cinema? Part of what makes *Les Pyramides (vue générale)* so distinct—and a contrast to the magic lantern show—is the presence of the travelers in the image, shown in a medium shot traversing the screen. Far from evacuating the image of people, as was the case in painting and photography, Promio's film capitalizes on the fact that motion and time are best apprehended through their presence. Promio's film indexes both the travelers' movement traversing the frame and the duration of the scene itself, something that earlier photographs had a more difficult time harnessing. This is not to say that Promio's film does not share the Orientalist legacy in its subject matter (especially with the costumes worn by those in the film), but that it does so with a difference. To make this claim is not to divorce this film from its colonial past, but to consider its potential caveat to the conventional narrative in its formal excess. Unlike photographers, who answered François Arago's call to use the camera to capture ancient monuments and scripts, Promio turns his cinematograph on the pyramids and captures time itself—that is, the duration of cinematographic capture as apprehended through the motion of human bodies.[6]

This chapter focuses on how a single 50-second film of the pyramids shot during Promio's world tour makes the site at Giza visible in particular ways. What the film offers is less the novelty of seeing the pyramids, which were often depicted in paintings, lithographs, and photography, than the novelty of seeing them in time. I argue that this early film transforms the pyramids from a mythologized and abstracted object into a temporal event seen over the course of the film's duration. Juxtaposing the film alongside David Roberts's painting, *Approach of the Simoon*, I first explore how the film shifts the relation to the historical past located in the distinction between restoration and preservation. Then, turning to André Bazin's "The Ontology of the Photographic Image" and Alfred North Whitehead's theory of the event, I address how the film's realism derives less from what it depicts than from the duration of depiction itself. I challenge the thematic discussion of film in terms of objects and places and invite us to consider the implications of cinematic time. I turn in the final section of the chapter to Youssef Chahine's science fiction rendering of Promio's film to weigh the postcolonial possibilities of reframing time itself. What is ultimately at stake is an effort to consider the interpretative world of this early film and the challenges it poses to a transnational history of film form.

Perfecting Place

Promio's film *Les Pyramides (vue générale)* was by no means novel for what it offered thematically to audiences, nor was it necessarily novel for being projected to audiences in Egypt. Its contents and the seeming continuity it performs with Orientalist painting make it appear little different from visual material that predates it. By the end of the nineteenth century, the pyramids, for audiences across the globe, were well known within the visual archive and travel writings on Egypt.[7] In fact, it was the prevalence of Egyptian motifs in art and architecture of this period that led Sir John Sloane to proclaim a predominant "Egyptian mania."[8] Artists ranging from David Roberts to Elihu Vedder sketched and painted the Sphinx and the pyramids years prior to Promio's cinematic depiction, and they often did so with stereotypically costumed figures as a condition of contextualization. From Jean-François Champollion's translation of the Rosetta Stone in 1822 to King Louis-Philippe's placement of the obelisk at the Place de la Concorde in 1833, Egypt came to be known through its objects, and these objects spoke of a particular land whose history was understood as much artistically and imaginatively as it was through archaeology and excavation.

It is likely because the content was well known that the film could astound audiences as it did. At a projection of the film held in Lyon on April 25, 1897, spectators supposedly marveled at what a Lyon-based newspaper described as "une idée si parfaite de ces antiques et majesteux monuments [so perfect an idea of these antique and majestic monuments]."[9] Even though these "majestic monuments" had often been the subject of representation, Promio's arrival signaled something different. Early spectators were able to behold perfection not simply as static depiction, but as vivid and animated duration.[10] The film provided the unique opportunity for audiences across the world to see these mythological monuments actually unfolding over time: that is to say, the pyramids and the Sphinx, glossed and refined for centuries in paintings, found, in 1897, their incarnation as history—or in the words of the French film theorist, André Bazin, "embalmed in time."[11] The awe that led European travelers for centuries to describe the sublime experience of seeing the pyramids was here approximated, as though magically, in time for audiences across the world.

That the account of the audience describes the film as "so perfect an idea [une idée si parfaite]" is quite revealing—perfection takes on particular significance when it comes to the viewing experience that film offered. Early spectators, as Tom Gunning's research adeptly points out, were *not* ignorant hordes duped into believing the illusion presented on-screen—instead, the arrival of film made possible an extensive discussion of what it is to see.[12] As early as July 1903, when the Arabic-language journal *al-Muqtataf* published a short entry on the cinematograph, it focused much less on any one film than it did on the trick of the eye that made it possible to see the illusion of movement over the duration of a film.[13] The entry discussed the technological dimensions of the moving picture alongside other phenomena, such as the magic lantern (*al-fānūs al-saharī*) and seemingly unrelated issues such as the cataract at Aswan (*shallāl Aswān*). What concerns the author is the illusion by which distinct images appear in a single moving picture (*ṣūra wāḥida mutaḥarrika*), and he describes the persistence of vision initially by pointing to the effect of spinning a lit match in a circle. In the article, he does not allude to any one particular film but tries to dissect the components of the cinematic illusion. He does not see films as a simple index of what is placed in front of the cinematograph, but rather as an occasion to consider how the image was made visible to the observer.

But even if early spectators were not duped into believing they were actually at the pyramids, what was the status of perfection that the film offered? If one answer focuses on technical discussions of seeing, then another answer focuses on how the film indexes the site, incarnating the here and now of the moment in 1897. In 1902, American, Austrian, German, Italian, and Egyptian teams, building on meticulous studies performed in the nineteenth century, set forth on a project to excavate the site of the Sphinx at Giza.[14] Working from preliminary mappings, in 1905, eight years following the Lumière film, one of the most monumental restorations began, lifting the sands around the base of the Sphinx and uncovering an entire landscape of temples that had been buried around the Sphinx's body. With the archaeological restoration of the landscape, the monument was perfected—differently. And with this perfection came a rather remarkable shift: From restoring the grandeur of these monuments through imaginative writings and travelers' accounts came the goal of restoring them from the weathering processes of history through archaeological excavation. The work of the numerous international teams brought the site into view in such a way as to restore how it might have appeared at the moment it was constructed.

Looking at the Lumière film now is to look upon a moment in the past when the landscape of the Sphinx lay partially covered by the weathering processes of time, hidden under the sands of Clio. In a curious twist, the film reveals the pre-restoration site at Giza and embalms the processes of history prior to the archaeological restoration. But the film also offers us a particular interpretative world, making the site visible in a particular way. Cast alongside the other films of the Lumière Brothers' global cinematic network, *Les Pyramides (vue générale)* becomes a sort of document to be viewed in the serialization of other global places. It does not possess its context, but becomes reproducible as an event within a series of these global films. It gestures at once to a moment in 1897 embalmed on celluloid and to a moment before the monumental restorations of 1905. We may speculate as to the terms of perfection that the film offered its audiences, but in doing so, it is worth considering another deserted history of an alternate interpretative world and an alternate relationship to the site.

Picturing the Past

In August 1838, the Scottish artist David Roberts departed from London for a journey to Egypt and then onward through the Holy Lands. He returned almost one year later with nearly three hundred drawings and three sketchbooks filled with material. With the help of Louis Haghe, a close friend and a liaison to the Moon publishing house, Roberts set out to transform his watercolors into lithographs, which were in turn reproduced and sold throughout Europe. From 1842 until 1855, Roberts's collection of paintings was issued in twenty parts and displayed at various locations in London and Edinburgh to help raise money to finance the project. By 1855, over ten years after Roberts's return, the lithographer successfully completed the 247 lithographs to be included in a version of the book, *The Holy Land, Syria, Idumea, Arabia, Egypt, and Nubia*.[15]

After arriving in Alexandria on September 24, 1838, Roberts journeyed up the Nile to Cairo, following a path similar to the journey Promio undertook years later. In fact, much like Promio, Roberts collected images from all over Egypt, and among a number of his trips, he too traveled to Giza where he produced images of the Sphinx and the Great Pyramid. Roberts's visits to various locations were remarkable in large part for the distinct visual form he offered to sites likely familiar to most of his public. His sketches, watercolors, and lithographs not only portrayed various historic scenes and monuments, but they assisted in the visualization of events known primarily through scripture and historical writings. Roberts's numerous on-site sketches served less as an index for what was present before his eyes than as a basis from which he could imagine how historical scenes might have looked. Engaged in a critical operation of visualizing and reconstructing the grandeur of a past moment, Roberts's sketches embellished what was seen with what effect it could produce, and the lithograph ensured the reproduction and printing of this material for a wide public.

Among a number of paintings from Giza, Roberts's *Approach of the Simoon, Desert of Gizeh* is perhaps his most famous, as well as one of the most romantically embellished (Figure 21). The painting depicts the Sphinx, staring to the left of the frame, with the pyramids in the background, filling the right side. A group of soldiers approaches from the lower-left corner and spans the bottom, while a large, circular sun, glowing in a golden red, fills out the left. Stunning as the composition of the painting is, it was not entirely accurate in a mimetic sense. The difficulty, as William Holman Hunt suggested to Charles Dickens, the painting's owner, is quite simply that the Sphinx faces the wrong direction. It is not possible to see the Sphinx from the perspective shown if the sun is rising or setting in the location indicated in the painting. Dickens, who admired the painting greatly, excused the re-facing of the Sphinx as "a poetical conception."[16] The truth, after all, was not embedded in the precise depiction of the objects as seen, but rather in a depiction evocative of the grandeur and scale of scenes described in sacred and historical writings.

In its evocation of the grandeur of these monuments, Roberts's painting embeds within it a certain relation to the past with implications for what it is to see, shifting toward what Philip Rosen notes as a distinction between restoration and preservation.[17] For Rosen, whereas preservation entails the effort to maintain a site in all of its contradictions, leaving bare the weathering of time as part of the site's specificity, restoration entails bringing the site itself back in

Figure 21. David Roberts, *Approach of the Simoon, Desert of Gizeh*, lithograph executed by Louis Haghe after Roberts, 1846–1849.

time, to its moment of functional novelty. Although Roberts's relationship to these sites predates the type of historical work described in Rosen's study, it does underscore a relationship to the past that is less the scientific approximation of what is than the effort to reconstruct what might have been. In this restorative process, the vision to which the scene corresponds is a vision furnished not through harnessing the scene empirically so much as through a recollection of its description in scripture and the historical record. It is this vision that makes Roberts's reorientation of the Sphinx an important part of rendering the affective history of the site.

Shortly following the publication of Roberts's work, one reviewer suggested that the compilation of lithographs and watercolors was "one of the most valuable publications of our day—vividly illustrating our readings in history, sacred as well as profane."[18] And yet another review, referring to the trips through the Holy Lands, suggested, "It has been the aim of Mr. Roberts to portray every object associated with Scripture—to bring vividly before us every architectural remain, and every feature of natural scenery which can give reality to the incidents of sacred writings, or impress us with deeper conviction of their truth, and elevate our reverential feelings."[19] For both of these reviewers, the strength of Roberts's work was not in its status as a document of what was there, but rather its remarkable manner of "illustrating our readings in history," an integral part of what was necessary to "impress" the viewer. In his sketches and paintings, Roberts went to great lengths to correct what was seen, embellishing sites with the addition of people to provide scale and shifting rocks and hills as suited the overall aesthetic arrangement of the artistic composition.

It is telling that contemporary reviewers of Roberts's work employed the terms "reality" and "truth" to describe his endeavor and that they used these terms *not* in reference to what his works portrayed, but to the "incidents of sacred writings." In the reviewers' understanding, the paintings' "reality" stands in relation less to some world to be known in synchronous geographic or spatial terms than to historical scenes described in scripture. When Roberts visited various sites throughout the Holy Lands, he looked upon them through a given framework: Their significance derived from the stories and traditions that made them meaningful. For the artist, as for his contemporary reviewer, the scenes come alive by virtue of what is known of them through knowledge of history and scripture. Much of what Roberts sees at the various sites entails a mode of sight not necessarily available to the naked eye, but integral to the trained sensibility. The realism implicit in these paintings points ultimately to a world whose truth resides less in empirical observation than in the supposed truth of scripture. The theory of representation is not mimetic so much as restorative, aspiring to reconstruct visually what is described in writing.

The frequent allusions to the truth of scripture both in reviews and in Roberts's own rhetoric demarcates a rather pronounced shift. Roberts's work inscribes a particular conception of artistic function and one whose terms do not graft so easily on discussions of realism. Roberts's artistic goal is to "elevate our reverential feelings" notably *not* for the scene itself, but for the "truth" of the sacred writings. For Roberts, the very terms of the world and what it means to represent it turn not toward a mimetic drive, but toward an affirmation of a truth whose basis is in scripture and historical writings. In this sense, Roberts's conception of artistic practice marks a relationship to the visual image that itself has a particular history.

Hans Frei offers a means of understanding this transformation regarding the place of truth in the analysis of scripture. In his work on biblical hermeneutics during the eighteenth and nineteenth centuries, he suggests that "the meaning of the text was no longer the text's depiction, even if it was agreed that the text was indeed realistic in character. Its realistic character was identified either with its factual reliability or with a unique realistic spirit in the tradition that produced the text."[20] Frei goes on to discuss how understanding "realistic features of biblical narrative" often entailed "encompassing them in a larger framework or category of explanation." He clarifies his point:

> If that interpretative framework was itself realistic it involved a historical reconstruction of the specific occurrences or general conditions from which the text arose. It meant bringing the world as a network of naturally explicable and undisrupted physical, mental, and social connections to bear on the text, on the assumption that this was indeed the real world into which the world of the text could be ranged by the appropriate reconstruction of the explicative sense.[21]

Frei's argument is attentive to histories of interpretation and notes how realism gives rise to a concept of "explicative sense," whose terms involve "a historical reconstruction of the specific occurrences or general conditions from which the text arose." In Roberts's lithograph, historical reconstruction runs a seemingly reverse course, grounding the reimagination of the scene in the world made thinkable in sacred readings.

To understand the gravity of the transformation from Roberts's lithographs to the Lumière film is to begin to explain how reference shifts from sacred writings to an observable world. Part of the transformation entails the displacement of truth from sacred writings to a world of peoples, places, and things. What is displaced, in other words, is the relationship between reference and object and ultimately the very relationship to the historical past. What we notice, then, as scholars analyzing these two texts, compels us to consider less the object depicted through the medium than the presumptions animated by the discourse in which the medium comes to be read. For Roberts, with his reorientation of the Sphinx, the art of historical restoration entails reimagination of the scene in its particularity during a moment in the distant past. In the film, we encounter a temporality of a different sort, embalmed in the play of light and shadows over the course of the 50-second projection.

The Image of Duration

When André Bazin published "The Ontology of the Photographic Image" (later included in his four-volume *What Is Cinema?*), he found at Giza the basis of his filmic theory of history. In this now-canonical essay, Bazin does not focus explicitly on the pyramids, but on their contents as figured in mummification and embalming. For Bazin, the novelty of cinematic realism lies in its capacity to stage duration, or as he writes, "Now, for the first time, the image of things is likewise the image of their duration, change mummified."[22] Oft quoted as this line is, it underscores part of an extended metaphor in which ancient Egypt serves as the origin of "the psychology of the image."[23] Throughout the first section of Bazin's essay, the photograph is integrally tied to mummification: "For photography does not create eternity, as art does, it embalms time."[24] Staged between embalming and mummification, Bazin's understanding of realism returns us to the site of the early Lumière film; and many of his reflections on time are themselves already theorized, or perhaps even embalmed, within this 1897 film.

Recent scholarship criticizes the tendency to see Bazin's essay as nothing more than naïve realism based on a reductive understanding of the index.[25] Against this line of argument, Daniel Morgan draws attention to the metaphors employed in Bazin's essay and notes that the examples of the snowflake and flower are not simple indices in the semiotic sense.[26] In a related claim, Tom Gunning argues that Bazin's essay does not rest on a correspondence theory between an object and its photograph.[27] But turning to Bazin's references to Egypt, we are led to consider the ways mummification and embalming animate the psychological dimensions in "the story of resemblance."[28] Bazin's often-shifting metaphors quite poetically draw us away from reference and lead us to consider realism as it is implicated in time. This axis of his essay is not so much overlooked by but subordinated in purely semiotic models. What Bazin finds at Giza is less the object world of ancient Egypt than a figure for considering relationships to time.

Whereas Roberts's painting locates the incidents from which to evoke the truth of sacred writings, Bazin's argument invokes the mythological Egyptian past differently. Bazin's essay begins with what he calls "the mummy complex," which he describes as the preservative impulse implicit in the practice of mummification:

> The religion of ancient Egypt aimed against death, saw survival as depending on the continued existence of the corporeal body. To preserve, artificially, his bodily appearance is to snatch it from the flow of time, to stow it away neatly, so to speak, in the hold of life. It was natural, therefore, to keep up appearances in the face of the reality of death by preserving flesh and bone.[29]

He notes, though, that terra cotta statuettes were placed alongside the mummies "as substitute mummies which might replace the bodies if these were destroyed."[30] He thus understands mummification less as an affirmation of the "ontological identity of model and image" than as a practice of a different sort. "It is no longer," Bazin tells us, "a question of survival after death, but of a larger concept, the creation of an ideal world in the likeness of the real, with its own temporal destiny."[31] Bazin's essay distinguishes between the aesthetic and the psychological in the plastic arts, and ancient Egypt functions as a point of departure in this broader "story of resemblance" that extends from perspective in fifteenth-century painting to the photographs of Nicéphore Niépce and the films of Lumière.[32] In this story, realism has less to do with the simple representation of an object than with the "creation of an ideal world . . . with its own temporal destiny."

What Bazin describes in his essay, replete as it is with references to Egypt, actually invokes a very different understanding of the historical past than does the Roberts's painting. If, for Roberts, the novelty of the realistic portrayal of the monument involves imagining a historical matrix within which to affirm the truth of scripture, then for Bazin, Egypt functions as part of an argumentative gesture toward the conception of time, preservation, and duration. The references to Egypt, in other words, are not to index some world whose verifiability is to be affirmed through excavation, but rather to describe a sensibility linked analogically to the emergence of photography and, as he states it, "the psychology of the image." Underscoring the durational aspects of the cinematic image, Bazin writes, "The cinema is objectivity in time":

> The film is no longer content to preserve the object, enshrouded as it were in an instant, as the bodies of insects are preserved intact, out of the distant past, in amber. The film delivers baroque art from its convulsive catalepsy. Now, for the first time, the image of things is likewise the image of their duration, change mummified as it were.[33]

When Bazin employs the term "change mummified," he invokes a curious shift between figural reading and literal reading, drawing upon Egyptian material in order to explain duration. It seems that Egypt, for Bazin, is less a place than the particularity of a historical practice of mummification, here decontextualized for the purposes of explaining the dynamics of duration. And yet it is difficult to ignore the extent to which Bazin's writings are themselves replete with references to Egypt.

Compelling arguments suggest that Egypt could not have been an entirely random example at the time when Bazin composed his essay. Antonia Lant points out that Bazin's remarks likely drew from a prevalent discourse linking Egypt and visual representation. She suggests that nineteenth-century Egyptomania "became essential to debates over cinema itself, and it was this legacy to which Bazin, inevitably, referred."[34] She gestures to debates on Bazin's realism in the pages of *Screen* during the 1960s and more recently in the work of scholars such as John Belton and Philip Rosen, but her intervention ultimately connects Bazin's rhetoric of Egypt to the "sheer extent of the evidence of the overlap between Victorian visions of Egypt and early motion picture culture."[35] Her claims address motion picture culture both in terms of film content and in terms of a visual history of material, including architectural design and urban monuments.

Taking Bazin's argument into account, what if the realism at the heart of his essay is concerned not so much with what is seen, but with its duration? What if, in other words, we understand Bazin's references to Egypt—in terms of mummification and embalming—not so much as thematizations of place but as a relationship to time? An exclusive emphasis on visuality tends to focus on the appearance of the image over and against the novelty of its duration, but Bazin is employing mummification and terra cotta statuettes less for the purposes of visuality than for an exploration of the psychological dimensions of time. For Bazin, in a curious figural twist, ancient Egypt disappears as a remnant of an argumentative example about the interactions between preservation, duration, and time.

Years before Bazin's essay, Alfred North Whitehead's *The Concept of Nature* also turned to the Great Pyramid as a "well-known fact" to which he could "safely appeal as an illustration."[36] The illustration he provided, however, was short-lived, and his essay went on to disarticulate the object in the language of the event, taking the so-called Great Pyramid from its status as a "well-known fact" to nothing less than an "illustration" animated with temporal disjunction.

> I have taken the existence of the Great Pyramid as a fairly well-known fact to which I could safely appeal as an illustration. This is a type of event which exhibits itself to us as the situation of a recognizable object; and in the example chosen the object is so widely recognized that it has received a name. An object is an entity of a different type from an event. For example, the event which is the life of nature within the Great Pyramid yesterday and today is divisible into two parts, namely the Great Pyramid yesterday and the Great Pyramid today. But the recognizable object which is also called the Great Pyramid is the same object to-day as it was yesterday.[37]

In this process, convoluted though it may seem, Whitehead conceptualizes the very grounds of knowing and naming by implicating perception and time in a newly forged language of the event. Deleuze would later describe Whitehead's work in his study of the Baroque, which charts a path for the reconsideration of history, predicated on a problem of knowing, naming, and being.[38]

The presence of the Great Pyramid in the theory of the event is by no means haphazard. In fact, in Whitehead's use of the Great Pyramid as an example, he throws into question not only the seemingly eternal history of the mythological monument, but also the manner by which it is perceived: Time transforms the object into a manifold scattering of objects, based on a manifold scattering of the "here and now." With this in mind, the object at stake in Whitehead's theory of the event is an object predicated on the particularity of time, to be known and perceived as such on the basis of its specific existence at a specific moment. When dealing with the Lumière film at Giza, we deal precisely in this realm of the today and yesterday, and we do so by virtue of the cinematic nature of the image, which provides an even more temporally bound understanding of the objects at stake on-screen, framed as they are in the language of the event.

There is a curious way in which cinema makes possible the theorization of the event upon which Whitehead embarks. His discussion of an object over time draws us back to studies of the moving image and the scrutiny of an object frame by frame. We might think here of the work of Eadweard Muybridge, whose motion studies entailed the disarticulation of a scene into discrete photographic moments.[39] The event, however, is not the moment of each frame, imperceptible as such, but the semblance of continuity: that is, the duration that makes this perception possible. The tension, then, between the momentary glance at the object and the frame-by-frame depiction of objects underscores a fundamental principle operative in *Les Pyramides (vue générale)*. In this film, far from observing a single object, we view the object in time; and it is precisely because it is seen in time that we can begin to speak of something such as an event, upon which the novel notion of duration emerges.

For Bazin as for Whitehead and ultimately Deleuze, the Great Pyramid is an occasion less for the reflection on Egyptian semiology (as it is for Vachel Lindsay's or Sergei Eisenstein's allusions to film hieroglyphics or Hegel's and Derrida's discussions of symbol) than for understanding the complex interactions of time, perception, and the event.[40] To speak, then, of the film as embedded in the object world of Egypt is to miss the particularity by which film makes thinkable Egypt in an entirely new manner: the transformation of the timeless, seemingly eternal Great Pyramid into the immediacy of the 50-second actuality film. What is theorized in this film, above and beyond the look at the pyramids, is the repetition of a procession across the bottom of the screen, which, more than ever before, alludes not mythologically to the monuments out there, but to the anti-monument that is the film. And perhaps even more than a photograph, embalming an instant upon it, the film of the pyramids monumentalizes neither the pyramids nor those traveling at the bottom of the screen, but the very dynamics of cinematic time.[41]

Cinematic Futures

In the 1995 film *Lumière et compagnie*, Youssef Chahine was one of over forty global directors commissioned to use the cinematograph to commemorate the centennial anniversary of the Lumière Brothers' first screening. For his contribution, Chahine focused his attention on the legacy of *Les Pyramides (vue générale)* in the history of Egyptian film, and he turned—as Promio had years before—to the pyramids at Giza.[42] As though re-creating the scene from 1897, Chahine's film puts on display the scene of filming the pyramids with a cinematograph. In a sort of wink at the audience, one filmmaker wears a black jacket with "LU" in white lettering and the other wears a white jacket with "MIÈRE" in black lettering. These two filmmakers, a playful nod to the Lumière Brothers themselves, are shot from a distance as part of the broader landscape, their figures framed against the backdrop of the three pyramids towering over them. Where Promio's film depicts travelers riding camels across the screen, Chahine opts to stage a spectacle that frames the act of filming. As the two figures in the foreground film the pyramids, a third figure slowly emerges from deep space, lumbering up a hill and toward the camera. In a fit of rage, this figure throws the cinematograph to the ground, stomps on it angrily, and then lumbers further forward, up a hill, and eventually off-screen. As this figure departs, the two filmmakers turn in disbelief, initially staring perplexed at each other and then at the figure running out of frame (Figures 22a, 22b, and 22c). Like the Promio film to which it pays homage, Chahine's film ends as the camera runs out of film, leaving the unexpected happening it has staged hanging indeterminately in the air.

What is remarkable about Chahine's short film is the reflexivity it offers not only with regard to the act of filming, but also to the collision of registers at stake in cinematic time. On a first level is the sort of mythological time of the pyramids, which serves as a sign of the location itself and as a testament to the monumental grandeur of the site. On a second level is the historical time of the two camera operators filming, which re-creates the scene of filming in 1897 as part of Promio's Egyptian series. And a third level involves Chahine's introduction of an element of science fiction—that is, the figure of the alien charging onto the scene. With this third level, Chahine puts into relief both the historical past of the image (in the mimicry of the formal style of the Lumière film, the thematic staging of the act of filming, and the monumental pyramids depicted) and the potential future (in the use of an alien arising from out of time and out of place). Where Promio's figures pass in front of the camera as part of the overall mise-en-scène, clad in costumes and atop camels, Chahine's figures are themselves estranged from the scene: The two camera

Figures 22a–c. Stills from Youssef Chahine's contribution to the 1995 commemorative film *Lumière et compagnie*: filming sequence, staged attack, and science-fiction vignette.

operators register as foreign to the scene just as the alien appears as otherworldly. In Chahine's iterative replay of Promio's film, we find less a preservative or restorative version of the past than a flirtation with a cinematic future, even if predicated on the destruction of the camera on-screen.

If we have considered Promio's film and Roberts's painting as different conceptions of history, then how might we understand what Chahine's film offers? It could well seem that Chahine highlights a certain nihilism through which to apprehend the destruction of the act of filming. Not only does he echo the historical scene, he twists it by allowing his 1995 centennial film to visualize the act of its destruction. And yet what this film visualizes, it should be noted, is not only the destruction of the cinematograph by the alien, but a perspective on this scene that persists beyond its end. Unlike Promio's film, Chahine's film includes a soundtrack. As the camera operator clad in the black jacket cranks the cinematograph, we hear the whirring of the camera, which registers as diegetic sound. When the alien attacks, or even a moment or two before, this whirring sound stops, and the scene proceeds without sound. Is this, we might wonder, the fate of cinema? What we have is the destruction of an apparatus (and its sound) that leaves in its wake the ubiquity of the vision. It takes cinema to witness the destruction of the cinematograph—far from visualizing the downfall of a medium or even its colonial history, we witness its end cinematically.

Alongside the restorative and preservative impulses of the historical approach to the image, then, Chahine's film reveals the possibilities of the future of cinema. In the context of *Lumière et compagnie*, his film does not begin or end with the black-and-white vignette. Before it appears, there is an image of Chahine directing the film. "Al-Taṣwīr ḥarām," a voice calls out, as we see the film proceed in its own way. This science fiction version of the pyramids reveals less the miracle of the cinematograph than a cinematic perspective of its destruction. In seeing the cinematograph on-screen, we both witness a scene of recording and its end—and we persist beyond the destruction we behold. Through Chahine's modern gaze, the pyramids creatively shimmer between past and future, the realism of the scene heightened by visualizing the apparatus fated to disappear.

Chahine's film is both a gesture to science fiction and a formal layering of cinematic time, which manages to enrich and complicate the horizon of the pyramids. In the emergence of various figures, the ultimate alien is the cinematograph, but in a curious twist, the vision it offers is what persists beyond its own destruction. This lesson, it seems, exceeds the thematic retribution visualized on-screen and positions Chahine himself as what we might call the triumphant visionary of the scene. There are echoes in this refrain to the work of

Gil Hochberg and Hoda El Shakry, who have each in different ways explored the possibilities of science fiction in the context of modern Arabic literature.[43] A filmmaker such as Larissa Sansour layers the complexities of archaeology and visuality in the context of Palestine, and the work of art, in these conversations, plays the remarkable role of visualizing both past and future differently.[44] In a popular context, Chahine here gestures to the mythology of the pyramids through the monument of the early Lumière film to imagine a particular retribution in a twist of speculative counterfactual history.

The Cinematic Event

To return to the Lumière Brothers' film, the single 50-second shot presents a number of objects, and these objects index a certain place, and this certain place emerges in an instant of historical filming on a day in 1897. Roberts's painting harkens back to a moment, restoring the pyramids to their past grandeur, while Bazin figures the pyramids as part of a theory of time, and Whitehead enfolds them in a theory of the event. The film, though, offers neither a history of the object nor the presentation of its mythological significance, but it stages a problem of seeing the mythological past in the 50-second duration of cinematic time. In the film, the mythological status of the pyramid is collapsed into the spectacle of duration.

Where the film *preserves* the image of the pyramids in 1897, embalming them in time, Roberts's painting *restores* the pyramids by imagining how they might have been at a moment referenced in the historical and scriptural record. The contrast between the two images lies in the following distinction: The film presents a set place, at a set time, and observable in the moving image for a global audience; and the painting relies upon a body of knowledge, gleaned from scripture and the historical record, that enables the vision presented. We have, in other words, one image, the Lumière film, which offers observation in time, and another image, the Roberts's painting, which offers an imaginative restoration of the scene according to historical writing and scripture. My argument has been that we need to read cinema not as a simple index of what is represented on-screen, but in terms of a relationship to time made thinkable in the visual encounter: Initially, the distinction between preservation and restoration, and then second, the logic of durational event as it plays out in the scattering of perception. This argument ultimately points us to the distinction between realism embedded in time and realism embedded in objects.

As film scholars, we often anchor our analysis in the object world of the text. A text like this early Lumière film, for example, could be read as an Egyptian film on account of what it presents on-screen. At the same time, it could be seen to shatter the boundaries of a national paradigm of intellectual inquiry. It is, after all, a film produced with the labor of a French production company, an Italian camera operator, and Egyptian assistants with an audience spanning the globe. But here I have outlined a different set of considerations focused on the perceptual world through which the site is made visible. *Les Pyramides (vue générale)* shares more in common with an emergent idiom of global representation (which links together all of these early Lumière films) than it does with the visual history of the site it documents. The film, then, cannot simply be situated as an Egyptian film of the pyramids—it offers us, instead, insight into the semiotic ideology of early cinema in its global travel. Undertaking a visual archaeology of the site and excavating the deserted histories of this Lumière film ultimately invites the challenge of charting a transnational history of film form.

In the following chapter, we track the cinematograph on a voyage from Jaffa to Jerusalem as it proceeds along a well-traveled railway route. What we see at this site is a world that expands with the backward movement of the camera, and what we encounter is a manner of seeing with an expanded frame. On a train departing the station in Jerusalem, Promio makes visible the basis for the epistemology of the tracking shot.

6
Tracks
Tracking the World in/as Cinema

It is perhaps surprising that Promio's trip through Ottoman Palestine includes so many films of the Jaffa-Jerusalem railway. The railway, heralded as the first of its kind in the Middle East, opened in 1892, just a few years before Promio's 1897 voyage. The construction was overseen by Yosef Navon, who initially sought financing in Istanbul before finally securing French support. The railway connected two major cities, the port city of Jaffa and the provincial capital Jerusalem, both of which served as strategic sites for the Ottoman government as well as part of a well-trodden pilgrimage route for tourists.[1] Of the fifteen films catalogued during Promio's visit to Ottoman Palestine, four feature this renowned trainline: an arrival of a train at the station in Jaffa (394), two films shot from the train en route to Jerusalem (399 and 400), and a final shot departing the station in Jerusalem (408). Add to this list a film of a boat (398) and a caravan of camels (407), and Promio's trek through the Holy Land is almost as committed to filming infrastructure and transport as it is the more iconic and expected scenes of the Church of the Holy Sepulchre (404) and the Via Dolorosa (403).[2] The novelty of Promio's train films was not simply that they depicted transport, but that they featured experiments in what it meant to see motion. In three of these train films, the cinematograph was mounted on the moving locomotive, employing a technique that would come to be known as the tracking shot and ultimately revolutionize how the world would be seen cinematically.

Of all the possible trains to address, I focus in this chapter on a comparative inquiry into two tracks in the history of world cinema, both drawn from the Lumière Brothers catalogue: the first, *Départ de Jérusalem en chemin de fer* (408), and the second, the famed *Arrivée d'un train à La Ciotat* (653). Allow me to place them in parallel here:

Figure 23. *Départ de Jérusalem en chemin de fer*, an 1897 Lumière film offering a panoramic view from the railway station in Jerusalem.

Track 1: Sometime in April 1897, Promio positioned his cinematograph on the back of a train departing a station in Jerusalem (Figure 23).[3] A row of five mustached men dressed in suits tip their hats to the departing train. With each passing moment, the film reveals more of the space and more of those gathered on the platform: a cluster of men, a woman with an ornate hat, then a man who crosses the track as others walk slowly forward, outpaced by the departing locomotive. Each tipped hat affirms the camera as a participant in the scene, one whose backward motion is a counterpoint to the speed of those walking. What is missing from this film is not the people (a common trope of the Orientalist landscape tradition), but the train itself. And yet its departure from the station reveals an entire world in the faces, clothing, and gestures of those bidding it farewell.

Track 2: Sometime in the summer of 1897, the Lumière Brothers shot one of three films documenting the arrival of a train at the station in La Ciotat, near their family summer residence (Figure 24). In contrast to the tracking shot from Jerusalem, here the camera is positioned at a stationary point on the platform as the train approaches from deep space. A porter appears with a

Figure 24. *Arrivée d'un train à La Ciotat*, the celebrated Lumière film of a train arriving at the station in La Ciotat.

cart in the foreground, and the train bellows smoke from its stack as it travels forward. Onlookers wait on the platform: an older woman in a plaid shawl, men clad in suits, and eventually a young girl in a white dress who crosses the line of those gathered for the train. Once the train pulls into the station, passengers file from the exits, while those waiting on the platform eventually find their way on board. With these various layers and scales of action, we have what the early commentator Félix Regnault described with awe as a phenomenon in which "one has the impression of depth and relief, even though it is a single image that unfolds before our eyes."[4]

Where the train at La Ciotat has been read as a critical site in film theory, the train in Jerusalem disappears into the archive of Middle East films, its theoretical importance subordinated to its geographical location. Pairing these two paradigmatic trains, we confront contrasting afterlives of arrival and departure, film history and film theory, and contextual and formal reading. Crossing the tracks, as I hope to do in what follows, means engaging the world made visible at this intersection of La Ciotat and Jerusalem. I draw here from histories of the tracking shot but aim to expand the world of world cinema to question when, how, and where the techniques and principles of film form are made thinkable. What is it to place the history of the tracking shot in the context of Middle East visual culture? How might we reconcile the specificity of place with the common emergence of formal visual techniques?

The answer to these questions is not an origin story—or at least not one that places the Middle East at its center. As any good film historian knows, Promio's supposed invention of the tracking shot took place not in Jerusalem, but in Italy, where, months prior, he had mounted the cinematograph on a gondola passing through the Grand Canal. "It was in Italy," Promio writes in his travelogue, "that I first had the idea of making panoramic views [*vues panomariques*]."[5] He continues, "When I arrived in Venice and went by boat from the train station to my hotel on the Grand Canal, I watched the banks fleeing in front of the gondola, and I thought that if the immobile cinema allows us to reproduce moving objects, then perhaps we could turn the proposal around and try to reproduce immobile objects as mobile with the help of the cinema."[6] And then, moving from idea to implementation, he sought approval for this new technique from the Lumière company: "I immediately made a reel that I sent to Lyon with a request to tell me what Mr. Louis Lumière thought of this experiment. The response was positive."[7] It is this published recollection, part of the travelogue in Coissac's book, that helps memorialize Promio as the inventor of what we now call the tracking shot.

Beyond the framework Promio's travelogue provides, it is worth noting how he highlights a broader tension between mobility and immobility. Most obvious is that Promio describes the physical scene in Venice as he travels from the train to his hotel by boat along the Grand Canal. Here we encounter world cinema as the movement of the camera operator from one physical location to another thanks to the underlying mobility of the cinematograph. There is, however, an additional register that Promio offers in his recollection—namely, a move from idea to action. This second move arises as he recounts his thought pattern while traveling on the gondola. His travelogue shifts in the description from terms of his location—"I arrived . . . and went"—to terms of observation and reflection—"I watched"—and ultimately—"I thought." His thinking offers a curious inversion of mobility and immobility: "If the immobile cinema allows us to reproduce moving objects, then perhaps we could turn the proposal around and try to reproduce immobile objects as mobile with the help of the cinema."[8] It is this flip, which makes immobile objects mobile, that transforms the static world into a world in motion and that has such broad implications for how we see. I underscore these various movements (of location and of thinking) because of what they reveal about world cinema not simply as a matter of location, but as an animation of the world in motion and time.

The seismic implications of Promio's technique—thought and idea, mobility and immobility—are by no means lost upon subsequent film historians. Georges Sadoul would eventually reproduce Promio's lines in his own discussion of the tracking shot: "We could perhaps turn the proposition around and reproduce immobile objects using mobile cinema."[9] At the time of Sadoul's writing in 1949, the tracking shot was already a common film technique, and it was prescient that even years earlier Promio had understood the implications of the mobile camera as he had. Like Sadoul, Jean Mitry would also return to Promio's famous film from the gondola in Venice, and he would add to his reflections an analysis of a film shot from the téléphérique at Mont Blanc.[10] Whether gondola, train, or téléphérique, each of these modes of transport puts the camera in motion to reveal the world anew, and whether Promio, Sadoul, or Mitry, each of these commentators highlights the intellectual implications of this shot as an important step within the history of cinema.

Traveling onward from Italy, Promio would go on to reproduce his technique for the mobile camera at other sites around the world, notably, for our purposes here, on his trip from Jaffa to Jerusalem. *Départ de Jérusalem en chemin de fer* is not itself foundational, nor even referenced in Promio's travelogue, and that might in fact be the point. What the film highlights is the ubiquity of a certain way of seeing the world—from Venice to Mont Blanc to Jerusalem. Already when Promio shot his film in 1897, there was elsewhere the phenomenon of the phantom ride, which involved a camera mounted to the front of a train. This technique is often credited to the American Mutoscope's 1897 film *The Haverstraw Tunnel* as its origin, and it was reproduced quite widely and not always with direct acknowledgment that such experiments were occurring across the world.[11] In fact, it would be echoed in two films that Promio shot from the rear of the train during his trip from Jaffa to Jerusalem. In the lore of early cinema, much has been made of the mounted camera technique as a proto-tracking-shot, but much less has been discussed of the relationship that this technique has to the various sites where it was filmed. How, we might wonder, does place matter in the history of film form?

The overall generalizability of the train in film history derives from its status as an optical experience that reframes the position of the traveler to the landscape. In his gloss of Wolfgang Schivelbusch's epic study *The Railway Journey: Trains and Travel in the Nineteenth Century*, Charles Musser emphasizes the reconfiguration of space in the modern age:

> The sensation of separation which the traveler feels on viewing the rapidly passing landscape has much in common with the theatrical experience of the spectator. Separation joins discontinuity as one of

the fundamental conditions of the new mode of perception which the cinema was to introduce into modern society and help to institutionalise as "natural."[12]

Here the train stands at the intersection of theater and cinema, and separation joins discontinuity in a radically new mode of perception. What is at stake is not simply the emergence of new modes of travel and new technologies, but an entire perceptual paradigm through which the modern world comes to be seen. Whether in the work of Paul Virilio, Daniel Morgan, or Jordan Schonig, the train features prominently within these broad stories of cinematic seeing, and within this history, the famed train at La Ciotat—as much as the gondola in Venice—remains a sort of urtext for film historians.[13]

As we will discover, this exploration of two tracks in early cinema ultimately reveals two frameworks for film analysis. Here at the crossroads of La Ciotat and Jerusalem are the implications of a world that comes alive in cinema and an entire way of seeing that the tracking shot makes possible. What happens when we reckon with the site at which film techniques are made visible? How do we reconcile the world system of early cinema (the various sites of the Lumière catalogue) with the cinematic world it brings into sight (in this case, the tracking shot)? In the arrival at La Ciotat and the departure from Jerusalem we find the potential history of a future for world cinema predicated less on composite shot structures than on the embodiment of cinematic motion, less a matter of breaking frames than capturing motion within the frame.

Placing Perceptual Paradigms

The iconic scene at La Ciotat—much like *La Sortie de l'usine*—exists in multiple forms. Louis Lumière is said to have shot the first version sometime between January 16 and February 3, 1896, during a visit to the family residence, which stood on 222 acres near Marseille. A second version of the film has a less determinable source, other than that it was also shot during the winter months. But it is the third version that is the most widely distributed and stands at the core of this chapter. Although it shares similar shot angles to the first and second, it was shot during the summer of 1897, a few months following Promio's voyage to the Middle East. An announcement for the screening of this third version appears in the *Lyon républicain* from October 10, 1897.[14] Lumière likely had a direct hand in coordinating and rehearsing the scene to be shown. Martin Loiperdinger notes that those leaving the train rarely look at the camera, either because they had been directed not to look or because they had become habituated to the camera operator on the platform.

One exception, of course, is a small child who clutches her aunt's hand and peers directly at the cinematograph. This two-year-old child was Madeleine Koehler, Louis Lumière's niece, and the two women alongside her are Rose (Louis Lumière's wife) and Marguerite Lumière (his sister-in-law). The scene on the platform also includes Louis Lumière's three-year-old niece Suzanne, his five-year-old nephew Marcel Koehler, as well as his mother Joséphine, who wears an iconic plaid cape.[15] With these recognizable figures, *Arrivée d'un train à La Ciotat*—like *Repas de bébé* and other renowned films from the Lumière estate—is a sort of family film, and the local scene it offers plays out in the lore of early cinema and across generations of film scholarship.

Whether in La Ciotat, Jerusalem, Alexandria, or Nagoya, the train is more than a fleeting motif in early cinema—it is part of its founding mythology. It was a train, after all, that gave rise to the legend of spectators so overcome by the realism of a film that they supposedly fled the theater. In an important and corrective gesture, Loiperdinger traces responses to *Arrivée d'un train à La Ciotat*, including those of Félix Regnault and Maxim Gorky, to help reassess the origins and faults of this "panic legend."[16] With attention to historical sources, Loiperdinger constructively points out the empirical grounds on which the stories of panicked spectators would have been impossible. For one, he notes, the size of the Salon Indien in Paris (where the film was initially screened) was so small that had audiences attempted to run, there would have been reports of trampling. Second, he acknowledges that advertising promoting the film already featured an image of a train projecting from the screen, which he takes to underscore how pervasive the panic legend was even at the time. Tom Gunning, addressing the persistence of this foundational story in early film, offers the following account of its resonance: "According to a variety of historians, [as the train appeared on screen] spectators reared back in their seats, or screamed, or got up and ran from the auditorium (or all three in succession)."[17] Gunning understands that this moment points to the "unprecedented realism" of cinema: "The image had taken life, swallowing, in its relentless force any consideration of representation—the imaginary perceived as real."[18] The permeation of the train myth is so extensive that even though disproven, it remains a prominent force for considering the dynamics of reception, and however false in itself, it has come to attest to the fundamental realism of the medium.

Shuttling between this cinematic primal scene and general theories of spectatorship, Lynne Kirby insightfully connects spectators and passengers to highlight what she describes as "parallel tracks" of cinema and trains. Like Schivelbusch before her, she offers a framework linking the train as a technological feat to the viewing experience it provides the passenger:

As a *perceptual* paradigm, the railroad established a new, specifically modern mode of perception that the cinema absorbed naturally. In other words, the kind of perception that came to characterize the experience of the passenger on the train became that of the spectator in the cinema.[19]

She continues by expanding her claim about the experience trains provided—both as a mode of panoramic perception that annihilates coordinates of space and time and as a radically new time consciousness of simultaneity with the institutionalization of standard time in 1883.

Besides the shock of temporal disorientation in relation to speed, acceleration, and simultaneity, the spectator-passenger was susceptible to the shock of surprise during the train journey (as emblematized by the accident) and the film journey (exemplified by rapid point of view shifts within the frame and across different shots). An unstable western subject, embodied concretely in passengers and spectators was created—one anticipating, yet immune, to shock. This was the modern urban subject jostled by forces that destabilized and unnerved the individual, creating a hysterical or, in nineteenth-century terms, "neurasthenic" subject.[20]

She emphasizes "speed, acceleration, and simultaneity" as well as "rapid point of view shifts within the frame and across different shots" as she details the experience of "the spectator passenger." In a shift from the response of audiences, Kirby helps to detail the parallel dimensions of train travel and the viewing experience—or what she describes so vividly as a "perceptual paradigm."

For all of the incredible richness such a pairing provides, I cannot help but wonder about the location of Kirby's claim about the spectator-passenger. Is Kirby's "unstable western subject" the audience in Jerusalem, Barcelona, or Paris? To what extent does the vocabulary of the spectator-passenger make sense for films whose fate was ultimately worldly in another sense—that is, always already firmly inside and outside of time and place? Kirby, Loiperdinger, and Gunning all address the novelty of an emergent perceptual paradigm that the convergence of trains and cinema offer, but they leave relatively open, empty, or imagined who is doing the perceiving and where. In pairing the train films from Jerusalem and La Ciotat, it is hard *not* to notice how and where they take place. For one, those standing on the platform in Jerusalem interact with the cinematograph, acknowledging the scene of filming, and even at La Ciotat, the look of Lumière's niece draws attention to the presence of the camera operator.

And second, these two films were regularly projected beyond where they were initially filmed. The Jerusalem train, for example, was screened May 9, 1897, in Barcelona, and again on October 22, 1898, at the Grand Café in Paris, and each time with an indication of place in the title. The train at La Ciotat regularly featured in Lumière programming in Lyon, Paris, and across the world. Both of these films are unto themselves traveling films—they offer thematic treatments of travel, provide formal instantiations of the tracking shot, and serve as texts circulated beyond their original site of production.

The critical claim to be made here is that a quest to decolonize film theory is not a matter of extending its purview to some imagined elsewhere (Jerusalem instead of La Ciotat, for example), but recognizing instead how at the colonial core of early cinema are the potentials of an alternate story, one predicated not on East and West, but on the dimensions of a medium as foreign in Montreal and Beirut as it is in Paris and Tokyo. The historical gravity of La Ciotat—its translation as a theoretical framework for contemporary film scholarship—derives in part from the situation it has within the history of cinema, but this situation is itself repeated, iterated, reframed, and projected across the world. Following the tracks it offers means traveling comparatively across other trains in world cinema, each of which reveals the world to new audiences in novel ways.

Middle East Trains

If we see in La Ciotat both the intimacy of a family film and a perceptual paradigm informing the correlation of trains and cinema, then we might wonder about the status of the numerous other trains in the Lumière catalogue. Katherine Groo draws our attention to Lumière films of trains in New York City; Melbourne, Australia; Kingstown, Ireland; and Nagoya, Japan. We might add the train at Ramleh Station from Promio's trip to Alexandria (Egypt), as well as the train sequence from his trip to Jaffa and Jerusalem (394, 399, 400, and 408). As Groo has it, "These visual repetitions affirmed the 'sameness' of life elsewhere, or perhaps the equivalent strangeness, as cities across the globe digested new forms of technology and travel and the Lumière brothers synchronized their appearances on-screen."[21] For all of the potential sameness in the repeated motif, each of the train films is titled according to its location and sequenced alongside its geographical and historical coordinates. The films of the Jaffa-Jerusalem train, for example, appear sequenced alongside other films from Promio's journey. Only La Ciotat seems to escape its locality to serve as a paradigmatic text within the annals of film theory.

Thus far, I have pointed to the persistence of La Ciotat for general theories of film form, and I have questioned the grounds on which claims are made for "western" spectators. To what extent does the perceptual paradigm derived from *Arrivée d'un train à La Ciotat* extend beyond France? Does *Départ de Jérusalem en chemin de fer* bespeak an alternate modernity? Given that *Départ de Jérusalem en chemin de fer* was filmed prior to the third and most famous version of *Arrivée d'un train à La Ciotat*, how might we understand the theoretical generalizability of the one over the other? One tendency would be to point to the exceptionality of the Middle East films by suggesting that they belong to an ethnographic branch of the Lumière catalogue, one that speaks to the exotifying look of a foreign camera operator. And yet, like Groo, I share in a resistance to this particular Orientalizing approach. The various films capture more than a camera operator might have intended, and their critical afterlife extends well beyond what might have initially been imagined for them. That said, we might still question the terms that film historians and theorists derive from local scenes (such as the family film from La Ciotat) to make claims about spectatorship more broadly.

Middle East trains were hardly the sole provenance of non-Western subjects, and it is important to acknowledge the imbrication of many kinds of actors in their construction. In Alexandria and Jaffa, trains were often financed by Britain and France with concerted interests in a sort of Mediterranean domination.[22] Already in 1892, published accounts of the Jaffa-Jerusalem railway herald its "promptness and rapidity" and its role "as an annihilator of space."[23] The train's journey proceeded from the coast of Jaffa, which notably does not have a harbor, across the various landscapes and hills to the Plain of Rephaim and eventually to Jerusalem, which stands at an elevation of 2,480 feet above the station at Jaffa. An international team of engineers from Poland, Switzerland, and Austria, and workers from Egypt, Algeria, and Sudan built the railway with financing from France, tracks from Belgium, and oversight from Ottoman authorities.[24] In the history of Ottoman railways, it is known that the British and the French had competing interests to generate rail lines that would facilitate the permeation of transit inland from the coast, and the Jaffa-Jerusalem railway was part of this imperialist vision.[25] By contrast, when the Hejaz railway was built in 1908, the Ottoman empire sought a route from Damascus to Medina, connecting inland sections of its empire.[26]

Orientalist travelogues commenting on train travel across the region seeming to underscore the shifting perceptual paradigms outlined by Kirby. The historian On Barak, for example, describes trains that traversed the Egyptian desert to highlight transformations that this form of travel introduced to perceiving the landscape. He writes, "Only when the active, dangerous, and bouncy crossing of the desert on camelback or cart was replaced by a relatively smooth, linear, and passive movement through the landscape could the landscape be viewed *as landscape*—an image set apart from its observer." Like Schivelbusch and Kirby before him, Barak helps us think critically about how the experience of train travel in the Middle East transformed perception:

> Looking at the desert through the train's window (window seats were always in high demand) revealed an Egypt that was flying past as a spectacle. Westerners were now looking at it with the kind of gaze they developed to circumvent the nausea of motion sickness: fixing their eyes on a distant stable point in the landscape, through which they saw Egypt moving like a diorama. The gaze from the train's window was predicated on the incorporation of a passive observer inside the optical mechanism. A sovereign external gaze was replaced by a new episteme that regarded the eye as part of the field of vision, problematizing the neat separation of subject and object. The train was an optical device that seemed to put things in perspective, creating the distance from the object and its picturesque effect: "You only need a mosque with a minaret and a few saints' tombs with whitewashed domes, built of mud, to make a picture," one railway passenger remarked. Or as another passenger put it, "[An Arab village] is hardly distinguishable from the land, certainly not in color. . . . However, a clump of palm-trees near it gives it an air of repose, and if it possesses a mosque or a minaret it has a picturesque appearance, if the observer does not go too near."[27]

Though he does not make an explicit connection to cinema (as Kirby does), there is something implicitly cinematic in the optical relationship the passenger has to the space outside the window: "A sovereign external gaze," Barak suggests, "was replaced by a new episteme that regarded the eye as part of the field of vision." If I dwell at length on this passage, it is because, even as Barak too invokes "Westerners" looking out a train window, he highlights the train as an optical mechanism. These observations lead him to make a claim about landscape:

> Indeed, the power of such pictures to bring the landscape into focus should be understood within the temporal structure of vision. The movement of the train did not allow extended viewing; it presented snapshots quickly flying past. In this speed the familiar—the contours of which the eye recognizes—was always the first to present itself.[28]

The eye, the train, and the landscape arise for Barak as inseparable from the broader contours of the eighty-four-mile Overland Route connecting Cairo to Suez. At stake is not only an image of the world, but the world with a difference—a world in which "a mosque with a minaret and a few saints' tombs constitute a picture."[29] The formal dimensions of looking are here inseparable from the permeation of the site.

In *Départ de Jérusalem en chemin de fer*, the train functions as a different sort of optical device and offers a different sort of perspective. Promio mounts the cinematograph atop the train and faces backward, filming those on the train platform bidding farewell as the train departs the station. Part of what distinguishes this film from *Arrivée d'un train à La Ciotat* is how the background eventually envelops the people on the platform—that is, they become smaller as the camera captures a wider field of vision. The train in Jerusalem engulfs its subjects into a broader landscape and eventually depicts the train station, ruins, and windmills in the background. The place is not inconsequential to the scene, nor is it possible to ignore the various indices of place that lend the film its particularity within the archive. Nicholas Baer helpfully describes what appears before our eyes: "Capturing men, women and children of varying ethno-religious backgrounds, who wear a mix of modern dress and traditional religious garb, the film depicts a veritable Altneuland, with old ruins alongside the Montefiore Windmill and the Jerusalem Railway Station."[30] These coordinates, visible in the background of the departing train, are as much a part of situating the place of the film as is the title. Less the horizontality of landscapes unfurling before a passenger looking out a train window, *Départ de Jérusalem en chemin de fer* expands and reveals coordinates of place spatially and in depth as it expands the visual field from the train leaving the station.

And yet when it comes to the film on the platform in Jerusalem, even more of the world is revealed by the situation of the film. There is a sort of visual breakdown according to styles of dress and classes of passengers, each of which delimits the mixing of social and religious contexts accentuated by the motion of the film. Where the arriving train in La Ciotat situates bodies in the foreground alongside the ever-growing locomotive, the departing train in Jerusalem depicts clusters of onlookers bidding the train farewell. In this process, what emerges is a distinction among various classes, indexed both by dress and location on the track, allowing for the shot itself to track from one social class to the next. As the shot begins, various onlookers greet the camera in Western dress of suits and hats. We then see urban effendis clad in the tarbouche and Ottoman dress, and as the shot withdraws even further, we see a cluster of men, assumedly of more rural stock, wearing more traditional turbans. On one single track of a railway connecting Jaffa to Jerusalem, the film reveals the cosmopolitanism of the region, all part of an

Figures 25a–c. Three stills from *Départ de Jérusalem en chemin de fer*, showing three styles of dress among those gathered on the platform.

expanding scope, a world revealed from a departing train (Figures 25a, 25b, and 25c).

In his study of Palestine around the world wars, Salim Tamari turns to archival photographs to analyze the mixing of social classes in public spaces. He begins by contrasting two photographs to note "the emergence of 'secular' space free from religious ritual; the mixing of men and women outside the domain of ceremonial processions; the new hybridity in attire for children and both sexes; and—most notably—the creation of a space for urban 'leisure time.'"[31] He attends to the clothing on display in the image and the particular arrangement of space: "Men's attire ranges from the traditional *qumbaz* and *laffeh* (head turban) to European hats and trousers—but most men are wearing the *tarbush*. A significant number of women in the image are wearing European clothes; few are wearing the traditional *mallayeh*. This is most likely a marker of their bourgeois standing."[32] He moves to a third image, which stands in contrast to the first two. "To appreciate this class factor," he writes, "consider the third photograph, which was taken during the same period inside the city in a public square in which a markedly plebeian crowd gives a more "representative" picture of the public dress code of the period."[33]

> The occasion in this case is the arrival of the *kasweh* (the ornate cover of the holy Ka'bah in Mecca) from Hijaz in 1914. The Jerusalem public, and peasants from neighboring villages, are out to greet the mufti of Jerusalem and the Ottoman governor accompanying the *kasweh*. Here, both men and women are predominantly in *qanabeez* and *mallayehs*, with very few European men's hats and women's dresses. The variation in headgear is much richer here than in the previous two images and gives us clear indications about the social background of the men in the crowd. Aside from Ottoman soldiers in their drab uniforms, we note the urban effendis in *tarabeesh*, peasants in *hattas*, Ashkenazi Jews in European hats, and "Arab Jews" in North African fezzes.[34]

I focus here on Tamari's description of the photograph to highlight a particular contrast in the manner of reading an archival image. On the one hand, we have the sort of analysis that Barak invites of a perceptual voyage framing the Arab landscape for the traveler, and on the other hand, we have the detailed analysis of the photograph as a document that Tamari engages. Where in Cairo we had seen *Le Khédive et son escorte*, which documented the departure of the *kiswah* from the Citadel, here in Jerusalem we have its arrival at the Jaffa Gate. The photograph for Tamari functions as a portal onto this moment and a reflection of clothing, social space, and the mixing of classes, even for an event coded as ceremonial. It is a document that serves as the index of a moment and a record of those who, unlike the writers of Orientalist travelogues we encountered in Barak's study of train optics, might not have left their written account behind.

In *Départ de Jérusalem en chemin de fer*, we have a visual document, but it is notably a document doubly in motion—as a film and as a camera mounted on a train. Engaging with this particular film means reckoning both with the perceptual paradigm as well as the blending of social classes that the train offers in its combination of city, country, bureaucrats, tourists, and laborers. Location is here both the indexical site captured on the camera and the formal signature of the film itself—a traveling shot. This composite image derives from the visualization it offers of a multinational infrastructure project (the Jaffa-Jerusalem railway) filmed on a multinational camera (the cinematograph). The ground of the image, we could say, is both *what* it presents in the various layers of its activity and *how* it depicts this world, in motion and time.

The World in/as Motion

I return now to our opening question: What happens to the history of world cinema if we reckon with the site at which a concept becomes thinkable—not simply La Ciotat and Jerusalem, but the birth of the tracking shot? In addition to serving as a framework for connecting trains and perception, La Ciotat has emerged as a framework for the potential history of cinema in its own right. Much of what makes La Ciotat such an iconic site in the history of cinema derives from the account Georges Sadoul offers in his *Histoire du cinéma mondiale*.[35] For Sadoul, spectatorship in La Ciotat is a matter of identification—he suggests that the film aligns the audience with the perspective of the camera.[36] Breaking the film into constituent parts, he notes the impressive number of shot types employed all in one short sequence, and he describes the feat of La Ciotat as a sort of inverted tracking shot (une sorte de *travelling* inverse).[37] In this short film, Sadoul reveals an entire cinematic grammar. It is as though La Ciotat contains unto itself the history of film form.

As though drawing the implications of Sadoul's claim to their logical conclusion, Vincent Pinel expands the horizons for La Ciotat. He sees in the film a sort of anachronistic culmination of three achievements of modern cinema: "This short film of only 50 seconds unites with disarming effectiveness three achievements of modern cinema: the 'realism' of deep focus, the dramatic impact of the sequential shot [*plan-séquence*] with a fixed camera, and the random principle of *Direct Cinema*."[38] Loiperdinger's account builds on Pinel's claim and helps explain La Ciotat as a miracle of deep focus:

> While our eyes continually adjust focus on objects at different distances, the Cinématographe Lumière Zeiss lens keeps everything before it from three feet to infinity in focus. Along the diagonal axis of the rails, the viewer perceives the long, extended spatiality of the platform at one glance. From the extreme foreground to the background, everything is equally in focus, a cinematic effect that cannot be achieved by the naked eye. The fixed frame and the deep focus make the back-and-forth on the platform appear even more complex than it actually is. The audience in the darkened projection room lacks the familiar spatial orientation in reality that is achieved by constantly refocusing the eyes, by changing visual fields through head movement, and, let's not forget, by hearing. Thus, it is not only the distorted proportions of the train's arrival that offer contemporary audiences unfamiliar perceptual experiences.[39]

From montage to deep focus, the travel of La Ciotat through the annals of film theory extends all the way to questions about narration. André Gaudreault, for example, reads in the film a broader theory of narrativity, one he places at odds with Marshall Deutelbaum's reading of the film as invested in the overall coherence of the pro-filmic event. Elsaesser glosses Gaudreault's position as follows: "Distinguishing between the mobility of the represented subjects, which regulates the succession of images, and the mobility of spatiotemporal segments, which governs the succession of shots, Gaudreault sees the two levels of narrativity (the one inherent in any moving image and the other initiated by any kind of shot-change) as dialectically intertwined."[40] What this means, Elsaesser suggests, is that "since every shot-change implies the intervention of a narrator, the single-shot film constitutes a mode which is already narrative, even if it is one without a narrator."[41]

Of all of the various approaches to the film, it is Philippe Dubois who rather critically points out that Sadoul's grammatical reading of shot structures overlooks the importance of movement in the sequence.[42] The Lumière film, for Dubois, asks that we understand the shot not *in* the movement, but *as* movement. It is in its consistent movement (as the train tracks forward) that this film disrupts notions of cinema as a series of cuts. "The movement of the train," Dubois tells us, "is unto itself the movement of cinema." We move from La Ciotat to the optics of trains more generally to a broader theory of cinema, but Dubois highlights the critical investment that the film offers for a general theory of movement.

Among various models for analyzing La Ciotat, I take this emphasis on movement rather than cuts as a key aspect of world cinema. There is a geographical model for world cinema that pieces together films from across the world (France, Algeria, Egypt, etc.), and there is a formalist model of film analysis that addresses the film as a composite of photographic instances documented sequentially (the 800 photograms captured on the cinematograph). And yet what the train film reveals, by contrast, is how motion allows for the apprehension of the world in a particular way—not as a sequence of proto-cinematic cuts, but as the embodiment of traveling, literalized in the tracking shot. Whether the approach of the train at La Ciotat or the departure of the train in Jerusalem, what we confront in both is the tracks as the site of a particular type of motion: the scale of the locomotive approaching the camera at La Ciotat and the ever-broadening landscape in the departure of the mounted camera at the station in Jerusalem. In either instance, we confront the marvel of the tracking shot wherein mobility and immobility reveal the dynamics that the camera makes possible.

What might it mean to compare La Ciotat and Jerusalem? Is such a comparative endeavor, one that I have placed at the heart of this chapter, itself a form of montage? Is world cinema a composite montage of various films from across the world? I embrace here the proposition that the tracking shot, "le traveling," is itself a matter of non-montage. What might it mean, then, to track from one site to the next (from Jerusalem to La Ciotat) without a cut, without breaking the seamless depth that these two films help to make thinkable? This sort of thinking, one that takes scale, mobility, and perception into account, is, we might suggest, less a world composed as a series of comparative sites than a world perceived with dimension and in depth. It is this continuity that the tracking shot allows us to question. What is it to read the moving image without the logic of the cut, the juxtaposition, or the comparison? In each train film is a pedagogy for how to think the poetics of place in world cinema—not a matter of location, but the apprehension of space and time itself, cinematically, as a matter of grappling with a world in motion.

Arriving at a Farewell

Allow me to emphasize in closing that these two films help us reckon with cinema not simply as an apparatus but as a mode of apprehension—one that makes visible certain worlds through the dynamics of motion. The novelty of world cinema lies not simply in the places depicted in films so much as in the traveling of the film itself across the world to audiences near and far. Locomotion is a motif literalized at La Ciotat and Jerusalem, and it is motion that becomes a structural component of the formal qualities these two sites make thinkable as a traveling/tracking shot. The contrast between La Ciotat, in which the camera stands on the platform, and Jerusalem, in which it is mounted on the train, derives from how the apparatus takes place. These are not simply matters of perspective or points of view, but movements that frame spectatorship itself. Both films offer a perspective on perspective.

In 1898, the Lumière Company shot *Passage d'un tunnel en chemin de fer (pris de l'avant de la locomotive)* (931), in Lyon, France, between the tunnel of Caluire and the station Lyon-Saint-Clair.[43] Unlike the departing train in Jerusalem, the train shot in Lyon features a camera strapped to the front of the locomotive as it proceeds forward, reversing the spatial arrangement that the train in Jerusalem offered—and aligning it, in the annals of film history, more properly with the characteristics of what would come to be known as the phantom ride.[44] By 1898, this shot structure was quite a bit more common, with Méliès famously shooting *Panorama pris d'un train en marche* (Star Film 151), which was filmed on the Chemin de der de Petite Ceinture as it passed through the Bel-Air-Ceinture station.[45]

Prior to these two moments—and prior to the departure of the train from Jerusalem—two additional train films attributed to Promio's visit to Ottoman Palestine exist in the Lumière catalogue. Both of the two filmic panoramas feature landscapes that are animated by the moving camera as it travels along the tracks. In the first, *Panorama en chemin de fer* (399), we have a tracking shot from right to left as the train passes quickly through a station; and in the second, *Panorama en chemin de fer (collines)* (400), we have a reverse tracking shot akin to the shot from Jerusalem, but revealing landscape. It is shot directly from the back of the train as it passes through the dry hillsides on the approach from Jaffa to Jerusalem (Figures 26a and 26b). While these two films might mimic the Orientalist trope of depicting landscapes without people in the Middle East, they combine in the process a particular technique rarely seen. Landscape paintings meant to depict a timeless and ancient Holy Land are here confronted with a model of visualization linked not only to the novelty of the train line and its rapid and disorienting frameworks for traversing the country, but to the modern technology of the cinematograph.

If this chapter has moved from two contrasting tracking shots to this detour through the phantom ride, I have done so to highlight the motion staged within each film as an integral dimension to the world it makes visible. Shuttling between local scenes and general theories of film, as well as specific places and the dynamics of film technique, I have tried to demonstrate some of the possibilities and limits of thinking world cinema through the poetics of motion rather than the logic of cuts and juxtapositions.

Figures 26a–b. *Panorama en chemin de fer* and *Panorama en chemin de fer (collines)*, 1897 Lumière films shot from the train to Jerusalem.

Allow me, then, to take a turn here away from the two tracking shots from which we began. I end here not with landscapes, but with a cinematic detail that returns us back to the station at Jerusalem. At various points in the film of the departure, those on the platform observing the cinematograph tip their hats (Figure 27). In his analysis of the film, Baer writes, "The illusion of movement produced by the filmic medium is duplicated not only through the camera's backward tracking movement but also through the forward motion of the individuals within the train, many of whom direct their gaze at the camera and raise their hats to the departing passengers."[46] In this simple gesture is an ambiguous sign, one given over to being read either as a greeting or farewell. It is a gesture that positions the film to be observed in a unique manner, dependent in part on an understanding of the social code that the tipped hat makes thinkable, a social code that registers differently even among those whom the camera slowly reveals in its reverse tracking. Only those wearing Western style caps tip them to the operator, those in the tarbouche and the turban either wave or simply stare back at the camera. The gesture, however, is one that the cinematograph captures differently than it does a landscape—the gesture is made to speak, we could say, in the film differently than the movement of the hills.

Against the backdrop of the various landscapes, the departure of the train from Jerusalem stands apart. Where the magic of La Ciotat stems from ignoring the camera, here in Jerusalem we confront the apparatus anew and yet see people bidding it farewell. I mention this all because the gesture's significance, its legibility as farewell, derives from the motion of the camera, an apparatus addressed by the onlookers, but not shown to the film spectator. It highlights a sort of visual ellipsis wherein we are led to identify with the camera itself. What ultimately matters here is what we see, but crucially how we are in turn addressed—as camera and as spectator. The gesture points us, in closing, to the challenge and the possibility of world cinema. The composite framework is not only a matter of visualizing worlds, but inscribing the conditions of intelligibility, a mode of address and identification as much as a text to be read. In the tip of a hat, then, is less a question of depicting worlds, people, or locations, than of framing movement, seeing the platform, those walking, and those gesturing toward us in a new fashion. In the departure of the train, we see the arrival of world cinema.

We move in the closing chapter from this gesture of farewell, the embodiment of motion through the mounted camera, to weigh yet one more refraction of what it is to see the world. In a film at the Jaffa Gate, we zoom in on a face when a pedestrian approaches the cinematograph. Far from making the immobile object mobile, here the pedestrian faces the camera and brings into

Figure 27. Still from *Départ de Jérusalem en chemin de fer* showing a man tipping his hat.

relief the contours of a personal history inscribed in the encounter. In the final chapter, then, we encounter both the particularity of a specific face at the Jaffa Gate and an encounter with the dynamics of seeing a detail in a system — the very crux of determining what it means to apprehend something as elusive as the world.

7
Scale
The World as Close-Up

On the last stop of our journey, we arrive on the streets of Jerusalem and encounter a face that is both memorable and anonymous within the annals of film history (Figure 28). The film in which it appears, *Porte de Jaffa: côté est*, listed as 401 in the Lumière catalogue, is one of at least fifteen films from Promio's trip to Ottoman Palestine during the month of April 1897.[1] Here specifically, we are at the east entry of the Jaffa Gate in Jerusalem. Over the course of the nearly 50-second film, this particularly prominent face emerges on the scene, notable, in large part, for its scale. The technique that Promio employs, turning the handle of the cinematograph and doing so on a public street, served at least two functions: recording the sights and people of the location visited and promoting the new technology in a sort of public display of the apparatus. In this instance, an onlooker approaches the cinematograph, or at least its operator, and lingers for a few moments before eventually crossing out of frame. His motion forward produces the unique effect of enlarging his scale, bringing into relief his face from among the passing pedestrians. His look at the cinematograph places him in film history as one of the first faces to be presented at a scale that would eventually come to be known as the close-up.

Forty years later, in an interview, Louis Lumière highlighted the crucial role that the close-up had played in the history of cinema: "I believe that cinema only took off at the moment that close-ups were created, from the moment the public was allowed to see the actors, the stars, from a wider angle than usual, which captures the subtleties of their expressions in ways that we do not see in the theater where there is a smaller angle."[2] As he continues his comments, he grows even more prophetic: "I believe [the close-up] is one of

Figures 28. *Porte de Jaffa : côté est*, an 1897 Lumière film of a street scene at the eastern gate of Jerusalem.

the important elements of the success of cinema." Lumière is apt to recognize that scale helps to distinguish theater and cinema, rehearsing a distinction that would play out in the writings of subsequent film theorists, including, quite famously, André Bazin.[3] But the status of the face before us at the Jaffa Gate is not that of a star, nor someone ordinarily recognized as having much significance beyond the site at which he appears. It is only looking back at *Porte de Jaffa: côté est* recursively that this face comes to matter in the ways that it does—that is to say, the appearance of the face at this scale is formally innovative as a precursor to the close-up in a future history of cinema.

Already on the street at the Jaffa Gate we discover at least two frameworks for looking. As a historical document, *Porte de Jaffa: côté est* attests to the appearance of the Jaffa Gate a year prior to its alteration to accommodate the arrival of the German Kaiser Wilhelm II. As part of the plans for his visit, he demanded a breach be cut in the wall to facilitate his triumphant entrance into the city.[4] What is captured on camera on one particular day in April 1897 reveals how the site appeared, what people wore, and ultimately how they walked—that is, before the moat was filled, before the gate itself was removed, and before the adjacent wall was lowered. In this manner of looking, the film serves as an indexical trace of a world in front of the cinematograph on the day of its filming. At the same time, seen as a formal document, *Porte de Jaffa: côté est* offers us one of the earliest instances of what would come to be known as a close-up. Unintentional though it might have been, we have here a face taking up much of the screen before passing out of the frame. The use of the close-up becomes commonplace in the narrative dimensions of silent film, and practices of editing help to situate this one style of shot within a broader narrative grammar and the coordinates of time and space. Properly speaking, then, what we have here at the Jaffa Gate is not a close-up so much as its prehistory, an anticipation of what was to come.

As part of this microhistory, I focus on the scale of the face to ask what it might mean to take a detail (this face at the Jaffa Gate) as a point of departure for an inquiry into world cinema. Does a close-up on this one detail bespeak some exemplarity for this face, this film, this location, this camera operator, this site? What are the conditions of its generalizability? Discussions of world cinema necessarily grapple with networks, systems, and structures, and yet the close-up, which extracts and magnifies, makes the detail a spectacle that collapses the dimensions of deep space.[5] When thinking of a global history of film, what does the close-up reveal? How does it collapse the spatial logic often at play in the study of here and there, near and far? How does it collapse the historical logic of then and now? What is the time and place of the close-up without recourse to a distant, contextual, or serialized reading? What might it mean to offer a close-up on world cinema?

The answer to these questions points to a broader methodological question at stake in the analysis of specific films for conjectures about world cinema. Notice that even in posing these questions I have already strayed from the image, the film, the face. Part of the magic of *Porte de Jaffa: côté est* is that this face offers a particularity beyond the generalizable abstractions of historicism and formalism. What matters is the legibility of the lines on the forehead, the clothing, the appearance of the eyes—in a word, the look. In this particular close-up, we both look at the face and the face looks back at us. As I hope to show in what follows, looking at this face already entails a reflection not only on seeing, but on general principles of observation. We are here torn between looking at someone on-screen and being seen through the camera. This tension, which draws us to the objectifying gaze characteristic of ethnography and the dislocating look at the camera itself, stages one of the key features of this close-up. The optics of the image push us beyond a simple matter of seeing the Jaffa Gate. Here in this archival Lumière film, we are already entangled in the poetic encounter of facing the past differently. The look is alive in cinematic form.

In the story this chapter tells, I will be offering reflections drawn from Ottoman Palestine, but I will be focusing, as you will see, on a particularly cinematic feature: the question of scale. What follows is an exploration of the critical tension between the sites of early film history and general theories of film form—or, perhaps even more explicitly, the detail of a single shot within a network of early cinema. To tell this story, we will be shifting between various scales: the particularity of this specific cinematic face alongside generalized theories of scales, worlds, and systems.

The Figure in the Carpet

In the opening paragraphs to the English version of *The World Republic of Letters*, Pascale Casanova offers us a reading of a detail from Henry James's "The Figure in the Carpet."[6] James, she suggests, affirms two fundamental principles: first, that there is an object to be discovered in each work, and second, that this secret is not unsayable: "James's metaphor of the figure, or pattern, in a carpet... was meant to suggest that there is something to be sought in literature that has not yet been described."[7] In a story that might well be understood as a reflection on literary hermeneutics, it is telling that Casanova brackets the interpretative debate and quickly focuses on the visually apprehensible dimensions of the carpet. She does so by citing a dialogue:

> "There's an idea in my work," replies the novelist, "without which I wouldn't have given a straw for the whole job. It's the finest, fullest intention of the lot." This, the critic finally succeeds in working out, is something "in the primal plan; something like a complex figure in a Persian carpet." The "right combination" of patterns "in all their superb intricacy" remains—like the purloined letter—exposed for all to see and yet at the same time invisible.[8]

In a shift from detail to system, from cognitive discovery to visual apprehension, she takes the Persian carpet to be emblematic of world literary space more generally. Seeing James's figure, she suggests, is a matter of perspective:

> If one is prepared to shift one's perspective, to step away from a particular text in order to examine it in relation to other texts, to try to detect similarities and dissimilarities between them and look for recurring patterns—in short, if one tries to take in the composition of the carpet as a whole, to see it as a coherent design, then it becomes possible to perceive the particularity of the pattern that one wishes to make appear.[9]

Expanding further, she ultimately argues that "understanding a work of literature, then, is a matter of changing the vantage point from which one observes it—of looking at the carpet as a whole." She later adds, "The singularity of individual literary works therefore becomes manifest only against the background of the overall structure in which they take their place. Each work that is declared to be literary is a minute part of the immense 'combination' constituted by the literary world as a whole."[10]

I am drawn to this detail in Casanova's work for a number of reasons. I admire the dexterity by which her reflections move from an astute reading of a specific figure to an assertion about the nature of world literature. And yet I wonder: Is it a performative contradiction that a treatise on world literary systems begins with this minute textual detail drawn from a single passage from a short story from a single writer? From what perspective is a world system visible? Must we take a step back in order to see a figure at a distance? These questions intrigue me because they seem central to a framework that positions the spectator between and among multiple national traditions. And yet, quite remarkably, Casanova makes the carpet itself visible by casting it against the backdrop of her own project. Little could James have suspected that this masterful critic could weave his carpet into her own work—that, through her, his story, his figure in the carpet, would become emblematic of twenty-first-century debates in world literature. Despite all the claims about seeing the big picture, the figure in the carpet shuttles between the radical particularity of James's story and the world literary system outlined in Casanova's book.

Through the astute eye of the literary critic, the detail in the carpet draws attention to seeing, apprehending, and making sense of broader systems and structures, all predicated on shifting perspective. There is a striking visual dimension to understanding the relationship connecting the detail to the system, and a detail is only ever a detail when framed as a matter of scale. At the heart of Casanova's treatise on world literature, then, is what we could almost see as a miracle of camerawork. The figure in James's carpet comes to make sense when the broadened perspective of the zoom-out reveals the system anew. World cinema is admittedly not world literature, even though debates in world literature permeate the field. Robert Stam's *World Literature, Transnational Cinema, and Global Media* is explicit about its borrowings from questions of translation, adaptation, and the remix to weigh the challenges and potentials of reading across media. Lúcia Nagib's *Theorizing World Cinema* as well as Shekhar Deshpande and Meta Mazaj's volume *World Cinema* draw explicitly from comparative literature and debates in world literature to elucidate the circulation of texts beyond national contexts.[11] What arises in these conversations is less an effort to distinguish literature from film than shared frameworks through which to engage transnational cultural production, postcolonial media, and translation. Each of them shares in discerning the figure in the carpet as a necessary step to recognizing the specific details out of which patterns arise.

When it comes to questions of scale, the literary scholar Nirvana Tanoukhi constructively points to relationships among literature and space, and she shifts the terms of Casanova's visual apprehension. In place of the visual emphasis, she offers an argument for what she describes as "a literary phenomenology of the production of scale":

> We are at a juncture where we must pursue directly a literary phenomenology of the production of scale, which can begin to elucidate the diverse forms of entanglement between literary history and the history of the production of space—and the function of literary criticism as an intermediary poetics.[12]

Tanoukhi's critical emphasis on production, which is here connected both to scale and to space, leads her to the function of literary criticism as "an intermediary poetics." Against this backdrop, she differentiates schoolchildren, "for whom scale is the relation between distance on a map and distance in reality," from "the literary comparatist," who centers scale as "the social condition of a landscape's utility."[13] Tanoukhi's reading emphasizes connections among history and social conditions, and places emphasis on the role of the critic to weigh how scale works within a text.

Anne-Marie McManus goes even further in drawing out the implications that these observations have in the classroom, especially when it comes to materials in Arabic. For McManus—as for Tanoukhi—the question of scale is not only an abstract system, but one that overlaps with a history of representational practices:

> Scholars routinely perform a bridging work to address these afterlives in the classroom, teaching the skills to read a translated novel through national histories and iconographies while simultaneously deconstructing a specter that so often lurks in worldly readings of Arabic novels: Orientalism.[14]

The intermediary poetics that Tanoukhi describes is actualized in the scenario articulated by McManus—namely, national histories and iconographies that serve as antidotes to the specter of Orientalism. This latter framework often serves as an explanatory matrix within which details become comprehensible. There may be a carpet visible in this system, and it is often as fanciful as Aladdin's magic carpet—which is to say, detached from the social conditions of historical production and tied to the fantasies about how and what it means to understand an aesthetic work within a regional designation.

A focus on the particular face in *Porte de Jaffa: côté est* is neither an effort to claim Lumière films for the Middle East, to regionalize and indigenize them, nor an effort to abstract them from what they show. Instead, reading in detail, tracking the face eclipsing the landscape means reckoning with scale as we reckon with place—not as a given, but as rendered intelligible. The film puts a world into relief, and the image comes alive at the moment it animates a system within it. And so, looking at the face looking at the operation of being filmed means reckoning both the dynamics of scale and the dynamics through which the face is made visible. At the scale it is shown, the face might be legible as part of the social world of Jerusalem in 1897, but it is equally part of eclipsing the dimensions, depth, and landscape of which it is a part. Unlike the figure in the carpet, which shifts according to how the reader views it, here in *Porte de Jaffa: côté est* the face actively takes place in the film, shifting, moving, and eclipsing aspects of the world made visible and foreclosed. No longer does the face index the social world in which it is embedded, it also occludes the coordinates through which its position is measured as part of the landscape.

The Close-up at a Formal Distance

Let us return, though, to our close-up. Staring at the scene of pedestrians strolling on the street, we find ourselves with a point of view characteristic of Promio's other films. The shot frames not only the Jaffa Gate in the background, but also the activities of those on the street. There is a sign for a barber to the left of the gate and a white awning for the Grand New Hotel that blows in the breeze on the right side of the frame (Figure 29a). With the cinematograph positioned curbside, pedestrians stroll both in the center of the street and along the elevated sidewalk: Two men approach and turn to the right; a man stands at a table between the gate and the cinematograph; two women pass on the left side; a man carrying chairs proceeds past the cinematograph; and two children spotting the operator sway back and forth in a playful game. The face that emerges on camera is but one of many faces that are captured in the scene and but one detail among many activities transpiring on the street that day in 1897 (Figure 29b).

Like other Lumière films shot on public streets, *Porte de Jaffa: côté est* favors a long shot of what it depicts, shooting bodies in full and highlighting various layers of activity to avoid a flattened-out image. And yet of all the various details that might capture the eye, what sets this film apart is the

Figures 29a–b. *Porte de Jaffa : côté est*, an 1897 Lumière film of a street scene at the eastern gate of Jerusalem.

presence of one pedestrian who initially crosses the frame to appear in close-up before disappearing off-screen in a sort of cinematic trick. The curiosity this particular face poses is that it seems to interrupt the camera operator. The face appears on the right side of the frame, pauses a moment, and then crosses off to the left before disappearing. What is at stake is not solely what is seen (the street scene, the man's face, and the Jaffa Gate), but how it is visualized (in time, with movement, and a distinct sense of the film's frame). And unlike portraiture and painting, the scale of the face as a close-up is here only legible in the context of a sequence that ensures its duration on-screen. In its brief moment of arrest, the face eclipses everything else onscreen and becomes a sort of spectacle unto itself. This face both sees and is seen, and it is indelibly linked to the apparatus through which filming itself occurs.

As though echoing Louis Lumière's observation, the film theorist Mary Ann Doane notes that the close-up is "one of, if not *the* most recognizable units of cinematic discourse, yet simultaneously extraordinarily difficult to define."[15] She draws together a number of writers who have reflected on the definitional problem of the close-up, from Jean Epstein (the French filmmaker of the 1920s renowned for his reflections on *photogénie*), Sergei Eisenstein (the Soviet filmmaker and theorist integral for analyzing the close-up as a unit of montage), and Béla Balázs (the Hungarian philosopher who explores the close-up as a sort of extrication) to the more recent reflections of Gilles Deleuze (with his concept of *visageficaton*) and Jacques Aumont (who glosses the sensible and legible role of the face in cinema). Each of these writers, she notes, helps animate a broader understanding of the close-up as a shot that stands outside of the film's narrative, as a "potential semiotic threat to the unity and coherency of cinematic discourse"—a detail in excess, be it the twitch of an eye, the subtle grimace, the alabaster-esque face of Garbo in the final scene of *Queen Christina*, or the shot of a sneeze in an early Edison film. The close-up is an image saturated in affect, exceeding the parameters of a part/whole relationship and ultimately actualizing the affective potentials of film as a medium. "Of all the different types of shots," Doane tells us, "it is the close-up that is most fully associated with the screen as surface, with the annihilation of a sense of depth and its corresponding rules of perspectival realism."[16] She notes: "The image becomes, once more, an image rather than a threshold onto a world. Or rather, the world is reduced to this face, this object."[17]

At the crux of her argument, Doane observes that most theorists of the close-up analyze it synchronically, emphasizing its extractability from the film's narrative. She reads a number of classical films to highlight the embeddedness of close-ups within the narrative structure. In doing so, she cites Carl Dreyer's *The Passion of Joan of Arc* (renowned for its composition almost entirely of facial close-ups), Rouben Mamoulian's closing shot of Greta Garbo's face in *Queen Christina* (described at length in Roland Barthes's essay "The Face of Garbo"), Cecil B. DeMille's use of Sessue Hayakawa in *The Cheat* (orchestrated within a careful construction of space), and Hitchcock's close-up of a knife in *Sabotage* (highlighting the significance of an object). Casting all of these examples of the close-up against the precedent in film theory, she then asks, "But does the close-up really produce the effects that are assigned to it? Does it look at us? Does the close-up extract its object from all spatiotemporal coordinates? Does it constitute a momentous pause in the temporal unfolding of the narrative?"[18] In contrast to those who see the close-up as external to narrative, she insists on analyzing it within the context of the narrative and as it is situated in a network of gazes (integral to the continuity of space and the grammatical intelligibility of the shot).

If I dwell at length at Doane's astute reading of the close-up within film history, it is because I wonder to what extent the Lumière film at the Jaffa Gate complicates the reflections that film theory would eventually offer for making sense of such images.[19] Prior to the conventions of narrative cinema and amid an almost neorealist long shot of a street scene, we encounter a gaze at the camera and the appearance of a face in close-up. In the film closely linked to the Jaffa Gate, the close-up takes place in a rather unique manner: both because the adornment of the face indexes a location and because its scale draws attention to the apparatus through which we look.

Looking closely at how this shot transpires reveals a rather fascinating effect. Notice in the first image (Figure 30a) the framing of the scene with the depth of space. As the camera operator cranks the camera, the pedestrian on the left side of the frame crosses the camera, staring all the while at it and making his way to the right side (Figure 30b). Then, crossing back in front of the camera, the pedestrian appears fully in close-up (Figure 30c).

Of the many aspects to notice in the shot (the Jaffa Gate, the clothing, and the activities of those within it), we are drawn from the close-up to its disappearance on the left side of the screen. Far from being a moment of extreme realism (indexing a site in time), the film demonstrates a sort of trick of the eye, keeping the Jaffa Gate steady in the background while effectively erasing the onlooker in the movement off-screen—and ultimately drawing our attention to the activity of filming and being filmed. The close-up, in other words, frames the operations of both production and disappearance, refracted as it is through a rare moment tangled in the network of gazes. In a certain sense, we

Figures 30a–c. *Porte de Jaffa : côté est*, an 1897 Lumière film of a street scene at the eastern gate of Jerusalem.

could say that the close-up serves to block the view, to obscure what is seen, and to reflect on the conditions of the camera itself. What we see on-screen is likely a result of the camera operator accosted by the onlooker. But what is made visible in the end is the novelty of a medium capable of close-up and its eventual passage to off-screen space.

There has been a tendency to read Promio's street scenes in the context of ethnographic films. In line with critical dimensions of documentary studies, these films tend to be understood either for their emphasis on landscape or for the objectifying positioning of the camera. Katherine Groo insightfully situates Promio's films from Egypt and Tunisia alongside the Ashanti films, noting the aesthetic implications of positioning the camera as Promio does. She highlights the formal features and aesthetic implications of these films:

> Promio placed the camera in the center of the streets, facing the action of oncoming foot traffic. Not only does this particular position flatten the frame and its visual contents; it also creates multiple visual obstructions. Individuals and animals emerge out of and disappear into the camera.[20]

She then goes on to note the social implications of this camera placement:

> The placement and proximity of the *cinématographe* also draws attention to the curious machine and the operator in everyone's way. Many films among the Egyptian and Tunisian collections capture little more than the exchange between subjects and camera.[21]

Groo's remarkable reading of the single shot allows for a formal and critical understanding of the street scenes, and she moves from the landscape to the body as she weighs the exchange between subjects and camera. As her analysis continues, she accentuates how the films not only highlight proximity and distance, but bodies and space, which she ultimately understands as a move toward abstraction:

> The returned gaze only confirms the disorienting presence of Promio in the streets, disrupting the city's daily traffic, trying to get close. Indeed, these films reflect a compulsion toward proximity and immediacy. They turn away from urban geography and engage the body, its physicality and force, the minutiae of its movements, and the surface of its skin. We lose visual coherence for abstraction; we lose the body for parts; and we lose the long shot for the extreme close- up.[22]

Her argument leads her to what she describes as a type of haptic looking:

> This visual surplus communicates a kind of no-place-and-time, a flattened surface of unreadable texture that intersects with the visual approach that Laura Marks describes as "haptic." She writes, "Optical visuality depends on a separation between the viewing subject and the object. Haptic looking tends to move over the surface of its object rather than to plunge into illusionistic depth, not to distinguish form so much as to discern texture. It is more inclined to move than to focus, more inclined to graze than to gaze."[23]

Both Groo and Laura Marks help us look differently at these scenes of looking, and each constructively shifts from the sort of visual command assumed in discerning the figure in the carpet. As bodies pass in front of, alongside, and behind Promio's camera on the street, the film, it would seem, flattens out the relationship of bodies and space, offering "a flattened surface of unreadable texture."

And yet if we turn from a collection of films to *Porte de Jaffa: côté est*, then we necessarily confront a scene of a different sort—less a body than a face, and less a face as a surface than a face as an encounter. It is worth noting that at the Jaffa Gate there is an exchange that interrupts what we see. What is remarkable about the interruption of the filming at the street in front of the Jaffa Gate is not simply the scale at which the face appears, but that in this scale the camera is made visible anew. If there is a disorientation, it is less on the part of the pedestrians on the street than it is on the part of the spectator in the theater who has been called out, interrupted, accosted, and for whom this being seen looking is a reminder of the scene itself. Here observation is turned back upon itself. Where looks at the camera are not uncommon in any of the Lumière films, the look in *Porte de Jaffa: côté est* transpires at a scale that others do not—it is both an approach and an interruption.

When we move from general theories of the close-up to the particularity of the face in the archival view from *Porte de Jaffa: côté est*, we confront a cacophony of temporalities and the anachronism entailed in the Lumière film. In this close-up, I have suggested, is both the revealing of a face and the eclipsing of a scene—in everything made legible at a large scale is a world behind the face made illegible. This move is not a poetic gesture, but is rather literalized in the motion of the body across the field of vision. From a world of depth, highlighting the distance of the cinematograph to the gate, the face brings radical surface to bear, collapsing the distance. In its movement across the frame and then back out of frame, it is obscured by motion, and in this

Figure 31. Filmed figure shielding his face from the camera in Jerusalem.

act, the interruption becomes the possibility of a blur. A surface, yes, but a surface that obscures both all that is behind it and, in its motion, its own legibility. What it reveals, in turn, is the act through which the filming occurs and the anonymous singularity of the pedestrian's face.

Looking and Masking

It has been noted that looks at the camera are not entirely uncommon. Even in what we have seen thus far, *Le Débarquement du congrès de photographie à Lyon*, *Marché arabe*, and *Départ de Jérusalem en chemin de fer*—all involve extensive looks and even waves at the camera. Here, though, at *Porte de Jaffa: côté est* the look functions not only as an eyeline match in a narrative world, but an encounter with the cinematograph. In this heavily mediated site, we are led to consider the dynamics of a close-up (possibly the first close-up) as a fold within the scene of filming. Anachronistic as it may be to say so, the close-up in this instance is a moment of non-continuity editing, an almost Brechtian moment in a sort of Godardian cinematic trick, drawing attention less to what the camera sees than to making the camera itself visible.[24]

Here is yet another face from yet another early film from Ottoman Palestine (Figure 31). As a figure descends a staircase, the face is obscured by a hand, attempting to avert the gaze of the camera and refusing the reciprocal

SCALE: THE WORLD AS CLOSE-UP

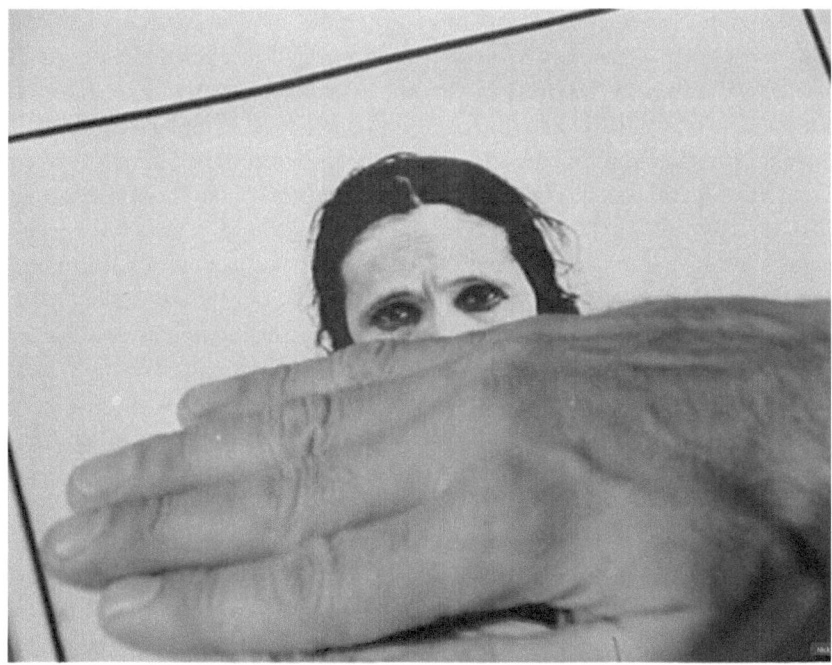

Figure 32. Still from Harun Farocki's *Bilder der Welt und Inschrift des Krieges* featuring an Algerian facing the camera.

look that we are offered in the film at the Jaffa Gate.²⁵ The fingers shield the eyes from recognition as the palm obscures the legibility of the face it covers.

It might be tempting to see in this gesture a sort of subversion, or resistance, to the observational camera. And yet this moment recalls Roland Barthes's reading of Duane Michals's portrait of Andy Warhol in *Camera Lucida*: "I have no desire to comment intellectually on this game of hide-and-seek," Barthes tells us, "since for me, Warhol hides nothing; he offers his hands to read quite openly."²⁶ Other hands appear prominently in Harun Farocki's discussion of Marc Garanger's photographs of Algerian women in *Bilder der Welt und Inschrift des Krieges* (Figure 32). We see on-screen a collection of photographs of women's faces, all shot from the same viewing angles and assembled in order on a table. The voice-over tells us, "The veil covers mouth, nose and cheeks and leaves the eyes free. The eyes must be accustomed to meet a strange gaze. The mouth cannot be accustomed to being looked at."²⁷ And just as the voice-over delivers these words, Farocki's hand covers aspects of Garanger's photos, recropping the faces that had been stripped for the gaze of the police camera and identity cards.

Alongside these tactics for avoiding the camera, what makes the Jaffa Gate film exceptional—in contrast to these faces engaged in games of hiding and revealing—is that on the street in 1897 the observed pedestrian interrupts the filming and effectively blocks the scene, flipping the script, looking at the camera and, over one hundred years later, at us looking at him. As I have suggested here, the film's close-up offers less the contemplative moment of *photogénie* than an interruption, the disappearance of the scene and the appearance of the act of filming.[28] It may remain part of the optical unconscious of film studies, but it is by no means canonically situated within any particular national cinema.[29] And although we may feel that the close-up no longer interrupts the act of filming or disappears the subject being observed off-screen, it remains nonetheless integral to the formal dimensions of viewing the world through the camera and the aesthetic possibilities implicit in facing the camera differently.

In the cataloguing of faces arises a particular challenge. In *Invisible Cities*, Italo Calvino describes a tendency by which a face shifts into a mask: "You reach a moment in life when, among the people you have known, the dead outnumber the living. And the mind refuses to accept more faces, more expressions: on every new face you encounter, it prints the old forms, for each one it finds the most suitable mask."[30] Calvino shifts here from the language of encounter ("on every new face you encounter") to that of printing ("[the mind] prints the old forms"), and he attributes to the mind the activity of finding a comparable visage that both resembles and masks the present one. In every accumulated face, then, is a sort of social projection.

Calvino's observation serves as the basis for Roland Barthes's encounter with Avedon's portrait of William Casby in *Camera Lucida*. In a transmedial shift to photography, Barthes writes, "Photography cannot signify (aim at a generality) except by assuming a mask." He continues, "It is this word which Calvino correctly uses to designate what makes a face into the product of a society and of its history. As in the portrait of William Casby, photographed by Avedon: the essence of slavery is here laid bare: the mask is meaning, insofar as it is absolutely pure (as it was in ancient theater)."[31] Where Calvino emphasizes an activity of the mind, which prints old forms and finds suitable masks, Barthes attributes a direct relation between masking and photography in relation to meaning.

> Society, it seems, mistrusts pure meaning: It wants meaning, but at the same time it wants this meaning to be surrounded by a noise (as is said in cybernetics) which will make it less acute. Hence the photograph whose meaning (I am not saying its effect, but its meaning) is too impressive is quickly deflected; we consume it aesthetically, not politically.[32]

From Casby's face, he turns our attention to August Sander's notary about which he writes,

> The Photograph of the mask is in fact critical enough to disturb (in 1934, the Nazis censored Sander because his "faces of the period" did not correspond to the Nazi archetype of the race), but it is also too discreet (or too "distinguished") to constitute an effective social critique.[33]

If I dwell on this move from faces to masking, it is to underscore a certain tendency for dealing with faces in the catalogue of world cinema. Untethered from the page, projected onto a screen in motion and time, the face at the Jaffa Gate acts, but it is equally available to be seen as a detail in a system: a face from Ottoman Palestine in a Lumière film, a harbinger of cinema in Palestine and Israel, a trace of a social world prior to the modern state and prior to the rise of film culture.

In the iterative framing of cinema, the local, national, transnational, and global dimensions of filmmaking mask the face in their own ways. The face becomes an index of place, and we gain through it the sort of reflection of what we already assume we know. As Palestinian cinema has emerged, Promio's films have receded from most accounts and been replaced with the basic components of a national film history. In *Palestinian Cinema: Landscape, Trauma, Memory*, for example, Nurith Gertz and George Khleifi make only a brief allusion to the early Lumière films, situating them as a moment prior or as a prehistory to their gloss of four different periods of Palestinian cinema.[34] Their account, following in line with the commonly told story, points to the genesis of Palestinian cinema with Ibrahim Hassan Sirhan's 1935 documentary of the arrival of Prince Saud to Jerusalem and Jaffa. Sirhan would go on to help found Studio Palestine in 1945, recruiting the assistance of the filmmaker Ahmad Hilmi al-Kilani, with whom he eventually established the Arab Film Company Production Studio. Both as a director and an early advocate of local production, Sirhan was and remained part of what these scholars refer to as the origins of Palestinian cinema. Gertz and Khleifi's periodization begins with Sirhan's film in 1935, and then proceeds with the silent films of 1948–67, the films of the Palestinian Revolution (1968–1982), and feature-length films of the contemporary period (1980–present) dominated by auteurist cinema and the directors Michel Khleifi, Rashid Masharawi, Hany Abu-Assad, Nizar Hassan, Mai Masri, and Elia Suleiman.

The national model of film scholarship, which often focuses primarily on feature film production (as in Gertz and Khleifi, as well as the classic studies of Georges Sadoul, Viola Shafik, and Roy Armes), is helpful for analyzing the consolidation of an industry and a film culture within a national space, but it somehow falls short of providing an adequate framework for analyzing the film at the Jaffa Gate. The thematic approach, in contrast, which analyzes films on the basis of what they depict (as in Lina Khatib's *Filming the Modern Middle East*) might appear better suited to Promio's films, but it fails to account for the fact that these early films were often viewed less in terms of what they showed to audiences than to the technical manner of presentation.[35] Each of the iterative frames—be it the national production model or the thematic model—provides a sort of mask through which the face can be understood. Refracted through the system of regionalization and periodization, the mask makes the face a figure in the carpet, woven into a tapestry of adjacent references.

And yet, as I have tried to suggest here, taking stock of the face from the Jaffa Gate means confronting a different game of hide and seek, one predicated on the challenge the face itself poses. From *Porte de Jaffa: côté est* we can derive something like a method for understanding what it means to look back at national cinema before national cinema. In the look back at the camera is an action that obscures the mask and that complicates the dynamics through which the recognition occurs. Against the backdrop of world cinema, here the face that stares at the camera might either be understood as a mask of Ottoman Palestine, the mythological groundwork of cinema in the Holy Lands, or, perhaps more ambiguously, as the radical particularity of a face unassimilable to the objectifying gaze of the camera, of the researcher, and of the legibility of the cinematic space of which it was part.

Zoom Out: Facing the Globe

In a gesture of framer framed, we encounter the basis of a world cinema that breaks the conditions of being displayed and that shatters the transparency through which an audience beholds what is represented. This cinema of attractions differs from the wave at the camera seen in many of these early films insofar as it marks an interruption. The scale of the face not only eclipses the scene, but also interrupts the filming, and it renders ever more specific the poetics of place that the film puts on display. In the approach we detect both a look and an apprehension, a turn of the face and a framing of the dispositif.

To zoom out at a further remove, to shift from the scale of the face to the broader collection of films, is to aim for a figure in the carpet. We might say that the issue Promio's films raise is not only a matter of recognizing the global spread of the medium, but noting how the medium itself transforms the recognizability of the world. With footage drawn from seemingly all corners of the earth, audiences could behold a vision of distant lands in motion over time. The vignettes offered scenes well known in paintings, photographs, and lithography, but they brought these images to life differently. And attending to these differences means attending to the unique appearance of the world in film—that is, to the critical importance of the close-up.

Our story of the Lumière catalogue involves a retroactive reconstruction of the origins of cinema predicated on the aggregation of films from the various operators and their indexing within a broader system. The archive draws together various films, but it does not aggregate the experience through which these films were projected at various locations in the world. An emphasis on the archive makes Lyon an anchoring point for films that were otherwise meant to circulate and display the world to the world. In the end, then, the collection brings the face from Ottoman Palestine to Lyon with the iterative potential of a future history of this scene of looking at the camera.

It is striking that Doane's remarkable reflections on scale span a much wider field of cinematic production than this microhistory of the Lumière Brothers, and I cannot help but marvel at her turn to the distinctions among the world and the globe, something she initially undertakes with a turn to Peter Sloterdijk. She notes,

> For Sloterdijk, the globe became "the central medium of the new homogenizing approach to location," and its "monopoly on complete views of the earth's surface" was only broken late in the twentieth century by satellite photography. A sense of the world as globe ruptured the experience of location as potentially separate, isolated, and protected. No place was immune from the knowledge that there was more, outside, that one is caught within a global network.[36]

Like Casanova's reckoning with James, both Sloterdijk and Doane attenuate the visual dimension of apprehending a world system, or in this case, the globe. In drawing attention to the question of location, Doane elicits the assumptions embedded in Sloterdijk's parsing of the globe through recourse to cinema:

> Location, for Sloterdijk, is "not a blind spot in a field, but rather a place in which one sees that one is seen" as a consequence of globalization. In this sense, cinema is compensatory. For in the theater, the spectator sees that they are not seen; the credibility of the film's space depends upon it. The delocalization of the spectator (not necessarily their disembodiment) is the precondition for the intense production of location that is a crucial component of cinema.[37]

What is remarkable is that Doane's analysis does not settle on the globe as a particular object, but on the conditions of visibility it offers, something she frames in terms of the delocalization of the spectator. Her line of inquiry pushes even further by noting how the view of the globe does not simply contrast theater and cinema, but it fundamentally reshapes Renaissance perspective, in which the rule of the horizon is so crucial.

At the conclusion of her book, Doane addresses the globe in pondering scale, and in doing so, draws attention to the work of the artist and theorist Hito Steyerl.

> But there is another kind of perspective, or perhaps a paraperspective, that is associated with the accelerating proliferation of maps in media of all sorts, as well as the pervasiveness of the aerial view. Drones, surveillance cameras, military aerial photography, and the zooming and floating vision facilitated by Google Earth disconcert and disrupt the spatial regime of linear perspective. Hito Steyerl places what she calls "vertical perspective" (the view from above) in relation to a general condition of destabilization and displacement in contemporary life—free fall. This condition is linked to a general sense of political, moral, and metaphysical groundlessness, the inability to find a stable foundation for thought or observation. Spatially, this is manifested in the loss of the horizon.[38]

Reckoning with world cinema, then, is reckoning with a question of scale—the story of the face, a life inscribed on the surface of the skin, refracted through the lens and projected through the light of the camera onto a screen, and the story of the film as an object among objects, collected and held as a potential projection in the future. I tell this story, returning us to the face, because at the heart of world cinema is the scale of the face and the scope of the film, a part of a whole, a whole of a part, a capture and a projection of the world. Each of the films in this book, each chapter and each projection, reveals the world anew.

If I began with Casanova's reflections on perspective and followed with a close-up on the face at the Jaffa Gate, then allow me, in closing, to zoom out. Like Casanova and later Doane, Homay King begins *Virtual Memory* with a detail of global proportions. Taking a cue from Hannah Arendt's remarks on Sputnik, King arrests her attention on the famous image known as the Blue Marble (Figure 33).

> The image showed the earth as a nearly perfectly round disc, in color, surrounded by a black void. The planet was now visible from its good side, its face an evenly illuminated, vivacious circle, beautifully centered in frame. . . . Earth had finally appeared in the form that would earn it the nickname "the Blue Marble," as it was affectionately called in captions of similar pictures taken from space.[39]

SCALE: THE WORLD AS CLOSE-UP

In seeming contrast to the close-up, the Blue Marble allows for the visual apprehension of the planet from afar. The perspective it offers would seem to make possible an understanding of the figure in the carpet—that is, the attention to clarifying and refining various details on the earth surface to be visible as a whole would seem to facilitate the sort of systematic view that Casanova's reading of James embraces. In fact, Doane reads the Blue Marble through the work of Laura Kurgan and across its different versions (from the 1972 NASA image to the 2005 and 2012 versions) to note that the latter views become "composite images, generated by a patchwork of satellite data."[40] And yet King adeptly reads the 1972 image as revealing a contradictory set of options:

> On the one hand, if we identify with the small world represented by the blue dot, the image might invite the kind of caretaking attitude that Brand and his cohorts espoused. On the other hand, if we identify with the eye of the camera and the perspectival point from which the image was taken, we find ourselves at a great distance from the planet: exiled and painfully alone perhaps, or, alternatively, larger than life, a deity who could crush the little planet with just a thumb and forefinger.[41]

In recognizing that "the spatial distance becomes a metaphor for disconnection and indifference," King's reading opens up our possibilities for apprehending the world. What I admire is that distance is not necessarily figured here as the capacity to see, command, and understand the figure in the carpet, but as a potential place of exile—alienated, abstracted, and apart. She figures the ambivalence between proximity and distance less as a visual or hermeneutic phenomenon than as an ethical question.

It strikes me that the significance of the encounter with the face in the archive—the interruption on the street in front of the Jaffa Gate—actualizes this sort of encounter. Not the masking of a face within the historical and temporal coordinates of Ottoman Palestine, not the formal curiosity of scale, but an encounter with the practice of filmmaking. This turn, this encounter, this face-off reveals far more than the all-knowing paraperspective of the figure in the carpet. With almost Levinasian resonances, it opens up the implications of facing the camera, even as it turns the film, which might otherwise function as a screen onto a foreign land into a mirror—not of oneself—but of an encounter that makes visible the fact of seeing. It is in this way that *Porte de Jaffa: côté est* can be seen as a work of world cinema—as a work that locates the act of being seen in the world.

At a moment when our field has been turning to world literary systems, global media, or the conditions of planetarity, it strikes me that mediation itself is inseparable from the ethical valences that King helps illuminate. Whether

Figure 33. *The Blue Marble*, photograph of Earth captured by the Apollo 17 crew on December 7, 1972. (NASA/Apollo 17 mission)

through the figure in the carpet, the globe, or the Blue Marble, we encounter the conundrum of how best to see the world. And yet looking at the close-up from the Lumière films challenges us not only to look, but to be looked at—not only to see, but to be made aware of the apparatus of seeing. In this way, proximity to the camera at once forecloses the broader figure in the carpet, the globe, and the world, even as it reveals, as though through a mirror, the apparatus through which seeing has become possible. Inadvertent though it may have been, Casanova's move from the sayable to the seeable and from discovery to perspective reveals the world anew, allowing us to understand that in the world system, the detail matters. And so too here, facing the look of this Lumière film at the Jaffa Gate reveals the intermediary world between the screen, the camera, and the eye. This, we could say, is the ethics of world cinema.

EPILOGUE
Planet
Otherworldly Futures

In our journey from Lyon to Neuville-sur-Saône, Algiers, Cairo, Giza, Jaffa, and Jerusalem, we finally arrive back at the beginning, which is to say, at the curious ellipsis in Alexandre Promio's travelogue. With only a cursory mention of his time in North Africa and the Middle East, Promio leaves little by way of a written record of his voyage. And yet what he doesn't recount in his travelogue, he instead leaves behind as films now catalogued and preserved as part of the origins of world cinema. Across each of the preceding chapters, I have taken a number of Promio's films to explore the world they help make visible—whether the market in Algiers, the prayer on a rooftop, a shot of the Ottoman khedive in Cairo, the Great Pyramid at Giza, the Jaffa to Jerusalem train line, or a face at the Jaffa Gate. I have been struck by how each film—caught between the scene of production, the circuits of dissemination, and the site of projection—complicates and enriches the story told of these early moments of film history. Beyond an aesthetics of capture (wherein every scene is an objectification of those within its frame), I have emphasized the iterative and appropriative potentials of projection to unsettle the grounds of world cinema. From the Tousson Stock Exchange in Alexandria to the Hammam Schneider in Cairo, it is in projection that the Lumière Brothers films take place, and it is projection that offers them an afterlife beyond their colonial frame. In the work of filmmakers such as Merzak Allouache, Youssef Chahine, and Abounaddara, we find critical and imaginative engagements that reanimate these moving images and untether them from their past. From Algiers to Cairo to Jerusalem, exploring this microhistory of Promio's voyage has been an effort both to confront an ethnographic mirage and to imagine a future past for world cinema. Out of Promio's ellipsis, in other words, I have aimed for a vision of what world cinema can be.

In 1995 the centenary celebration of the Lumière Brothers' cinematograph in Lyon offered a particular understanding of a multicultural, global, and transnational history for cinema. Whether the global directors commemorated "Le Mur des Cinéastes" or the photograph of Mrinal Sen and Youssef Chahine walking arm in arm, each aspect of the Lumière Institute seems to honor a vision of world cinema as the union of national directors from all corners of the globe. At the same time, the commemorative project *Lumière and Company* handed the cinematograph to directors from across the world, each tasked with shooting a film on the device to be a constituent part of the commemorative anthology film.[1] Zhang Yimou, Sarah Moon, David Lynch, and Abbas Kiarostami are just a few of the forty directors invited to participate in the project. Like the interlocking arms in the photograph, each of the global directors in *Lumière and Company* functions as part of a broader global network in the history of cinema. Sutured together in this visual anthology, their various short films constitute not only an afterimage of the cinematograph, but one that draws its origins back to the worldly circuits of the Lumière Brothers camera operators. This vision, separated by one hundred years from the inaugural footage of workers leaving the factory, bespeaks a global imaginary distinct from the world at the end of the nineteenth century. Bidding farewell to the colonial discourse of the civilizing mission and the height of French imperialism, we encounter the advent of multiculturalism and the circuits of capital connected to a globalized film industry.

The labor of world cinema extends us from the factory gates in Lyon across the world with the cinematograph disseminated in the hands of camera operators and onward through the rise of global film culture. Soon after the first screening to audiences in Lyon, Alexandre Promio's voyage to Algeria, Egypt, and Ottoman Palestine reveals commonplace scenes anew and sets the groundwork for future filmmakers. Markets, trains, and ports are part of a shared repertoire within the global Lumière catalogue, and in specific films, details, accidents, and framings restage the logic of the cinematic encounter. In the scene of an Arab market in Algiers, we confront the dynamics of seeing and being seen as children pass in and out of the shadows, and at the Jaffa Gate in Jerusalem, we encounter an onlooker who approaches the operator to observe the cinematograph observing. In these various glances are echoes of the photographers at the Congress of Photography, often carrying photographic cameras, greeting the cinematograph as they leave their boat. The various interactions with the cinematograph are a reminder that Lumière films take place as an event of filming, indexing a given site in time. And yet as part of a medium meant for display, these Lumière films are also scenes of projection, destined to mirror back faces for audiences and to provide a window onto a place elsewhere in time. Out of Algeria, Egypt, and Ottoman Palestine, then, emerge both the basis of a local screening practice and the framework through which location comes to be understood. Films take place, I have argued, but in the dynamic interplay between capturing and projecting, they are always already dislocated from a fantasy of being situated.

As much as the cinematograph is itself an instrument of conquest (*à la conquête du monde*, as the slogan goes), so too is there hope to be had in the potential futures of its past—that is, in the projections, afterlives, and appropriations that its future iterations make possible. The various chapters have been united in connecting film history with film form in order to blur the relationship between the world and its various illusions. Captured on the cinematograph are both the figural dimension of what we see projected and an imagined relationship to a world onscreen. It is this latter investment in the world on and as screen that I have tried to trace across the work of artists and filmmakers. In the iterative play of screenings, appropriation, and digitization lies the hope of manifold future visions of what world cinema can be—that is, an archive alive in the persistence of its dissemination.

Toward a Planetary Cinema

It is striking that the preface to Georges-Michel Coissac's *Histoire du cinématographe de ses origines à nos jours* includes a reference not only to the universality of cinema but also to its planetary scope. Coissac notes that film appeals to all publics, and he cites M. Hamp, who refers to those working with the cinematograph as "mechanics of a universal language."[2] Promio's demonstrations in Algiers and Cairo could be understood to communicate beyond the constraints of particular languages, and already in 1925 when Coissac published his book, the network of Lumière camera operators could be understood as harbingers of a world cinema to come. But it is where Coissac moves from his observation that is so intriguing. "If we were to arrive on the planet Mars," he writes, "it is with the cinematograph that we would undoubtedly communicate most quickly and effectively with the inhabitants of the planet."[3] In what might appear a subtle nod to Georges Méliès's *Le Voyage dans la lune*, we arrive not only at the global dimensions of the cinematograph, but its potential connection to a beyond, an elsewhere, a planet that exceeds the stretches of empire.[4] Beyond the image of Youssef Chahine and Mrinal Sen walking arm-in-arm or even the image of the Blue Marble, Coissac's observation, almost a century earlier, is a gesture to a world beyond the

Figure 34. *Le Débarquement du congrès de photographie à Lyon*, still depicting the astronomer Jules Janssen among the delegates.

world—an effort to envision the cinematograph as the basis for an interplanetary language.

Among those crossing the gangplank in *Le Débarquement du congrès de photographie à Lyon* is the astronomer Jules Janssen whose proto-cinematic "photographic revolver" was used in 1874 to record the passage of the planet Venus (Figure 34).[5] As Janssen passes in front of the cinematograph that June morning in 1895, he clutches what looks like a telescope in his hands. Unlike those who confront the cinematograph with photographic cameras, he functions as a curious portal to the potentials of a planetary cinema. His appearance attests to a history of past experiments with motion photography and to a particular celestial vision. With Janssen, motion photography turned not simply to the world, but to its place among the planets. In 1870, during the Franco-Prussian war, Janssen escaped France in a balloon in order to observe the totality of the solar eclipse from the African continent.

A few years later, on December 8, 1874, Janssen then traveled to Japan, where he turned his photographic revolver to capture forty-eight exposures over the course of seventy-two seconds on a daguerreotype disc.[6] What he

PLANET: OTHERWORLDLY FUTURES 171

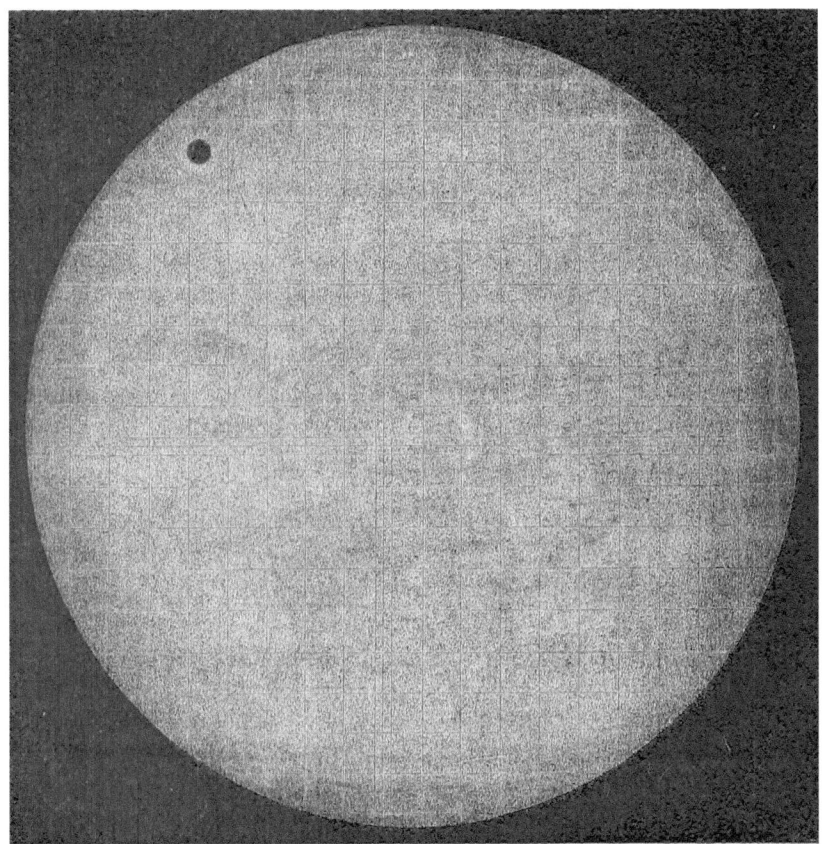

Figure 35. Jules Janssen, *Transit of Venus* (1874).

successfully recorded in this endeavor was the passage of Venus in front of the sun (Figure 35). This famed experiment was an accomplishment for astronomy as much as it was for photography—and as an experiment in motion photography, eventually cinema. Janssen would be enlisted by the Lumière Brothers during his visit to Lyon for an additional film (*Discussion de Monsieur Janssen et Monsieur Lagrange*), which was also shown to the audience at the Congress of Photography. All of this to say that Janssen was, even crossing the gangplank in 1895, a celebrity, and one whose recognition on-screen prompted an awareness of a world beyond earth, and earth as a planet among the stars.

In Janssen's appearance in *Le Débarquement du congrès de photographie à Lyon* is a refraction predicated not only on recognition, but on the embodiment of a technology that exists in excess of the photographer—that is, a vision through which to understand the eclipse of the planets. His image of Venus passing across the sun had already led him to share the results of the revolver with the Société Française de la Photographie in 1874 and then at Académie des Sciences in 1876. With his fame established, he went on to serve as president of the Société Astronomique de France (SAF) from 1895 to 1897, a title he would hold at the time of his visit to the Congress of Photography in Lyon.

What would it be to understand world cinema in the context of the celestial vision that Janssen makes imaginable? What is his place among the stars? These questions point both to Janssen's celebrity status and to the tensions his appearance rehearses between the radically local (one face among many), the universe to which it gestures (an astronomer in the history of photography and film), and the future possibilities of world cinema (envisioning earth among the planets). In this film of photography is encapsulated a broader vision for world cinema to capture not simply images of the world but also of the planetary. With Janssen, we encounter a vision for imaging and imagining a world in which earth is one among the planets, and the planets are multiple among the stars.

"The earth is not a planet," Frédéric Neyrat proclaims in his reading of philosophers of the Earth ranging from Husserl and Heidegger to Arendt.[7] Like others before him, Neyrat proposes a planetary philosophy "capable of thinking together the ecological emergency and the cosmological dimension," all part of a broader ethics he embeds in his call for celestial democracy.[8] From Copernicus to Lukáš Likavčan's "comparative planetology," Neyrat charts "how planetary thinking has passed from a metaphorical engagement with outer space to a material one embedded in Earth system science."[9] In this encounter with Janssen on-screen is a visual embodiment of an entire framework for visualizing the organization of the stars beyond the indexicality of worldly images. From eclipses to solar systems, Janssen embodies the potential of planetary cinema. At a time when photography and cinema were understood to capture images of the world for circulation across the globe, Janssen's composite photographs of Venus visualized the contingency of the planets in motion—a Copernican turn within world cinema.

Janssen's appearance in *Le Débarquement du congrès de photographie à Lyon* is a detail that not only highlights the film as an artifact (documenting his presence at the Congress of Photography in 1895) but also positions it as a mirror that stages a structure of recognition (for both Janssen as a historical figure and the history of the cinematograph). Through Janssen, we encounter a key to understanding the place of the planet in the local history of Lyon. The recognition of Janssen by those at the conference and by subsequent historians of cinema gestures to the possibilities of mirroring not simply in a psychoanalytic sense but also in the artifactual sense, in a way that sheds light on the place of the planet. The scene on display is less a matter of looking through the screen onto a foreign world than of seeing oneself rendered both familiar and technologically foreign. The estrangement is itself part of the enchantment, and the optical devices that Janssen had on display are here literalized in his cinematic incarnation. The historic figure responsible for imaging and imagining other planets is brought onto the screen for himself to behold as part of the audience. On the banks of the river, captured on an afternoon on camera, we encounter a basis for seeing the world, the planet, and the stars anew.

A crucial axis of the book has emphasized the aesthetics of capture (what the cinematograph records) as containing unto itself a potential history. There is an echo here of Francis Doublier, who appears on the bicycle in *La Sortie de l'usine* and who goes on to serve as a camera operator, bringing the cinematograph across the world before eventually assisting in the memorialization of the Lumière Brothers as part of the origins of cinema. We could also consider the Khedive 'Abbas Hilmi II, whose appearance in Cairo bespeaks a model of governance soon to be eclipsed, or the Great Pyramid at Giza or the Jaffa Gate, whose landscapes would shift in the years shortly following their being filmed. In each of these cases, films capture details, but the details themselves come to be reconfigured with the passage of time—which is to say, the situation of each film is only ever the potential of becoming anew. The task of unsettling world cinema—in Janssen's appearance and in that of the myriad other films—demands reckoning with the contingency of the coordinates of the here and now, the shifting grounds on which films take place.

Planetarity

In the preface to the twentieth anniversary edition of *Death of a Discipline*, Gayatri Chakravorty Spivak distinguishes the "planetary" from her term "planetarity." She turns, in doing so, to citations of her work that point to the term's fundamental untranslatability:

> Let me quote from my entry on "planetarity" as it is to be found in Barbara Cassin's *Dictionary of the Untranslatables*, as translated by Emily Apter: "My use of 'planetarity' . . . does not refer to any applicable methodology. . . . Planetarity is not susceptible to the subject's grasp [Begriff = the German word for concept, containing the metaphor of grasp = greifen]." And in this description, I give in

conclusion the double bind of the ruse of consciousness, faced with the untranslatability of the word planetarity: "We must persistently educate ourselves into the peculiar mindset of accepting the untranslatable, even as we are programmed to transgress that mindset by 'translating' it into the mode of 'acceptance.'" It is this "translation" that produces the reading practice welcomed by readers, mostly student readers. I finesse it by way of the uncanny, of figuration.[10]

Where Coissac embraces the cinematograph as "the mechanics of a universal language," one which is best equipped to communicate with a distant planet, we encounter in Spivak's work a question posed above and beyond such fantasies of transparent communication. When Spivak discusses translation, she recognizes a relation to life and language informed by the conception of fieldwork in the writings of the anthropologist Talal Asad. In the end, she welcomes the irreconcilable and ambivalent site of translation, and her reflections on planetarity lead her ultimately to embrace the importance of "translating": "May translating rather than translation," she proclaims, "be the future of the humanities."

> We will be a global community, each one of us globalizable, upstream from politics, an island of languaging in a field of traces. The trace of an "unknown" language is where we know meaningfulness is operating, but we don't know how. Our task as teachers and translators calls us into this challenge, the recognition that a fully translated globe is nothing that we should desire.[11]

I admire in Spivak's reflections a push against the simple understanding of the planet as a world or a figure; after all, as she tells us, "a fully translated globe is nothing that we should desire." For any of us trained as comparatists, Spivak's insistence on translating as a transitive verb gestures to the importance of resisting instrumentalized ways of knowing.

As Spivak continues to engage planetarity, she weaves together questions of language and knowing, and she returns to earth to embrace "island-thinking." She draws the term from the Caribbean philosopher Edouard Glissant and attributes its resonance to her year spent teaching at the University of Hawai'i. "We must displace the heritage of postcoloniality into island-thinking," she cautions, "[Viet Nam] can move into this with brilliance." It is curious that a parallel version of the essay, published not as the preface to her book but as an essay in the journal *Janus Unbound*, carries with it a less-than-subtle difference: "We must displace the heritage of postcoloniality into island-thinking. Japan can move into this with brilliance."[12]

In this scene of translating, how might we read these brackets around "Viet Nam"? Is there a substitutability of one term, one place, one country for another? Implicit in the move from Japan to Vietnam is a reading of a passage of Marguerite Duras's *The Sea Wall*. Spivak's citation functions differently in *Janus Unbound*, where Japan is at stake, but "Viet Nam" appears in her preface alongside her reflections on Duras. As she walks us through the passage, she invites a scene of translating:

> The comparative literary impulse reads translation translating; and notices that the echo of the sea—"la mer"—every time the book refers to the mother—the main character—as the generic unappropriated "la mère"—would be missed in English, even if it had translated the word generically rather than with the completely inappropriate "Ma."[13]

What follows is a proclamation in which Spivak ventriloquizes: "Learn French, the book says. Only then can we suspect that—in this text—the Anthropocene acts out its program of destruction."[14] It is in this context, the folds in a scene of translating, that Viet Nam and Japan are substituted one for the other in brackets. It is in translating that the citation travels from one location to another, each nation interchangeable in the grammar Spivak offers through her engagement with Duras's work.

When we bring Spivak into conversation with Coissac's fantasy of interplanetary communication ("it is with the cinematograph that we would undoubtedly communicate most quickly and effectively with the inhabitants of the planet"), we might wonder again about the stakes of translating. Does translating have a place among those mechanics of a universal language? I point to these instances to underscore what has been at stake across the various chapters of this book. Much as a film might seem to capture the duration of a moment in time, it lives on when projected, and in projection, it shifts the here and now of the moment it comes to be seen. In the context of Spivak's framework for translating, then, we are not in the realm of a universal language so much as we are at an encounter with how, when, and where a film takes place. Translating is the labor of engaging the taking place of world cinema in the ever-shifting circuits of dissemination—whether in Lyon, Montreal, or on Mars.

Translating—understood in its cultural, linguistic, and intermedial valences—means visualizing the world and the planets anew. And here I want to return us to Janssen's visualization of the eclipse. The magic of the image is not in its fantasy of an indexical having-been-there, but in the resistance to figuration. Whether Janssen's revolver or *Le Débarquement du congrès de photographie à Lyon*, what we encounter is the marvel of the technological—not as the naïve condition of being there, but in the critical question of how something is rendered visible. Part of the key promise of this moment of cinema lies in the enchantment it offers for the conditions through which the world comes to be seen—that is, the act of seeing as an act of translating, and the act of translating as an inquiry into the conditions of the illusion. Here we have an echo of Dai Vaughan and those spectators who investigate the boat in the harbor, and we have the conditions of translating world cinema. From Viet Nam to Japan in Spivak's essay, and from Algeria, Egypt, or Ottoman Palestine in this microhistory, there is a vision that translating makes possible: less a figure than an encounter, a face-off, and a scene of world cinema not as a knowable, but as a confrontation.

The Promise of a Future Planet

And yet another world is possible. Another glimpse at a planet. In the opening sequence of Larissa Sansour's *A Space Exodus* is an image of earth and eventually of the moon with the two round celestial bodies emerging in parallel alongside one another.[15] A soundtrack by Aida Nadeem blends the sonic dimensions of space travel with syncopated rhythms of Arabic music, and eventually the shot of the earth and the moon cuts to a sequence of an astronaut (Larissa Sansour) adjusting a control panel. The film shows her hands flipping switches before revealing the side of her face and panning down her arm to reveal her name tag and a Palestinian flag on the arm of her space suit. As the sequence continues, we see her look out into space, and as a shot reveals a close-up of her eye, we hear her voice on the soundtrack: "Jerusalem, we have a problem." Her face looks upward, illuminated by the light, and then a shot from behind depicts her hand adjusting a lever above. "No, everything is fine," we hear; "we are back on track." The eerie sounds of space combine with the clicks of levers and buttons, all toward a gradual crescendo as the moon appears on-screen, Sansour puts on the helmet to the spacesuit, and announces, "The sunbird has landed." The iconic soundtrack from Kubrick's *Space Odyssey* plays with an Arabic twist, and as a voice announces, "That is one small step for a Palestinian, one giant leap for mankind," we see Sansour descend the ladder of the spaceship, walk a few steps, and plant the Palestinian flag on the moon (Figure 36).

This sequence is revealing for the delicate interplay it offers of flags, music, names, and embroidery, all of which index Palestine, and the replay of the iconic lunar landing. The world is at stake—visible as it is in the opening shot of the film—and the world is also small, contingent, and somehow otherworldly at this moment. After planting the flag, Sansour is shown waving at

Figures 36. Still from Larissa Sansour's *A Space Exodus* depicting the raising of a Palestinian flag on the moon.

the earth in a shot over her shoulder (Figure 37). The camera, it seems, offers us an identification with her view of the earth as a distant planet—the abstraction that is the blue marble is here localized through the perspective of the Palestinian astronaut waving from afar. Unlike the iconic image of the earth as a marble, here it is cast in perspective. We cut from this over-the-shoulder shot to its obverse: Sansour's face as she waves. The face of the planet counters the face of the astronaut. Planetary cinema is localized.

In Sansour's gesture is a sort of greeting that we have seen across numerous films (including *Départ de Jérusalem en chemin de fer*), but here with a twist. Where those on the train platform in Jerusalem greet the camera with a wave, Sansour here greets the world itself with a gesture, all while claiming the otherworldly as a site for Palestine. In 2009, following the Oslo Accords, filmmaking makes thinkable a satirical and dark solution to the plight of the Palestinians, and in doing so, it helps provincialize the place of world cinema, extending politically and aesthetically the limitations of a discourse of multiculturalism. Alterity here finds itself outside of the worldly situation, and Palestine becomes the site from which to bid farewell to a world it leaves behind.

As the film continues, Sansour is shown running back across the screen as the film cuts to an image of the moon. The music fades as the moon passes to the left and Sansour reappears floating in space, upside down and in close-up on the right. She passes in front with the Palestinian flag on her sleeve and

Figures 37. Still from Larissa Sansour's *A Space Exodus* showing a wave at the planet Earth.

then her name tag shown prominently. The music crescendos, and she passes off the right side of the frame and reappears again on the right, floating against the backdrop of stars. The music continues, and a voice can be heard, "Jerusalem? Jerusalem?" as Sansour eventually floats into deep space, becoming ever smaller as the music fades and the film credits appear. In the end, there is no particular grounding for this astronaut beyond the disorientation of a world without gravity and the infinity of a deep space among the stars.

I draw our attention to this gesture toward planetarity not to allegorize Sansour's remarkable film, nor to uproot it from the critical attention it offers as part of a trilogy of films. Instead, it is precisely the location it offers—its rooting of the Middle East, of Palestine, and of the Arab world in the context of the abdication of the world that seems crucial. Sansour's face is both that of Palestine and that of a new world made possible. In the gesture of the wave, both a greeting and a farewell to the possibility of an earthly existence. A world cinema that is not.

A World beyond Compare

The Lumière catalogue offers a worldly text of a particular sort—and an invitation to consider the limits of national, linguistic, and historical frameworks for the global vision that Lumière's potential history of world cinema offers us. Jacques Deslandes's *Histoire comparée de cinéma* is itself not so much a comparative history of national cinemas as it is an effort to weigh the different trajectories that contribute to the phenomenon of a nascent cinematic culture.[16] Likewise, in the work of scholars such as film historians Sadoul and Coissac, we encounter less the telltale debates of comparative versus world literature than a media archaeology, one that reckons with the various dynamics of technology, culture, and transformative conceptions of art moving back in time.

From Janssen's eclipse to Spivak's planetarity to Sansour's wave at the planet earth, each offers a way to consider the contingency of a moment and the shortcoming of the multicultural constellation of national cinemas. Out of world cinema understood as regional puzzle pieces arises a dangerous bind, one constantly trapped in a regressive logic that masks the potential histories of every image. Planetary cinema is a cinema that takes comparison not as an analytical category but as an encounter with the elsewhere and an ethical limit to what can be seen, known, and understood. In the eclipse is a planet that, in obscuring the view, makes a new constellation visible, just as the face at the Jaffa Gate eclipses all that is visible behind it, but makes visible the scene of being filmed. The point here is that in cinema is made thinkable relationships in excess of juxtaposition—the movement of the camera as the train departs the station in Jerusalem makes visible a world in motion, and the film of the pyramids at Giza condenses mythological time into the vernacular duration of film. Across 800 photograms arises the possibility for seeing the world anew—the blur, the eclipse, the shudder emerge as sites from which translating can occur.

At stake in all that I have shared in this microhistory is neither simply a visualization of world cinema nor a globalizing corrective to early film history. Instead, I take seriously the complex life of an animated photograph, refracted and projected, in order to shed light on its sedimented histories for thinking the world—formally, historically, and otherwise. In the collection of Lumière films are manifold sedimented histories for thinking collective futures, the visualization of the planet, and the universalizing projection of a world beyond the literacies of particular languages. In Promio's ellipsis, then, we encounter a productive counterpoint to the listing of national cinemas with nothing less than the future of the world at stake.

Acknowledgments

Years ago, in a graduate seminar on film historiography, my professor posed a question: What might it mean to devote an entire seminar paper to the analysis of a single Lumière Brothers' film? Most of us laughed at the idea, but as I reflected on the task of committing to one 50-second shot, I eventually took it as a challenge. My professor's question invited us to explore the world made visible through attention to detail rather than through the accumulation of examples. In this practice of extended looking, I began to see film anew, not simply as a staged representation of an imagined elsewhere, but as a world brought to life in motion and time. The constraint of the seminar paper inspired me to engage what it means to see through the cinematograph. Weighing 5 kilograms, the portable device recorded films consisting of 800 photograms, 17 meters in length, which translated to roughly 50 seconds, depending on the speed at which the camera operator cranked the handle. For the seminar, I focused on a film shot in 1897 at the pyramids in Egypt, and this exercise eventually grew into an article and an overall inspiration for this book.

Over the years that followed, I have drawn from the Lumière Brothers catalogue to continue the practice of extended looking, selecting films for specific occasions: *Jaffa: Porte ouest* for an event in Oslo, Norway; *Prière du muezzin* for a talk in Rabat, Morocco; and *Marché arabe* for a talk at the University of Michigan. As I tracked the itinerary of the camera operator Alexandre Promio across North Africa and the Middle East, I turned to specific films that animate, in the interplay of light and shadow, the significance of film history, visual culture, and comparative literature. Since I first began working with this archive almost twenty years ago, I have been transformed by conversations and collaborations in locations ranging from Berlin, Berkeley,

Cairo, and Beirut, to Eugene, Rabat, Tunis, and Tangier. The pages of this book bear the trace of mentors, colleagues, and friends whose influence informs how I see both the worlds these films make visible and those they foreclose off-screen, out of focus, and beyond.

As I look back on when I encountered the Lumière Brothers, it was in Mary Ann Doane's class that the most iconic of their films played before my eyes for the first time. I was met initially with boredom staring at the various vignettes: workers leaving a factory, a baby being fed, a gardener with a hose, and a train arriving at station. And yet Professor Doane's lectures revealed how these films capture time and motion in unique ways, and her courses highlighted the philosophical and theoretical implications at stake in these images. Three years later, Kaja Silverman's seminar in film theory would extend what it means to see the world through film. She brought to life in her classroom the attentive and creative ways of looking that I so admire in her writing. And finally, a year later, it was Anton Kaes's seminar on film historiography that ultimately raised the question that set in motion the study that transpires in this book. From him, I learned what it means to see the world in a detail and to consider the critical role that stories play within and beyond the frame. I have a deep indebtedness to these three professors and to those others who helped train my eyes to see, especially Réda Bensmaïa, Karl Britto, Judith Butler, Rosalind Galt, Deniz Göktürk, Philip Rosen, Muhammad Siddiq, Joseph Slaughter, Ann Smock, Trinh T. Minh-ha, and Gauri Viswanathan.

The Forum for Transregional Studies served as my intellectual home as this book developed and took shape. Workshops in Alexandria, Beirut, Berlin, Cairo, Cape Town, Rabat, and Tunis have been invaluable in forming friendships, collaborations, and questions animated across various chapters. I have appreciated the support of the Alexander von Humboldt Foundation for extended stays in Berlin and visits to the Lumière Institute in Lyon. Foremost on an extensive list of friends and mentors is Georges Khalil whose leadership has served as a model for me of scholarly collaboration and generative discussions. I have been grateful to develop and learn from the numerous opportunities the Forum provided me, and I extend a very heartfelt thank you to Maha AbdelMegeed, Refqa Abu-Remaileh, Yvonne Albers, Rüstem Ertug Altinay, Elisabetta Benigni, Julie Billaud, Rasha Chatta, Islam Dayeh, Zeina G. Halabi, Hatim al-Hibri, Walid Houri, Ahmed Fekry Ibrahim, Christian Junge, Banu Karaca, Ramy Khouri, Gijs Kruijtzer, Anne-Marie McManus, Adam Mestyan, Mostafa Minawi, Lamia Moghnieh, Amir Moosavi, Rachid Ouissa, Friederike Pannewicke, Frode Saugestad, and Adania Shibli for friendships that have supported and sustained me over these years.

Early in the project, Kaveh Askari, Tarek El-Ariss, Omnia El Shakry, Peter Limbrick, and Daisuke Miyao helped guide my path with gracious engagement and intellectual inspiration. I have also benefited from the incredible modes of visionary looking made available to me by Siraj Ahmed, Samer Ali, Anjali Arondekar, Blake Atwood, Dima Ayoub, Nicholas Baer, Nima Bassiri, Omar Berrada, Hicham Bouzid, Rodrigo Brandão, Ali Cherri, Jenny Chio, Iggy Cortez, Pardis Dabashi, Elise Domenach, Amanda Doxtater, Emily Drumsta, Alex Dubilet, Karim Elhaies, yasser elhariry, Hoda El Shakry, Karen Emmerich, Samuel England, Samera Esmeir, Scott Ferguson, Hannah Freed-Thall, Joshua Gang, Bernard Geoghagen, Benj Gerdes, Amanda Jo Goldstein, Olivia Harrison, Gretchen Head, Charles Hirschkind, Daniel Hoffman-Schwartz, Elizabeth Holt, Louise Hornby, Tung-Hui Hu, Basit Iqbal, Kelda Jamison, Matthew Keegan, Charif Kiwan, Michael Kunichika, Jean-Michel Landry, Sido Lansari, Katherine Lemons, Anneka Lenssen, Sulgi Lie, Alice Lovejoy, Shaoling Ma, Tom McEnaney, Franklin Melendez, Pashmina Murthy, Julie Napolin, Jennifer Nash, Firat Oruc, Stefania Pandolfo, Kris Paulsen, Nimrod Reitman, Amy Rust, Jeffrey Sacks, Allison Schachter, Simona Schneider, Vanessa Schwartz, Stephen Sheehi, Tess Takahashi, Adam Talib, Kabir Tambar, Ben Tran, Barbara Turquier, Tobias Warner, Sarah Ann Wells, Karen Yekplé-Zumhagen, Damon Young, and Kamil Zapaśnik.

I have appreciated the community in the departments of Comparative Literature and Cinema Studies at the University of Oregon that has helped foster my intellectual life. I thank colleagues past and present: Peter Ailiunas, Michael Aronson, Mike Bray, Jon Crawford, Nissryne Dib, Nicholas Forster, Sangita Gopal, Erin Hanna, Masami Kawai, Dong Hoon Kim, Katherina Loew, Gabriela Martinez, Kevin May, Allison McGuffie, HyeRyoung Ok, Priscilla Peña Ovalle, Ari Purnama, Sergio Rigoletto, Jerell Rosales, André Sirois, Daniel Goméz Steinhart, Janet Wasko, and Colin Williamson. A heartfelt thank you to Aycan Akcamete, Monique Balbuena, Steven Brown, Katherine Brundan, Kenneth Calhoon, Roy Chan, Katya Hokanson, Dawn Marlan, Leah Middlebrook, Lanie Millar, Jenifer Presto, and Tze-Yin Teo. I owe a debt of gratitude to Musʻab Abdulsalam, Hadil Abuhamid, Anita Chari, Mai-Lin Cheng, Jasmine Chorley-Schulz, Miriam Chorley-Schulz, Palita Chunsaengchen, Jovencio De La Paz, Yewulsew Endalew, Baran Germen, Andréa Gilroy, Zachary Hicks, Jahn, Fatou Jobe, Lamia Karim, Anya Kivarkis, Yei Won Lim, Cintia Martinez Velasco, Sandra Mefoude, Fabienne Moore, Ahmad Nadalizadeh, Mariam Nadeem, Martha Ndakalako, Coosje Oldenhuis, Feba Rasheed, Untara Rayeesa, Tera Reid-Olds, Daniel Rosenberg, Leslie Rutberg, Cera Smith, Cynthia Stockwell, Laurel Sturgis-O'Coyne, Debarghya Sanyal, Kyle Shernuk, Casey Shoop, Jalen Thomson, Nicholas

Wirtz, Shuangting Xiong, and generations of students and colleagues from whom I have learned so much.

Catherine Grant and Jason Mittell helped facilitate an incredible summer session at Middlebury College that illuminated film analysis in new ways for me. I benefited richly from the opportunity to learn techniques of videographic criticism and from the remarkable group of scholars they drew together. Thank you to Dalia Davoudi, Shelleen Greene, and Salomé Aguilera Skvirsky, each of whom patiently watched and reflected on the Lumière Brothers films with me. Thank you to Pierre-Olivier Toulza for being the best lab mate imaginable and to Annette Davison, Roger Hallas, Olga Kim, Dayna McLeod, Isabelle McNeill, Katarzyna Paszkiewicz, Laura Caballero Rabanal, Will Scheibel, Charlotte Scurlock, Murray Smith, Daniel Goméz Steinhart, and Wanzhou Xiao for their camaraderie, insight, and advice.

Along this journey, I have appreciated the friendship and support of my postcolonial reading group: Sunayani Bhattacharya, Daniel Elam, Kritish Rajbhandari, and Akshya Saxena. To audiences at the University of Cape Town, EGE in Rabat, the Leibniz Center for Literary and Cultural Research in Berlin, Kenyon College, Georgetown University in Qatar, Emory University, University of Southern California, University of Michigan, University of Texas at Austin, Florida Atlantic University, University of Wisconsin at Madison, University of California at Davis, Yale NUS, University of Chicago, University of Texas at Dallas, Georgetown University, and University of Minnesota, I have been grateful for the questions and engagement you provided me. Excerpts of chapter 5 first appeared as "Deserted Histories: The Great Pyramid and Early Film Form," *Early Popular Visual Culture* 6, no. 2 (July 2008): 159–70, and I thank the journal for permission to publish this material. The Oregon Humanities Center has helped support this book with a generous subsidy toward its publication. Thank you to Paul Peppis, Leah Middlebrook, and the incredible staff for the seminars, events, and fellowship.

My deep gratitude extends to a number of friends who read and commented on the manuscript. A very heartfelt thank you to Travis Wilds, whose patience and keen eye proved invaluable to me as I revised. Karen Emmerich and Colin Koopman graciously read and commented on early chapters, and Pierre-Olivier Toulza assisted me on the quest for permissions. Alice Lovejoy and Masha Salazkina stepped in during the final weeks for a virtual manuscript workshop with generous insights and constructive feedback. I thank Zeina G. Halabi for her support and encouragement; Leah Middlebrook for her wisdom, insight, and advice; and Kenneth Calhoon for hallway conversations that helped sustain my thinking and writing. I extend a thank you to my editor Tom Lay for his confidence in this project, my copyeditor Teresa

Jesionowski for her discerning eye, and the incredible staff at Fordham University Press for their professionalism and support through the various phases of the publication process.

I owe a special thank you to Brent Eng, who inspired me with near daily consultations and whose friendship serves as a valuable reminder of what I appreciate most about thinking, writing, and learning. My chosen family has continued to grow over the years: Tadashi Dozono, Mayanthi Fernando, Rouven Guessaz, Banu Karaca, Milad Odabaei, Hannes Strätz, and Rocío Zambrana are all part of making this world a better place. Sunday river walks with Stacy Alaimo have been grounding for me, and swimming pool chats with Colin Koopman helped me arrive at my title. For concerts and conversations, I thank Tres Pyle, and for dinners and dog walks, I thank Kate Kelp-Stebbins and Marcel Brousseau. A heartfelt thank you to Tink Campbell, Erica Dillon, Melanie Krebs-Pilotti, Stephanie LeMenager, Armando Manalo, and David Marks—and to dear friends and family in Montreal, Chicago, Florida, Paris, and Virginia. To my immediate and loving triumvirate Keefie, Max, and Theo, I am indebted to you for the abundance of love, laughter, and purrs you bring to my life.

If this book focuses on a practice of extended looking, it also turns on the possibility of seeing the world in new ways. In the midst of writing, I was heartbroken to lose a dear friend and mentor through whom I had come to understand the dynamics of seeing and insight. Saba Mahmood remained for me an inspiration throughout the writing process, and her critical sensibility continues to illuminate how I understand the work we do. It was she who pushed me to question the connections of media and mediation, and it is through her that I grew attuned to the ethical stakes of looking. Even in the last few months of her life, Saba continued to teach and inspire me, offering me glimpses of how she valued the meaning of intellectual endeavors, their inseparability from life itself, and the place of work within it all. In her death, she revealed new paths for me to understand how we would remain in dialogue, and her lessons inform nearly every word of this book. For her friendship, her love, and her inspiration, I am deeply grateful. I dedicate this work to her memory and her abiding devotion to inquiry at once critical and compassionate.

Notes

Introduction. Microhistory: Envisioning Ellipsis

1. G.-Michel Coissac, *Histoire du cinématographe de ses origines à nos jours* (Paris: Éditions de Cinéopse, 1925), 194–99.

2. See Promio's account published in Coissac, *Histoire du cinématographe de ses origines à nos jours*. A translation exists by Gerard-Jans Claes; see Alexandre Promio, "A Travelogue," *Sabzian*, May 27, 2020, https://www.sabzian.be/text/a-travelogue. For an authoritative account of Promio's travels, see Jean-Claude Seguin, *Alexandre Promio, ou, Les énigmes de la lumière* (Paris: Harmattan, 1999), and references to Promio in Richard Abel, *Encyclopedia of Early Cinema* (London: Routledge, 2005), 13, 58, 92–93, 216, 485, 519, 540, 599, 615, 632.

3. It is worth noting here that Promio's claim, which avoids making the classic iconophobia argument, does manage to overlook the prevalence of photography in the Ottoman Empire. See Muhammad Isa Waley, "Images of the Ottoman Empire: The Photograph Albums Presented by Sultan Abdülhamid II," *British Library Journal* 17, no. 2 (1991): 111–27.

4. See Michelle Aubert et al., *La Production Cinématographique des Frères Lumière* (Paris: Librairie du Premier Siècle du Cinéma. Paris: Editions Mémoires de cinéma, 1996), as well as a website maintained by Manuel Schmalsteig (https://catalogue-lumiere.com/). For reference to Promio's activity in the Middle East specifically, see Viola Shafik's pioneering book, *Arab Cinema: History and Cultural Identity* (Cairo: American University in Cairo Press, 2007), as well as Michael Allan, "Deserted Histories: The Lumière Brothers, the Pyramids and Early Film Form," *Early Popular Visual Culture* 6, no. 2 (2008): 159–70, and Mohamad Soueid, "Documenting Lebanon," in *Documentary Filmmaking in the Middle East and North Africa*, ed. Viola Shafik (Cairo: American University in Cairo Press, 2022), 33–46.

5. Ariella Aïsha Azoulay, *Potential History: Unlearning Imperialism* (London: Verso Books, 2019), 288.

6. See, for example, Anjali Arondekar, *Abundance* (Durham, NC: Duke University Press, 2023).

7. See, for example, Ahmed al-Hadari, *Tarikh al-sinima fi Misr* (Cairo: Nādī al-Sīnimā bi-al-Qāhirah, 1989); Samy Helmy, *Bidayat al-Cinema Al Misriyya* (General Organization of Cultural Palaces, 2013); Samy Helmy, *Madrasat al-Iskandariyya lel-Tasweer al-Cinema'i* (Alexandria: Bibliotheca Alexandrina, 2013); and Shafik, *Arab Cinema: History and Cultural Identity*.

8. Fatimah Tobing Rony, *The Third Eye: Race, Cinema, and Ethnographic Spectacle* (Durham, NC: Duke University Press, 1996); Alison Griffiths, *Wondrous Difference: Cinema, Anthropology, and Turn-of-the-Century Visual Culture* (New York: Columbia University Press, 2001); and Jeffrey Ruoff, ed., *Virtual Voyages: Cinema and Travel* (Durham, NC: Duke University Press, 2006).

9. Among numerous possible sources exploring this connection, see Weihong Bao, "In Search of a 'Cinematic Esperanto': Exhibiting Wartime Chongqing Cinema in Global Context," *Journal of Chinese Cinemas* 3, no. 2 (2009): 135–47.

10. See *al-Ahram*, November 9, 1896, and *La Réforme*, December 1, 1896.

11. For coverage in the Algerian press, see *La Dépêche algérienne*, November 22 and December 16, 1896.

12. For an announcement of Promio's visit to Algeria, see *La Dépêche algérienne*, December 19, 1896, 3. For accounts of Promio's visit to Alexandria, see *La Réforme*, March 8 and March 9, 1897; for the trip to Cairo, see *al-Akhbar*, March 12, 1897.

13. I point here to a few sources that document this early history of cinema: Abdelghani Megherbi, *Les Algériens au miroir du cinéma colonial: (Contribution à une sociologie de la décolonisation)* (Alger: E.D.,1982); al-Hadari, *Tarikh al-sinima fi Misr*; Guy Hennebelle, *Les Cinémas Africains en 1972* (Paris: Société africaine d'édition, 1972); Lizbeth Malkmus and Roy Armes, *Arab and African Film Making* (London: Zed Books, 1991); and Shafik's remarkable *Arab Cinema: History and Cultural Identity*.

14. An important account of this mythology can be found in Christophe Gauthier's article, "Comment les Frères Lumière devinrent les pères du cinéma: La querelle des inventeurs," *Bibliothèque de l'École des chartes* 167, no. 1 (2009): 155–78.

15. Debates exist about the origins of film, but in nearly all accounts the Lumière Brothers are credited with having popularized the cinematograph and capitalized on its powers of projection to audiences in Lyon initially, then Paris, and eventually across the world. See George Sadoul, *Louis Lumière* (Paris: Seghers, 1964).

16. For a detailed account of these experiments, see Benoît Turquety, *Inventing Cinema: Machines, Gestures and Media History* (Amsterdam: Amsterdam University Press, 2019).

17. See Louis Lumière, "The Lumiere Cinematograph" in *A Technological History of Motion Pictures and Television: An Anthology from the Pages of the Journal of the Society of Motion Picture and Television Engineers*, ed. Raymond Fielding (Berkeley: University of California Press, 1967), 49–50.

18. Laurent Mannoni, *The Great Art of Light and Shadow: Archaeology of the Cinema* (Exeter: University of Exeter Press, 2000), 422.

19. See Mannoni, *The Great Art of Light and Shadow*, 422—as well as Bernard Chardère, Guy Borgé, and Marjorie Borgé, *Les Lumière* (Lausanne: Payot, 1985); Jacques Rittaud-Hutinet, *Le cinéma des origines: Les frères Lumière et leurs opérateurs* (Seyssel: Champ Vallon, 1985); and Vincent Pinel, *Louis Lumière: Inventeur et Cinéaste* (Paris: Nathan, 1994). Most of these accounts affirm that Charles Moisson produced the initial prototype used at the screening in 1895 (now housed at CNMN in Paris) and that Jules Carpentier helped to produce ten cinematographs at the outset of 1896. See George Sadoul's interview with Louis Lumière in *Sight and Sound*, 17, no. 66 (Summer 1948): 68–70.

20. A gloss of this particular statement generates a number of questions for Jean-Claude Seguin, who goes on to explore the record of how it was that Promio secured his position, especially when other operators had longer histories with the Lumière family. See Seguin, *Alexandre Promio, ou, Les énigmes de la lumière*, 19, 21.

21. Alexandre Promio, "A Travelogue" (https://www.sabzian.be/text/a-travelogue), May 27, 2020, with my own slight adaptation to the translation.

22. Promio, "A Travelogue."

23. See Rittaud-Hutinet, *Le cinéma des origines: Les Frères Lumières et leurs opérateurs* and Seguin, *Alexandre Promio, ou, Les énigmes de la lumière*.

24. See, for example, Félix Mesguich, *Tours de manivelle: Souvenirs d'un chasseur d'images* (Paris: B. Grasset, 1933), portions of which have been translated by Kevin Riordan and Corbin Treacy as "A Translation from Felix Mésguich's *Tours de manivelle*," *Modernism/modernity* 18 no. 2 (2011): 447–48. See Gabriel Veyre, *Dans l'intimité du sultan, au Maroc 1901–1905* (Paris: Librairie Universelle, 1905); Philippe Jacquier and Marion Pranal, *Gabriel Veyre, Opérateur Lumière: Autour du monde avec le Cinématographe, Correspondance (1896–1900)* (Lyon/Arles: Institut Lumière/Actes Sud, 1996); and Philippe Jacquier, "Un opérateur de la Maison Lumière, Gabriel Veyre," in *Le Cinéma Francais Muet Dans le Monde, Influences Réciproques*: Symposium de la FIAF (Paris: Cinematheque de Toulouse/Institut Jean Vigo, 1988). For general accounts of camera operators' experiences, see Dominique Moustacchia and Béatrice de Pastre, "De la solitude des premiers opérateurs à la mise en œuvre des équipes de tournage: Le cas des opérateurs Lumière," *La Revue Documentaires*, no. 26–27 (2016): 19–29, as well as Rittaud-Hutinet, *Le cinéma des origines*.

25. See, for example, Tom Gunning's entry on "Camera Movement," in *Encyclopedia of Early Cinema*, ed. Richard Abel (London: Routledge, 2005), 133.

26. Coissac, *Histoire du cinématographe de ses origines à nos jours*.

27. Carlo Ginzburg, "Carlo Ginzburg: 'In History as in Cinema, Every Close-Up Implies an Off-Screen Scene,'" *Verso Books*, June 6, 2023, https://www.versobooks.com/blogs/news/5536-carlo-ginzburg-in-history-as-in-cinema-every-close-up-implies-an-off-screen-scene..

28. Ginzburg, "In History as in Cinema."

29. Ginzburg, "In History as in Cinema."

30. Ginzburg, "In History as in Cinema"

31. Ginzburg, "In History as in Cinema"

32. Seguin, *Alexandre Promio*.

33. These questions are insightfully explored in Daisuke Miyao, *Japonisme and the Birth of Cinema* (Durham, NC: Duke University Press, 2020). For the Latin American context, see John Fullerton's "Creating an Audience for the *Cinématographe*: Two Lumière Agents in Mexico, 1896," *Film History: An International Journal* 20, no. 1 (2008): 95–114.

34. See Jack Shaheen, *Reel Bad Arabs* (New York: Olive Branch Press, 2012), as well as Melanie McAllister, *Epic Encounters: Culture, Media, and US Interests in the Middle East since 1945* (Berkeley: University of California Press, 2005).

35. I draw inspiration from the remarkable work of Laura Marks whose *Hanan al-Cinema: Affections for the Moving Image* (Cambridge, MA: MIT Press, 2015) models the experimental dynamism of independent Arab media art. Even though her work addresses experimental works from the last twenty-five years, it shares in its embrace of cinema as a site for unfolding and enfolding.

36. Alison Griffiths, *Wondrous Difference: Cinema, Anthropology, and Turn-of-the-Century Visual Culture* (New York: Columbia University Press, 2001), and Fatimah Tobing Rony, *The Third Eye: Race, Cinema, and Ethnographic Spectacle* (Durham, NC: Duke University Press, 1996).

37. It is worth noting that Promio may or may not have been the operator to have shot these films. Some ambiguity exists in the archival sources: "Alexandre Promio's travelogue remains to this day the only testimony that attributes these films to him, but one cannot rule out the possibility that Émile Lavanchy-Clarke, the brother of Lumière's concessionaire in Switzerland, may have operated the camera." https://catalogue-lumiere.com/series/alexandre-promio-a-geneve-1896. See, for example, Roland Cosandey, "Le catalogue Lumière (1896–1907) et la Suisse: Éléments pour une filmographie nationale," *1895, revue d'histoire du cinéma*, no. 15 (1993): 3–30.

38. Tom Gunning, "The Whole World within Reach," in *Virtual Voyages*, ed. Jeffrey Ruoff (Durham, NC: Duke University Press, 2006).

39. Edward Said, *Orientalism* (New York, Vintage, 1979); Timothy Mitchell, *Colonising Egypt* (Berkeley: University of California Press, 1991); Ella Shohat and Robert Stam, *Unthinking Eurocentrism* (New York: Routledge, 1994); as well as, more recently, Ali Behdad, *Camera Orientalis* (Chicago: University of Chicago Press, 2016); and Stephen Sheehi, *The Arab Imago* (Princeton, NJ: Princeton University Press, 2016).

40. See, for example, Hansmartin Siegrist, *Auf der Brücke zur Moderne Basels erster Film als Panorama der Belle Epoque* (Basel: Christoph Merian Verlag, 2019), https://www.tinguely.ch/en/exhibitions/exhibitions/2022/lavanchy.html as well as https://kinematografie.ch/blogeintrag-details/ein-phantom-der-filmgeschichte-f-h-lavanchy-clarke.html; https://catalogue-lumiere.com/series/alexandre-promio-a-geneve-1896/.

41. https://kinematografie.ch/blogeintrag-details/ein-phantom-der-filmgeschichte-f-h-lavanchy-clarke.html.

42. *Le Progrès*, Lyon, jeudi 31 juin 1895, and quoted in Bernard Chardère, *Lumières sur lumière* (Lyon: Presses universitaires du Lyon, 1987), 115.

43. For an account of tableaux vivants in early cinema, see Leah Lahmbeck, Britt Salvensen, and Vanessa Schwartz, eds., *City of Cinema: Paris 1850–1907* (Los Angeles: DelMonico Books, 2022).

44. Dai Vaughan, "Let There Be Lumière," in *Early Cinema: Space, Frame, Narrative*, ed. Thomas Elsaesser (Bloomington: Indiana University Press, 1990), 64.

45. Vaughan, "All the actors are in motion. Their smallest actions are so naturally reproduced that one wonders if there is any illusion."

46. Vaughan, "Let There Be Lumière."

47. Vaughan, "Let There Be Lumière."

48. Vaughan, "Let There Be Lumière."

49. Jordan Schonig, *The Shape of Motion: Cinema and the Aesthetics of Movement* (Oxford: Oxford University Press, 2021), 19, 21, 29–32.

50. See Philip Rosen, "Document and Documentary: On the Persistence of Historical Concepts," in *Theorizing Documentary*, ed. Michael Renov (London: Routledge, 1993).

51. Coissac, *Histoire du cinématographe*, v.

52. See Vanessa Schwartz, "On the Move: Seeing the World in Early Transport Films," in *Paris: City of Cinema* (Los Angeles: DelMonico Books, 2021), 120–53.

53. Tom Gunning, "The Cinema of Attractions: Early Cinema, Its Spectator, and the Avant-Garde," *Wide Angle* 8 (1986): 3–4, and André Bazin, "The Myth of Total Cinema," in *What Is Cinema?* vol. 1, trans. Hugh Gray (Berkeley: University of California Press, 1967).

54. See André Gaudreault et al., *The End of Cinema?: A Medium in Crisis in the Digital Age* (New York: Columbia University Press, 2015), as well as https://www.youtube.com/watch?v=w5Mjb-AqiMs&ab_channel=Numapresse and https://www.youtube.com/watch?v=uzKt4ogokAs&ab_channel=Centerfor21stCenturyStudies.

55. See Richard Abel, *The Ciné Goes to Town: French Cinema, 1896–1914*, updated and expanded ed. (Berkeley: University of California Press, 1998), 102–3.

1. World: The Labor of Representation

1. A filmed version of this event is available as the final film on *The Lumière Brothers' First Films* (New York: Kino International, 1996). The centenary

proliferated a number of conferences and books, among which *L'Aventure du cinématographe: Actes du congrès mondial Lumière* (ALEAS: Université Lumière, Lyon 2, 1995), and John Fullerton, ed., *Celebrating 1895: The Centenary of Cinema* (Sydney: John Libbey, 1998).

2. Institut Lumière, https://www.institut-lumiere.org/musee/discover-the-lumiere-site/the-hangar-du-premier-film.html.

3. The Archives françaises du film (AFF) in Paris has been restoring and making the films accessible to the public https://histoiredesarts.culture.gouv.fr/Toutes-les-ressources/Centre-national-du-cinema-et-de-l-image-animee-CNC/Le-projet-Lumiere). The work of Michelle Aubert and Jean-Claude Seguin, *La production cinématographique des Frères Lumière* (Paris: Éditions Mémoires de Cinéma, 1996), as well as Manuel Schmalstieg's website established with the Conception Multimédia de l'Ecole d'Arts Appliqués de la Chaux-de-Fonds provide valuable resources for understanding the scope and scale of the archive (https://catalogue-lumiere.com/).

4. See Malek Khouri's remarkable book, *The Arab National Project in Youssef Chahine's Cinema* (Cairo: American University in Cairo Press, 2010). For a general overview see Michael Allan, "Youssef Chahine's Iskandariyya . . . Leh?" in *Global Encyclopedia of Lesbian, Gay, Bisexual, Transgender, and Queer History* (New York: Charles Scribner's Sons, 2019), 847–51.

5. Eve Kosofsky Sedgwick, *Touching Feeling* (Durham, NC: Duke University Press, 2002), 8.

6. Samera Esmeir, "On Becoming Less of the World," *History of the Present* 8, no. 1 (April 2018): 88.

7. Esmeir, "On Becoming Less of the World," 90.

8. Esmeir, "On Becoming Less of the World," 90.

9. Masha Salazkina, "World Cinema as Method," *Canadian Journal of Film Studies/Revue canadienne d'études cinématographiques* 29, no. 2 (2020): 12.

10. Salazkina, "World Cinema as Method," 12.

11. For a thoughtful engagement with the convergence of world literature and world cinema, see Keya Ganguly, "World Literature, World Cinema, and Dialectical Criticism," in *The Cambridge Companion to World Literature* (Cambridge: Cambridge University Press, 2018).

12. Dudley Andrew, "An Atlas of World Cinema," *Framework* 45, no 2. (Fall 2004): 9–23.

13. Michael Gott and Thibault Schilt, eds., *Cinéma-monde* (Edinburgh: Edinburgh University Press, 2018); and Bill Marshall, "Cinéma-monde? Towards a Concept of Francophone Cinema," *Francosphères* 1, no. 1 (2012): 35–51.

14. Shekhar Deshpande and Meta Mazaj, eds., *World Cinema: A Critical Introduction* (New York: Routledge, 2018).

15. Robert Stam, *World Literature, Transnational Cinema, and Global Media: Towards a Transartistic Commons* (London: Routledge, 2019).

16. See, for example, Paul Cooke, *World Cinema's "Dialogues" with Hollywood* (Baskingstoke: Palgrave Macmillan, 2007); Stephanie Dennison et al., *Remapping*

World Cinema: Identity, Culture and Politics in Film (London: Wallflower Press, 2006); Rosalind Galt and Karl Schoonover, *Global Art Cinema: New Theories and Histories* (New York: Oxford University Press, 2010); Lina Khatib, *Storytelling in World Cinemas*, vol. 1–2 (London: Wallflower Press, 2012); Lúcia Nagib et al., *Theorizing World Cinema* (London: I. B. Tauris, 2012); Lúcia Nagib, *World Cinema and the Ethics of Realism* (New York: Continuum International, 2011); Rob Stone et al., eds., *The Routledge Companion to World Cinema* (Abingdon: Routledge, 2018).

17. Andrew, "An Atlas of World Cinema," 12.

18. Dudley Andrew, "Time Zones and Jet Lag in World Cinema, in *World Cinema/Transnational Perspectives* (London: Routledge, 2009).

19. Sadoul noted that Thomas Edison, William Kennedy, and Laurie Dickson predated the Lumière claims to the first film. See Georges Sadoul, *Histoire du cinéma mondial, des origines à nos jours* (Paris: Flammarion, 1968), 19. In the quest for origins stories, Louis Le Prince's "Groundhay Garden Scene" from October 14, 1888, is also seen to be the first. See David Nicholas Wilkinson's documentary *The First Film*.

20. See Jacques Aumont, "Lumière Revisited," *Film History* 8, no. 4 (1996): 416–30. See also Georges Sadoul's interview with Louis Lumière in *Sight and Sound* 17, no. 66 (Summer 1948): 68–70—also found in Harry Geduld, *Filmmakers on Filmmaking* (Blooomington: Indiana University Press, 1967). Harun Farocki, "Workers Leaving the Factory," trans. Laurent Faasch-Ibrahim, *Senses of Cinema*, no. 2 (July 2002), https://www.sensesofcinema.com/2002/harun-farocki/farocki_workers/ and George Didi-Huberman, "People Exposed, People as Extras," *Radical Philosophy* 156 (July/August 2009): 16–22.

21. See, for example, Marshall Deutelbaum's chapter in *Film before Griffith*, ed. John L. Fell (Berkeley: University of California Press, 1983).

22. More information on Francis Doublier, including cited interviews with him, can be found in Jay Leyda, *Kino: A History of Russian and Soviet Film* (Princeton, NJ: Princeton University Press, 1983), 18–23; Richard Abel, *The Ciné Goes to Town* (Berkeley: University of California Press, 1998), which on page 53 alludes to Doublier's work at Fort Lee; and Clara Auclair's talk, "In Focus: The Treasures of the Francis Doublier Collection," from the Eastman Museum on April 9, 2021 (https://www.youtube.com/watch?v=khiiz1RoVGc).

23. See the interview with Francis Doublier in Bernard Chardère, *Lumières sur Lumière* (Lyon: Institut Lumière: Presses universitaires de Lyon, 1987), 273.

24. A more detailed account of the various camera operators can be found in Jacques Rittaud-Hutinet, *Le cinéma des origines* (Seyssel: Champs Vallon, 1985).

25. For more detail on the memorialization, see Jacques Aumont, "Lumière Revisited," *Film History* 8, no. 4 (1996); Didier Caron, "L'in(ter)vention Lumiere," *Revue de la Cinémathèque*, no. 5 (Spring 1994): 104–16. Aumont distinguishes the Lumière-centric historians such as Coissac, Georges Sadoul, *Les pionniers du cinéma* (Paris: Editions Denoël, 1948), Henri Kubnick, Victor Perrot, Maurice Bessy

and Lo Ducca from the anti-Lumièrists such as Maurice Noverre, Jacques Deslandes, Laurent Mannoni, *The Great Art of Light and Shadow*, especially Chapter 16 (Devon: University of Exeter Press, 2000), and Vincent Pinel.

26. See Chardère, *Lumières sur Lumière*, 273–76. Doublier's account in the interview is at times at odds with more recent scholarship on the global travels of camera operators.

27. Debjany Ganguly, *This Thing Called the World* (Durham, NC: Duke University Press, 2016); and Pheng Cheah, *What Is a World? On Postcolonial Literature as World Literature* (Durham, NC: Duke University Press, 2016).

28. Tom Conley, *Film Hieroglyphs* (Minneapolis: University of Minnesota Press, 1991); and Edgar Garcia, *Signs of the Americas* (Chicago: University of Chicago Press, 2020).

29. I point here to the common trope in early postcolonial studies regarding mimicry. See Homi Bhabha, "Of Mimicry and Man," in *The Location of Culture* (London: Routledge, 1994); and Michael Taussig's *Mimesis and Alterity* (London: Routledge, 1993).

30. See Nicholas Mirzoeff's discussion of the plantation complex in *The Right to Look: A Counterhistory of Visuality* (Durham, NC: Duke University Press, 2011).

31. I refer here to a number of books that have informed my interest in these films: Fatimah Tobing Rony, *The Third Eye: Race, Cinema, and Ethnographic Spectacle* (Durham, NC: Duke University Press, 1996); Alice Maurice, *The Cinema and Its Shadow* (Minneapolis: University of Minnesota Press, 2013); Paula Amad, *Counter-Archive: Film, the Everyday, and Albert Kahn's Archives de la planète* (New York: Columbia University Press, 2010); Alison Griffiths, *Wondrous Difference: Cinema, Anthropology, and Turn-of-the-Century Visual Culture* (New York: Columbia University Press, 2001); Katherine Groo, *Bad Film Histories: Ethnography and the Early Film Archive* (Minneapolis: University of Minnesota Press, 2019), especially 64–73; and Ariella Aïsha Azoulay, *Potential History: Unlearning Imperialism* (London: Verso Books, 2019).

32. Harun Farocki, *Arbeiter verlassen die Fabrik* (film), and "Workers Leaving the Factory," *Senses of Cinema*, no. 21 (July 2002), https://www.sensesofcinema.com/2002/harun-farocki/farocki_workers/. See also Sarah Ann Wells, "At the Shores of Work," *Comparative Literature* 73, no. 2 (June 2021): 166–83.

33. Farocki, *Arbeiter verlassen die Fabrik*.

34. Farocki, *Arbeiter verlassen die Fabrik*.

35. Charlie Chaplin, *Modern Times*, United Artists, 1936; see Sianne Ngai's remarkable reading in the chapter "Animatedness" in *Ugly Feelings* (Cambridge, MA: Harvard University Press, 2005).

36. Jean-Marie Straub and Danièle Huillet's film *Too Early, Too Late*, Grasshopper Film, 1982.

37. See, for example, P. Adams Sitney's "A Cinema of Resistance," *Artforum*, May 2016; and Barton Byg, *Landscapes of Resistance* (Berkeley: University of California Press, 1995). Daniel Fairfax helps link "le plan Straubian" to debates over

people and draws in doing so from Helge Heberle and Monika Funke Stern, "Das Feuer im Inneren des Berges: Gespräch mit Danièle Huillet," *Frauen und Film*, no. 32 (1982): 10. See Daniel Fairfax, "Straub, Jean-Marie & Huillet, Danièle," *Senses of Cinema*, no. 52 (September 2009), https://www.sensesofcinema.com/2009/great-directors/jean-marie-straub-and-daniele-huillet/.

38. Stephen Best and Sharon Marcus, "Surface Reading: An Introduction," *Representations* 108, no. 1 (2009): 1–21.

39. Sergei Eisenstein, *Film Form: Essays in Film Theory*, ed. and trans. Jay Leyda (1949; San Diego: Harcourt Brace, 1977), 36.

40. Eisenstein, 36.

41. Eisenstein, 36.

42. Eisenstein, 37.

43. See Manon Demurger and Musée Albert Kahn, *Les Archives de la Planète*, ed. Valérie Perlès (Musée départemental Albert Kahn: LienArt, 2019); Isabelle Marinone et al., *Un Monde et son double: Regards sur L'entreprise visuelle des Archives de la Planète (1919–1931)* (Presses Universitaires de Perpignan, 2019); and Trond Bjorli and Kjetil Jakobsen, eds., *Cosmopolitics of the Camera: Albert Kahn's Archives of the Planet* (Bristol: Intellect Books, 2020).

44. Amad, *Counter-Archive*; Groo, *Bad Film Histories*.

45. Dziga Vertov, *A Sixth Part of the World* (Film & Kunst GmbH, 2010).

46. Lisa Parks, *Cultures in Orbit: Satellites and the Televisual* (Durham, NC: Duke University Press, 2005).

2. Location: Locating Looks in World Cinema

1. Tom Gunning, "The Cinema of Attractions: Early Cinema, Its Spectator, and the Avant-Garde," *Wide Angle* 8 (1986).

2. I point here to some excellent reflections that hit upon location in world cinema. See Kaveh Askari, *Relaying Cinema* (Oakland: University of California Press, 2022); Daniel Steinhart, *Runaway Hollywood* (Oakland: University of California Press, 2019); and Samhita Sunya, *Sirens of Modernity* (Oakland: University of California Press, 2022).

3. John David Rhodes and Elena Gorfinkel, *Taking Place: Location and the Moving Image* (Minneapolis: University of Minnesota Press, 2011), viii.

4. Rhodes and Gorfinkel, *Taking Place*, xvi.

5. Priya Jaikumar, *Where Histories Reside* (Durham, NC: Duke University Press, 2019), 30.

6. Priya Jaikumar, *Where Histories Reside*, 30.

7. See Nicholas Mirzoeff, *The Right to Look* (Durham, NC: Duke University Press, 2011); Ariella Azoulay, *Potential History* (London: Verso Books, 2019), 383.

8. Bridget Alsdorf, *Gawkers* (Princeton, NJ: Princeton University Press, 2022), 153.

9. I allude here to a wealth of scholarship on structures of identification in cinema. See, for example, Sergei Eisenstein, "Film Form: New Problems," and his

later essay, "Dickens, Griffith and the Film Today," in *Film Form: Essays in Film Theory* (San Diego: Harvest Books, 1949), 133, 249–51. See also Laura Mulvey, *Visual and Other Pleasures* (London: Palgrave Macmillan, 2009); Kaja Silverman on "Suture," which is Chapter 5 of *The Subject of Semiotics* (New York: Oxford University Press, 1983); and Mary Ann Doane, "Film and the Masquerade," *Screen* 23, no. 3–4 (1982): 74–87.

10. Livio Belloï, "Lumière and His View: The Cameraman's Eye in Early Cinema," *Historical Journal of Film, Radio & Television* 15, no. 4 (October 1995): 461–74.

11. Belloï, "Lumière and His View."

12. Belloï, "Lumière and His View."

13. Christian Metz, *The Imaginary Signifier: Psychoanalysis and the Cinema* (Bloomington: Indiana University Press, 1982), 45.

14. Metz, *The Imaginary Signifier*, 45.

15. Metz, *The Imaginary Signifier*, 45.

16. Metz, *The Imaginary Signifier*, 49. See also Kaja Silverman, *The Acoustic Mirror: The Female Voice in Psychoanalysis and Cinema* (Bloomington: Indiana University Press, 1988).

17. Hamid Naficy, "Theorizing 'Third-World' Film Spectatorship," *Wide Angle* 18, no. 4 (1996): 3–26.

18. Fatimah Tobing Rony, *The Third Eye: Race, Cinema, and Ethnographic Spectacle* (Durham, NC: Duke University Press, 1996), 6. See also Alice Maurice, *The Cinema and Its Shadow: Race and Technology in Early Cinema* (Minneapolis: University of Minnesota Press, 2013).

19. Scott Curtis, *The Shape of Spectatorship: Art, Science, and Early Cinema in Germany* (New York: Columbia University Press, 2015); Vance Kepley Jr., "Whose Apparatus? Problems of Film Exhibition and History," in *Post-Theory: Reconstructing Film Studies*, ed. David Bordwell and Noel Carroll (Madison: University of Wisconsin Press, 1996); and Haidee Wasson, *Everyday Movies: Portable Film Projectors and the Transformation of American Culture* (Oakland: University of California Press, 2020).

20. See Bernard Chardère, *Lumières sur Lumière* (Lyon: Presses universitaires du Lyon, 1987), 113–15.

21. See Anne Friedberg, *The Virtual Window: From Alberti to Microsoft* (Cambridge, MA: MIT Press, 2006).

22. A gloss of this particular statement generates a number of questions for Jean-Claude Seguin, who goes on to explore the record of how it was that Promio secured his position, especially when other operators had longer histories with the Lumière family. Jean-Claude Seguin, *Alexandre Promio, ou, Les énigmes de la lumière* (Paris: Harmattan, 1999), 19, 21.

23. G.-M. Coissac, *Histoire du cinématographe de ses origines à nos jours* (Paris: Éditions de Cinéopse, 1925), 195; M. François Pascal was an older teacher of the Lumière brothers at La Martinière, a school founded in Lyon in 1831 with

experimental pedagogical methods based on the work of Henry Tabareau, one of its directors. Promio would publish short entries on Pascal's photographic experimentation and another on the cinematograph itself.

24. See Jean-Claude Seguin, "Aux origines du cinéma en Algérie: Alexandre Promio," *Le Documentaire dans l'Algérie coloniale* (2014): 33.

25. Seguin, *Alexandre Promio*, 83 (my translation).

26. See Charles Musser's remarks on John Stoddard in *The Emergence of Cinema: The American Screen to 1907* (Charles Scribner's Sons, 1990). See also Charles Musser, "Documentary's longue durée: Beginnings, formations, genealogies," NECSUS (Autumn 2020), https://necsus-ejms.org/documentarys-longue-duree-beginnings-formations-genealogies/.

27. Tom Gunning, "The Whole World within Reach," in *Virtual Voyages*, ed. Jeffrey Ruoff (Durham, NC: Duke University Press, 2006), 27.

28. Gunning, "The Whole World within Reach," 29.

29. Abdelkader Benali, *Le cinéma colonial au Maghreb* (Paris: Éditions du Cerf, 1998), especially the first chapter, "De la peinture au cinéma: Naissance d'une mythologie colonial."

30. See Rony, *The Third Eye*; Alison Griffiths, *Wondrous Difference: Cinema, Anthropology, and Turn-of-the-Century Visual Culture* (New York: Columbia University Press, 2002); Jennifer Lynn Peterson, *Education in the School of Dreams* (Durham, NC: Duke University Press, 2013); Paula Amad, *Counter-Archive: Film, the Everyday, and Albert Kahn's Archives de la planète* (New York: Columbia University Press, 2010).

31. Rony, *The Third Eye*, 4, 16; see also Pierre Leprohon, *L'exotisme et le cinéma: Les "chasseurs d'images" à la conquête du monde* (Paris: J. Susse, 1945).

32. Griffiths, *Wondrous Difference*, 186.

33. Griffiths, *Wondrous Difference*, 195–96.

34. Azoulay, *Potential History*; and Mirzoeff, *The Right to Look*.

35. Félix Mesguich, *Tours de manivelle: Souvenirs d'un chasseur d'images* (Paris: B. Grasset, 1933); see also https://www.la-belle-equipe.fr/2020/12/20/felix-mesguich-le-premier-chasseur-dimages-du-cinematographe-lumiere/.

36. Peterson, *Education in the School of Dreams*, 218.

37. Described in Seguin, *Alexandre Promio*, 82–83.

38. *La Dépêche algérienne*, December 19, 1896, 3 (my translation).

39. Gunning, "The Whole World within Reach," 39.

40. Gunning, "The Whole World within Reach," 39-40.

41. Gunning, "The Whole World within Reach," 40.

42. Belloï, "Lumière and His View."

43. Belloï, "Lumière and His View."

44. See Malek Alloula and Barbara Harlow, *The Colonial Harem*, trans. Myrna Godzich and Wlad Godzich (Minneapolis: University of Minnesota Press, 1986); Ali Behdad, *Camera Orientalis: Reflections on Photography of the Middle East* (Chicago: University of Chicago Press, 2016); and Stephen Sheehi, *The Arab Imago:*

A *Social History of Portrait Photography 1860–1910* (Princeton, NJ: Princeton University Press, 2016).

45. I draw here from Jennifer Fay's brilliant engagement with portals. In a twist on Arundhati Roy's use of the term, Fay insightfully engages how Tsai Ming-Liang's films function as "a portal between worlds, a medium that exposes conditions as they are and provides an immersive image of the world as it could be." See Jennifer Fay, "A Portal to Another World: On Cinema, Climate Change, and a Good Apocalypse," in *What Film Is Good For: On the Values of Spectatorship*, ed. Julian Hanich (Oakland: University of California Press, 2023), 14.

3. Frames: De-Centering Orientalist Optics

1. *The Lumière Brothers' First Films* (New York: Kino on Kino, 1997).
2. *The Lumière Brothers' Films*.
3. See *Prière du muezzin*, https://catalogue-lumiere.com/priere-du-muezzin/.
4. I refer here to René Magritte's *La Trahison des images* (1929). See also Michel Foucault, *This Is Not a Pipe* (Berkeley: University of California Press, 1983).
5. For insightful analysis of framing in cinema, see: Patrick Keating, *The Dynamic Frame: Camera Movement in Classical Hollywood* (New York: Columbia University Press, 2019); Gerald Mast, "On Framing," *Critical Inquiry* 11, no. 1 (1984): 82–109; Constantine V. Nakassis, *Onscreen/Offscreen* (Toronto: University of Toronto Press, 2023); Eyal Peretz, *The Off-Screen: An Investigation of the Cinematic Frame* (Stanford, CA: Stanford University Press, 2017).
6. Anne Friedberg, *The Virtual Window* (Cambridge, MA: MIT Press, 2006).
7. See Jean-Louis Baudry and Alan Williams, "Ideological Effects of the Basic Cinematographic Apparatus," *Film Quarterly* 28, no. 2 (1974): 39–47; Stephen Heath, "Narrative Space," *Screen* 17, no. 3 (Autumn 1976): 68–112.
8. Friedberg, *The Virtual Window*, 85.
9. Georges Sadoul, *Histoire du cinéma mondiale, des origines à nos jour* (Paris: Flammarion, 1949), 20. Sadoul's early descriptions of the Lumière films highlight many elements that later film theorists subsequently embrace (depth of field, rising smoke, and rustling leaves).
10. See Noël Burch, *Theory of Film Practice* (Princeton, NJ: Princeton University Press, 1981).
11. Noël Burch, "Primitivism and the Avant-Garde: A Dialectical Approach," in *Narrative, Apparatus, Ideology: A Film Theory Reader*, ed. Philip Rosen (New York: Columbia University Press, 1986), 486.
12. Burch, "Primitivism and the Avant-Garde," 486–87.
13. Burch, "Primitivism and the Avant-Garde," 486–87.
14. Livio Belloï, "Lumière and His View: The Cameraman's Eye in Early Cinema," *Historical Journal of Film, Radio and Television* 15 (October 1995): 461–74.
15. Belloï, "Lumière and His View."

16. Tom Gunning, "'Primitive' Cinema: A Frame-up? Or the Trick's on Us," *Cinema Journal* 28, no. 2 (1989): 10.

17. Gunning, "'Primitive' Cinema," 10.

18. Gunning, "'Primitive' Cinema," 10.

19. Sadoul, *Louis Lumière* (Paris: Seghers, 1964.) 1964, 100.

20. Sadoul, *Louis Lumière*, 1964, 100.

21. See Sadoul, *Histoire du cinéma mondial, des origines à nos jours*; Vincent Pinel, *Louis Lumière: Inventeur et Cinéaste* (Paris: Nathan, 1994); and Noël Burch and Ben Brewster, *Life to Those Shadows* (Berkeley: University of California Press, 1990).

22. Dai Vaughan, "Let There Be Lumière," in *Early Cinema: Space, Frame, Narrative*, ed. Thomas Elsaesser (London: British Film Institute, 1990), 65.

23. Vaughan, "Let There Be Lumière," 65.

24. Vaughan, "Let There Be Lumière," 65.

25. Ali Behdad, *Camera Orientalis: Reflections on Photography of the Middle East* (Chicago: University of Chicago Press, 2016), 38.

26. Behdad, *Camera Orientalis*, 38.

27. Linda Williams, "Film Body: An Implantation of Perversions," *Cine-Tracts* 12 (1981): 22.

28. Williams, "Film Body," 22.

29. Williams, "Film Body," 22.

30. Williams, "Film Body," 22.

31. Edward Said, *Orientalism* (New York, Vintage, 1979), 21.

32. Said, *Orientalism*, 21.

33. Said, *Orientalism*, 21.

34. Said, *Orientalism*, 21.

35. Said, *Orientalism*, 21.

36. *Bab El Oued City*, directed by Merzak Allouache (Médiathèque des Trois Mondes, 1994). Another example could be seen in the work of Zineb Sedira, especially in her work "Saphir" (https://www.fvu.co.uk/projects/saphir), described in Richard Dyer, "Zineb Sedira: Saphir," *Nka: Journal of Contemporary African Art* 24 (2009): 116–19.

37. See Nathalie Goedert and Ninon Maillard, "Culture visuelle du territoire (I): *Pépé le Moko* et l'invention de la frontière," https://imaj.hypotheses.org/1229.

38. For reference to the phrase "invention without a future," which is attributed to Louis Lumière, see James Naremore, ed., *An Invention without a Future: Essays on Cinema* (Berkeley: University of California Press, 2014), 19; and Tom Gunning, "New Thresholds of Vision: Instantaneous Photography and the Early Cinema of Lumière," in *Impossible Presence: Surface and Screen in the Photogenic Era*, ed. Terry Smith (Sydney: Power, 2001), 71.

39. See *Le Photorama Lumière*, https://www.institut-lumiere.org/musee/les-freres-lumiere-et-leurs-inventions/photoramas.html.

40. William Henry Jackson, *Algiers—The Embankment and Boulevard de la République* (photograph), published as halftone in *Harper's Weekly*, 1895, 229. https://www.loc.gov/item/2004707259/.

41. Denise Oleksijczuk, *The First Panoramas: Visions of British Imperialism* (Minneapolis: University of Minnesota Press, 2011), 55; see also Angela L. Miller, "The Panorama, the Cinema and the Emergence of the Spectacular," *Wide Angle* 18 no. 2 (1996): 34–69; and Brooke Belisle, "Nature at a Glance: Immersive Maps from Panoramic to Digital," *Early Popular Visual Culture* 13, no. 4 (2015): 313–35.

42. See, for example, Erwin Panofsky, *Perspective as Symbolic Form*, trans. Christopher S. Wood (New York: Zone Books, 1991); Hubert Damisch and John Goodman, *The Origin of Perspective* (Cambridge, MA: MIT Press, 1994); and Friedberg, *The Virtual Window*.

43. *Chamber's Journal of Popular Literature, Science and Arts* 33–34, no. 316 (January 21, 1860): 34; as quoted in Erkki Huhtamo, *Illusions in Motion: Media Archaeology of the Moving Panorama and Related Spectacles* (Cambridge, MA: MIT Press, 2013), 16.

44. Behdad, *Camera Orientalis*, 53–54.

45. See the chapter "Colonial Panorama" in Roger Benjamin, *Orientalist Aesthetics: Art, Colonialism, and French North Africa, 1880–1930* (Berkeley: University of California Press, 2003), 114; and Miller, "The Panorama, the Cinema and the Emergence of the Spectacular."

46. I point here to the insightful essays gathered in *On the Viewing Platform: The Panorama between Canvas and Screen*, ed. Katie Trumpener and Tim Barringer (New Haven, CT: Yale University Press, 2020).

47. André Bazin, "The Myth of Total Cinema," in *What Is Cinema?*, vol. 1, ed. and trans. H. Gray (Berkeley: University of California Press, 2005).

48. André Bazin, "Painting and Cinema," in *What Is Cinema?*, vol. 1, ed. and trans. H. Gray (Berkeley: University of California Press, 2005), 166.

49. Julien Duvivier et al., *Pépé le Moko* (Criterion, Janus Collection, 1937/2006); Gilles Pontecorvo, *Battle of Algiers* (Casbah Films, Kanopy Streaming, 1966); Merzak Allouache, *Bab El Oued City* (Médiathèque des Trois Mondes, 1994).

50. Lina Khatib, *Filming the Modern Middle East: Politics in the Cinemas of Hollywood and the Arab World* (London: I. B. Tauris, 2006); and Derek Gregory, *The Colonial Present: Afghanistan, Palestine, and Iraq* (Malden, MA: Blackwell, 2004).

4. Sovereignty: Iterations of Cinematic Statecraft

1. See Jean-Claude Seguin, *Alexandre Promio, ou, Les énigmes de la lumière* (Paris: L'Harmattan, 1999), 55–91.

2. Antonia Lant, "The Curse of the Pharaoh, or How Cinema Constructed Egyptomania," *October* 59 (1992): 101.

3. See Lant, "The Curse of the Pharaoh"; and Robert Birchard, "Kalem Company, Manufacturers of Moving Picture Films," *American Cinematographer* 65 (1984).

4. "Un curieux voyage en Egypte.—Le monde entier paraît devoir devenir bientôt la conquête du Cinématographe Lumière, à en juger par le nombre considérable de scènes animées nouvelles prises sur l'ancien et le nouveau continent que la maison Lumière reçoit constamment de ses habiles opérateurs . . ." from the *Lyon républicain*, Lyon, April 18, 1896; quoted in Michelle Aubert et al., *La Production Cinématographique des Frères Lumière*, Librairie du Premier Siècle du Cinéma (Paris: Editions Mémoires de cinéma, 1996), 72.

5. The Italian expatriate Henri Dello-Strologo arranged these screenings and also hosted Promio's Egyptian tour. For histories of early Egyptian cinema, see Hamid Hamzaoui, *Histoire du cinema égyptien* (Paris: Autres Temps, 1997); Jacob M. Landau, *Studies in the Arab Theater and Cinema* (Philadelphia: University of Pennsylvania Press, 1958); Lizbeth Malkmus and Roy Armes, *Arab and African Film Making* (London: Zed Books, 1991); Georges Sadoul, *The Cinema in Arab Countries* (Beirut: Interarab Centre of Cinema and Television, 1966); Viola Shafik, *Arab Cinema: History and Cultural Identity* (Cairo, Egypt: American University in Cairo Press, 1988); Sa'id Shimi, *Tarikh al-taswir al-sinima'i fi Misr, 1897–1996* (Giza: Cinefilm, 1997).

6. Lehnert & Landrock, "Ramleh Station," Alexandria, Egypt, https://dp.la/item/a93b698873def3200153532c3b70c8cf. See also Stephen Grant collection. https://africa.si.edu/2020/02/the-stephen-grant-postcard-collection-digitization-project/.

7. See Adam Mestyan, "Khedive," *Encyclopaedia of Islam, Three* (Leiden: Brill, 2020).

8. This procession has been well documented historically in paintings, prints, and descriptions. Its cinematic versions exist in the Lumière catalogue and later in the British Pathé newsreel film, "Procession of the Carpet" from 1926. More details on its history can be found at Fatma Fowzy and Doaa Kandil, "Re-Constructing Old Mahmal Procession Route through Consulting Contemporary Visual Sources," *Journal of Arts, Architecture, and Humanistic Sciences*, 10.21608/MJAF.2023.174654.2901.

9. See Mary Roberts, "Ottoman Statecraft and the 'Pencil Of Nature': Photography, Painting, and Drawing at the Court of Sultan Abdülaziz," *Ars Orientalis* 43 (2013): 10–30, http://www.jstor.org/stable/43490307, and "The Limits of Circumscription," in *Photography's Orientalism: New Essays on Colonial Representation*, ed. Ali Behdad and Luke Gartlan (Los Angeles: Getty Research Institute, 2013). See also Muhammad Isa Waley, "Images Of The Ottoman Empire: The Photograph Albums Presented by Sultan Abdülhamid II," *British Library Journal* 17, no. 2 (1991): 111–27, http://www.jstor.org/stable/42554325. In the context of the Qajar dynasty, see Layla Diba, "Images of Power and the Power of Images: Intention and Response in Early Qajar Painting," in *Royal Persian Paintings: The Qajar Epoch, 1785–1925*, ed. Layla Diba (Brooklyn Museum of Art in association with I. B. Tauris Publishers, 1998); and Ali Behdad, *Camera Orientalis* (Chicago: University of Chicago Press, 2016), especially the fifth chapter.

10. David Bordwell, *On the History of Film Style* (Cambridge, MA: Harvard University Press, 1997),158.

11. Here I am thinking of artists such as Louis Béroud and Ludwig Deutsch, but also photographers, such as Underwood and Underwood, who arrive years later (https://www.gettyimages.ch/detail/nachrichtenfoto/the-holy-carpet-parade-with-the-mahmal-cairo-egypt-nachrichtenfoto/463998199?language=fr), or British Pathé films https://www.youtube.com/watch?v=bw-as8q9Ais.

12. See, for example, Ifdal Elsaket, "Projecting Egypt: The Cinema and the Making of Colonial Modernity 1896–1952," diss., University of Sydney, 2013; Karim Elhaies, "When Old Cinema Was New: The Media Making of Modern Egypt and Its Early Cinema," PhD diss., New York University, forthcoming; Ilhami Hassan, *Tarikh Al-Cinema Al-Masriyya (1896–1970)* (Cairo: Ministry of Culture, 1995); Samir Farid, ed., *Tarikh Al-Cinema Al-Arabiyya Al Samita* (Cairo: General Union of Arab Artists, 1994); Viola Shafik, *Arab Cinema* (Cairo: American University in Cairo Press, 2007); Georges Sadoul, *Les cinémas des pays arabes* (Beirut: Centre interarabe du cinéma et de la télévision, 1966); and Ahmed al-Hadari, *Tarikh al-sinima fi Misr vol. 1* (Cairo: Nādī al-Sīnimā bi-al-Qāhirah, 1989). See also Hamid Hamzaoui, *Histoire du cinema égyptien* (Paris: Autres Temps, 1997); Sa'id Shimi, *Tarikh al-taswir al-sinima'i fi Misr, 1897–1996* (Giza: Cinefilm, 1997); Lizbeth Malkmus and Roy Armes, *Arab and African Film Making* (London: Zed Books, 1991).

13. See Valentina Vitali, ed., *Theorising National Cinemas* (London: Routledge, 2019); Richard Abel, Giorgio Bertellini, and Rob King, eds., *Early Cinema and the "National"* (Bloomington, IN: John Libbey, 2008); Will Higbee and Song Hwee Lim, "Concepts of Transnational Cinema: Towards a Critical Transnationalism in Film Studies," *Transnational Cinemas* 1, no. 1 (2010): 7–21; Mette Hjort and Scott Mackenzie, eds., *Cinema and Nation* (London: Routledge, 2000); and Andrew Higson, *The Instability of the National* (London: Routledge, 2000).

14. Seguin, *Alexandre Promio*, 48–49.

15. See Aubert et al., *La Production Cinématographique des Frères Lumière*.

16. Royal Collection Trust, "Abbas II Hilmi (1874–1944), Khedive of Egypt," accessed October 20, 2025, https://www.rct.uk/collection/search#/8/collection/403802/abbas-ii-hilmi-1874-1944-khedive-of-egypt.

17. See Samy Helmy, *Bidayat al-Cinema Al Misriyya* (Alexandria: General Organization of Cultural Palaces, 2013); and *Madrasat al-Iskandariyya lel-Tasweer al-Cinema'i* (Alexandria: Bibliotheca Alexandrina, 2013).

18. See, for example, Viola Shafik's entry in Richard Abel, *Encyclopedia of Early Cinema* 309, "A Chronology of Firsts in Alexandria," https://www.bibalex.org/alexcinema/historical/chronology.html; see also Samy Helmy, "Start Up City: Alexandria, The Cradle of Egyptian Cinema," *Rawi*, no. 9 (2018), https://rawi-publishing.com/articles/startup-city?lang=en. An account can also be found in Marta Petricioli, *Oltre il mito: l'Egitto degli italiani* (Milan: B. Mondadori, 2007), 277.

19. I allude here to al-Hadari's account in *Tarikh al-sinima fi Misr vol. 1*, pp. 3 and 78.

20. Frank Kessler, "Images of the 'National' in Early Non-Fiction Films," in *Early Cinema and the "National,"* ed. Abel, Bertellini, and King, 22.

21. Kessler, "Images of the 'National,'" 25.
22. Kessler, "Images of the 'National,'" 25.
23. Stephen Bottomore, "She's Just Like My Granny," in *Celebrating the Centenary of Cinema*, ed. John Fullerton (London: John Libbey, 1998).
24. Bottomore, "She's Just Like My Granny," 172.
25. Bottomore, "She's Just Like My Granny," 172.
26. Bottomore, "She's Just Like My Granny," 174.
27. Bottomore, "She's Just Like My Granny," 173.
28. Ernst Kantorowicz, *The King's Two Bodies: A Study in Mediaeval Political Theology* (Princeton, NJ: Princeton University Press, 1957); and Giorgio Agamben, *The State of Exception* (Chicago: University of Chicago Press, 2005).
29. It is worth noting here Viola Shafik's remarkable study of Mohammed Bayoumi whose films of Sa'ad Zaghlul provide a contrasting framework for reflections on sovereignty in cinema: see "Cameramen, Their Heroes and the Expansion of Time," in Viola Shafik, *Resistance, Dissidence, Revolution: Documentary Film Esthetics in the Middle East and North Africa* (London: Routledge, 2023).
30. See, for example, *'Abd al-Rahman al-Jabarti's History of Egypt. 'Aja'ib al-Athar fi 'l-Tarajim wa 'l-Akhbar*, ed. Thomas Philipp and Moshe Perlmann (Stuttgart: Franz Steiner Verlag, 1994), vol. 3, part II, section 31.
31. See, for example, Daniela Potenza, "Literary Trajectories of Sulaymān al-Ḥalabī, a Hero Who Was Born a Criminal," *Annali di Ca' Foscari. Serie orientale* 56 (2020): 81–104.
32. See André Gaudreault, "Showing and Telling Image and Word in Early Cinema," in *Early Cinema: Space, Frame, Narrative*, ed. Thomas Elsaesser and Adam Barker (London: British Film Institute, 1990), 274–28; and Tom Gunning, "An Aesthetic of Astonishment: Early Film and the (In)Credulous Spectator," *Art and Text* 34 (1989): 31–45.
33. Valentine Robert, "La part picturale du *tableau-style*," in *The Image in Early Cinema*, ed. Scott Curtis et al. (Bloomington: Indiana University Press, 2018), 289.
34. Robert, "La part picturale du *tableau-style*," 291.
35. Leah Lehmbeck's chapter "Fine Art on Film" as part of the *City of Cinema: Paris 1850–1907*, ed. Leah Lehmbeck, Britt Salvesen, and Vanessa Schwartz (Los Angeles: Delmonico Books, 2022), 90–91; and Charles Musser, "A Cinema of Contemplation: A Cinema of Discernment: Spectatorship, Intertextuality and Attractions in the 1890s," in *The Cinema of Attractions Reloaded*, ed. Wanda Strauven (Amsterdam: Amsterdam University Press, 2006), 161–78.
36. Abounaddara. "Dignity Has Never Been Photographed." *documenta 14*, June 2017. https://www.documenta14.de/en/notes-and-works/15348/dignity-has-never-been-photographed; for the scandal in the French press, see responses in reference to the article "Inside the Mind of French General Kléber's Killer," by Gilles Paris (https://www.lemonde.fr/en/history/article/2023/03/21/inside-the-mind-of-french

-general-kleber-s-killer_6020110_157.html); "Fanaticism on Screen," at the Institute for Ideas and Imagination of Columbia University in May 2021 (https://ideasimagination.columbia.edu/events/abounaddara).

37. See, for example, Anne-Marie McManus, "On the Ruins of What's to Come, I Stand," *Critical Inquiry* 48, no. 1 (2021): 45–67, the fourth chapter of Ryan Watson, *Radical Documentary and Global Crises* (Bloomington: Indiana University Press, 2021); Chad Elias, "Emergency Cinema and the Dignified Image: Cell Phone Activism and Filmmaking in Syria," *Film Quarterly* 71 (2017): 18–31; and Anneka Lenssen, "The Filmmaker as Artisan," *Third Text* 34 (2020): 159–71.

38. Lenssen, "The Filmmaker as Artisan," 168.

39. Lenssen, "The Filmmaker as Artisan," 170–71.

40. Moustafa Bayoumi, "The Civil War in Syria Is Invisible—but This Anonymous Film Collective Is Changing That," *The Nation*, June 29, 2015, https://www.thenation.com/article/archive/the-civil-war-in-syria-is-invisible-but-this-anonymous-film-collective-is-changing-that/.

41. Bayoumi.

42. Abounaddara, *In Search of the Syrian Fanatic* (https://vimeo.com/819559793); and for an article alongside the film, see https://www.alquds.co.uk.

43. See, for example, Paula Amad, *Counter-Archive* (New York: Columbia University Press, 2010).

44. Jacques-Alain Miller, "Sovereign Image," *Lacanian Review: Hurly Burly*, no. 5 (Summer 2018): 42.

45. Roland Barthes, *Camera Lucida*, trans. Richard Howard (London: Vintage Classics, 1993), 4.

46. Ariella Aïcha Azoulay, *Potential History: Unlearning Imperialism* (London: Verso, 2019), 391.

5. History: The Duration of Myth

1. The film is now known by the title, *Les Pyramides (vue générale)*, and is catalogued at the Lumière archives as 117 (381).

2. See *The Lumière Brothers First Films* (DVD) (New York: Kino Films, 1996) and *Lumière and Company* (videorecording) (Fox Lorber, 1995), in which Youssef Chahine mimics this shot by choosing the pyramids as the backdrop for his own short film shot on a Lumière camera.

3. Quoted in Julia Ballerini, "Orientalist Photography and Its 'Mistaken' Pictures," in *Picturing the Middle East: A Hundred Years of European Orientalism*, ed. Henry Krawitz (New York: Dahesh Museum, 1995), 22–23. See also Larry Schaaf, "Charles Piazzi Smyth's 1865 Conquest of the Great Pyramid," *History of Photography* 3, no. 4 (October 1979): 331–54.

4. Ali Behdad, *Camera Orientalis* (Chicago: University of Chicago Press, 2016), 33–34.

5. Kathleen Stewart Howe, *Excursions Along the Nile: The Photographic Discovery of Ancient Egypt* (Santa Barbara: Santa Barbara Museum of Art, 1994), 21.

6. See Michael Allan, "Picturing Other Languages: Reflections on Photography and Philology," *College English* 82, no. 1 (2019).

7. See Elliott Colla, *Conflicted Antiquities* (Durham, NC: Duke University Press, 2007) as well as "The Measure of Egypt," *Postcolonial Studies* 7, no. 3 (2004): 271–93.

8. Brian Curran, "Review of *Egyptomania: Egypt in Western Art 1730–1930*," *Art Bulletin* 78, no. 4 (1996).

9. *Lyon républicain*, Lyon, May 2, 1897, in which the entire entry reads:

Devant le grand succès obtenu par la magnifique vue du convoi de chameaux passant devant le Sphinx et les pyramides d'Égypte, cette scène animée, qui donne une idée si parfaite de ces antiques et majestueux monuments, figurera encore toute la semaine avec les nouvelles vues qui seront visibles à partir d'aujourd'hui au Cinématographe Lumière.

An earlier article from April 25, 1897, also alludes to the film in these terms:

C'est ensuite devant le Sphinx que le Cinématographe conduit le spectateur et un convoi de chameaux défilant devant le monstre de pierre permet d'avoir une idée très exacte de ses dimensions géantes.

See Michelle Aubert et al., *La Production Cinématographique des Frères Lumière*, Librairie du Premier Siècle du Cinéma (Paris: Editions Mémoires de cinéma, 1996), 76.

10. Tom Gunning, "An Aesthetic of Astonishment: Early Film and the (In)Credulous Spectator," *Art and Text* 34 (1989): 31–45.

11. André Bazin, *What Is Cinema?* ed. and trans. Hugh Gray (Berkeley: University of California Press, 1967).

12. Gunning, "An Aesthetic of Astonishment: Early Film and the (In)Credulous Spectator," 34–35.

13. "al-Simenatoghraf," *al-Muqtataf*, July 1903. In the initial titling, the term, "cinematograph," is typographically twice misspelled (al-simenatoghraf), only later to be corrected in an article on the cinematograph in medicine (al-sinematoghraf fi al-tibb) published in January 1904.

14. Christiane Zivie-Coche, *Sphinx: History of a Monument* (Ithaca, NY: Cornell University Press, 2002). Although previous excavations had uncovered portions of the Sphinx's body, they were not as comprehensive as the 1905 excavation.

15. For descriptions of the travel and plates of some of the images, see David Roberts et al., *David Roberts* (Oxford: Phaidon Press and Barbican Art Gallery, 1986).

16. The Scottish Arts Council, *Artist Adventurer David Roberts* (Edinburgh: Ivanhoe, 1981), 17.

17. Philip Rosen, *Change Mummified: Cinema, Historicity, Theory* (Minneapolis: University of Minnesota Press, 2001). Rosen draws a distinction between historiography (the text written by the historian), history (the object of the text), and historicity, which he describes as "the particular interrelations of the mode of historiography and the types of construction of history related to it" (xi).

18. See "Roberts' Pictures of the Near East," in Roberts et al., *David Roberts*, 72.

19. "Roberts' Pictures of the Near East," 72.

20. Hans Frei, *The Eclipse of Biblical Narrative: A Study in Eighteenth- and Nineteenth-Century Hermeneutics* (New Haven, CT: Yale University Press, 1974), 220.

21. Frei, *The Eclipse of Biblical Narrative*, 220-221.

22. Bazin, *What Is Cinema?* 15.

23. Bazin, *What Is Cinema?* 13. It is worth noting that Bazin emphasizes realism as a property not intrinsic to the image itself, but structured in the relationship of the viewer to the image.

24. Bazin, *What Is Cinema?* 14.

25. For two insightful examples critical of the older paradigm of Bazin scholarship, see Daniel Morgan, "Rethinking Bazin: Ontology and Realist Aesthetics," *Critical Inquiry* 32, no. 3 (2006): 443–81; and Tom Gunning, "Moving Away from the Index: Cinema and the Impression of Reality," *differences* 18, no. 1 (2007): 29–52.

26. Morgan, "Rethinking Bazin," 448.

27. Gunning, "Moving Away from the Index: Cinema and the Impression of Reality," *differences* 18, no. 1 (May 2007): 31: "Bazin's account of the realism of photography rests less on a correspondence theory (that the photograph resembles the world, a relation Peirce would describe as iconic), than on what he describes as 'a transference of reality from the thing to its reproduction,' referring to the photograph as 'a decal or approximate tracing.'"

28. Bazin, *What Is Cinema?* 10.

29. Bazin, *What Is Cinema?* 9.

30. Bazin, *What Is Cinema?* 9.

31. Bazin, *What Is Cinema?* 10.

32. Bazin, *What Is Cinema?* 10.

33. Bazin, *What Is Cinema?* 14–15.

34. Antonia Lant, "The Curse of the Pharaoh, or How Cinema Contracted Egyptomania," *October* 59 (1992): 90.

35. Lant, "The Curse of the Pharaoh," 90.

36. Alfred North Whitehead, *The Concept of Nature, Tarner Lectures Delivered in Trinity College, November, 1919* (Cambridge: The University Press, 1920).

37. Whitehead, *The Concept of Nature*, 77.

38. Gilles Deleuze, *The Fold: Leibniz and the Baroque*, trans. Tom Conley (Minneapolis: University of Minnesota Press, 1993).

39. See Tom Gunning, "Never Seen This Picture Before: Muybridge in Multiplicity," in *Time Stands Still: Muybridge and the Instantaneous Photography Movement*, ed. Phillip Prodger (New York: Oxford University Press, 2003), 222–72.

40. See Chapter 8 of Vachel Lindsay's *The Art of the Moving Picture* (New York: Macmillan, 1915); Sergei Eisenstein, *Film Form: Essays in Film Theory* (1949; San Diego: Harcourt Brace, 1977); and Jacques Derrida's remarks in "The Pit and the Pyramid: Introduction to Hegel's Semiology," in *Margins of Philosophy*, trans. Alan Bass (Chicago: University of Chicago Press, 1984).

41. It is worth noting the rich insights of Karl Schoonover and Rosalind Galt, who in Chapter 6 of *Queer Cinema in the World* help explore the dynamics of queer time. Their work along with that of Jean Ma and Bliss Cua Lim further opens up the question of cinema and time. See Karl Schoonover and Rosalind Galt, *Queer Cinema in the World* (Durham, NC: Duke University Press, 2016); Jean Ma, *Melancholy Drift: Marking Time in Chinese Cinema* (Hong Kong: Hong Kong University Press, 2010); and Bliss Cua Lim, *Translating Time: Cinema, the Fantastic, and Temporal Critique* (Durham, NC: Duke University Press, 2009).

42. A collaboration of thirty-nine directors, each of whom was tasked with shooting a film on cinematographs, *Lumière et compagnie* commemorates the centenary of the Lumière Brothers. See https://vimeo.com/479280814 (56:50).

43. See Hoda El Shakry, "Palestine and the Aesthetics of the Future Impossible," *Interventions* 23, no. 5 (2021): 669–90; Gil Hochberg, *Becoming Palestine: Toward an Archival Imagination of the Future* (Durham, NC: Duke University Press, 2021).

44. Larissa Sansour and Søren Lind, *In the Future They Ate from the Finest Porcelain* (SciFi Trilogy, 2015), as well as Larissa Sansour, *A Space Exodus* (Mec Film, 2008) and with Søren Lind, *Nation Estate* (Mec Film, 2012). See also the interview with Larissa Sansour, "Time, Nationhood, Resistance: Larissa Sansour's Latest Film *In the Future They Ate from the Finest Porcelain*," interview, *Art Radar Journal*, February 1, 2016, http://www.artradarjournal.com/2016/02/01/palestinian-artist-larissa-sansours-interview.

6. Tracks: Tracking the World in/as Cinema

1. Salim Tamari, *The Great War and the Remaking of Palestine* (Oakland: University of California Press, 2017), especially chapter 3, which elaborates on Ottoman urban planning and what Tamari terms the "triadic modernity" connecting Jaffa, Jerusalem, and Beersheba. See also Joseph Glass, "The Biography in Historical-Geographical Research: Joseph Novon Bey—A Case Study," in *The Land That Became Israel*, ed. Ruth Kark (New Haven, CT: Yale University Press, 1990), 77–89.

2. References to the films can be found at https://catalogue-lumiere.com/.

3. For more scholarship on the tracking shot, see Daniel Morgan, *The Lure of the Image* (Oakland: University of California Press, 2021), 31–36. On the tracking shot in Pontecorvo's *Kapo*, especially Serge Daney's rejection of it, see Serge Daney, "The Tracking Shot in *Kapo*," in *Postcards form the Cinema*, (London: Berg / Bloomsbury, 2007), 17–35; Sam Di Ioro, "Three Tracking Shots," *Contemporary French Civilization* 32, no. 2 (July 2008): 86; Patrick Keating, *The Dynamic Frame: Camera*

Movement in Classical Hollywood (New York: Columbia University Press, 2019); Jordan Schonig, The Shape of Motion: Cinema and the Aesthetics of Movement (Oxford: Oxford University Press, 2021); and Damon Young, Making Sex Public, and Other Cinematic Fantasies (Durham, NC: Duke University Press, 2018), 270 n23.

4. Félix Regnault, L'Illustration, May 30, 1896, 446–47. This description is cited and translated in Lynne Kirby, Parallel Tracks: The Railroad and Silent Cinema (Durham, NC: Duke University Press, 1997), 271n211, and most likely refers to number 8 in the Lumière catalog. Gunning notes that this panic is described as though inscribed in the image rather than referring to audiences.

5. G.-Michel Coissac, Histoire du cinématographe de ses origines à nos jours (Paris: Éditions de Cinéopse, 1925), 194–99, and in translation by Gerard-Jans Claes, Alexandre Promio, "A Travelogue." Sabzian, May 27, 2020. https://www.sabzian.be/text/a-travelogue.

6. Coissac, Histoire du cinématographe, 195.

7. Coissac, Histoire du cinématographe, 195.

8. Coissac, Histoire du cinématographe, 195.

9. Sadoul, Histoire du cinema mondial, 24, Promio on the traveling: "on pourrait peut-être retourner la proposition et reproduire à l'aide du cinéma mobile les objets immobiles."

10. Jean Mitry, Histoire du Cinéma (Paris: Éditions universitaires, 1967), 113.

11. See https://archive.org/details/haverstraw_tunnel.

12. Thomas Elsaesser and Adam Barker, Early Cinema: Space, Frame, Narrative (London: BFI Pub., 1990), 20.

13. See Paul Virilio's chapter, "Cinema and Tracking Shot," in War and Cinema: The Logistics of Perception, trans. Patrick Camiller (London: Verso, 1989), 11–30, 69–95. See also Daniel Morgan's recent book, The Lure of the Image (Oakland: University of California Press, 2021); and Jordan Schonig's chapter on the locomotive in Deep Mediations: Thinking Space in Cinema and Digital Cultures, ed. Karen Redrobe and Jeff Scheible (Minneapolis: University of Minnesota Press, 2020).

14. Martin Loiperdinger and Bernd Elzer. "Lumière's Arrival of the Train: Cinema's Founding Myth," Moving Image 4 (2004): 103.

15. Loiperdinger, "Lumière's Arrival of the Train," 110.

16. Loiperdinger, "Lumière's Arrival of the Train," 99.

17. Gunning, Tom. "An Aesthetic of Astonishment: Early Film and the (In) Credulous Spectator." Art and Text 34 (1989): 31–45.

18. Gunning, "An Aesthetic of Astonishment," 115.

19. Kirby, Parallel Tracks, 7.

20. Kirby, Parallel Tracks, 7.

21. Katherine Groo, Bad Film Histories: Ethnography and the Early Film Archive (Minneapolis: University of Minnesota Press, 2019), 64–65.

22. See Paul Cotterell, The Railways of Palestine and Israel (Abingdon: Tourret, 1984).

23. See Selah Merrill, "The Jaffa Jerusalem Railway," *Scribner's Magazine* 13, no. 3 (March 1893).

24. Merrill, "The Jaffa Jerusalem Railway."

25. See Zachary Lockman, *Comrades and Enemies: Arab and Jewish Workers in Palestine, 1906–1948* (Berkeley: University of California Press, 1996). See also "Railway to Jerusalem," Conrad Schick, accessed October 23, 2025, https://conradschick.wordpress.com/geography/railway-to-jerusalem/..

26. See On Barak, *Powering Empire: How Coal Made the Middle East and Sparked Global Carbonization* (Oakland: University of California Press, 2020), 219–21.

27. Barak, *Powering Empire*, 35.

28. Barak, *Powering Empire*, 39.

29. Among numerous sources, see *The Egyptian Railway; or, The Interest of England in Egypt* (London: Hope and Co., 1852).

30. Nicholas Baer, "Transnational Imaginaries: The Place of Palestine in Gershom Scholem, Franz Kafka, and Early Cinema," in *Transnational German Studies*, ed. R. Braun and B. Schofield (Liverpool: Liverpool University Press, 2020), 224.

31. Tamari, *The Great War and the Remaking of Palestine*, 55–56.

32. Tamari, *The Great War and the Remaking of Palestine*, 55–56.

33. Tamari, *The Great War and the Remaking of Palestine*, 55–56.

34. Tamari, *The Great War and the Remaking of Palestine*, 55–56.

35. Georges Sadoul, *Histoire du cinéma mondial: des origines à nos jours* (Paris: Flammarion, 1949), 20–21; see also Georges Sadoul, *Histoire générale du cinéma. Tome 1: L'invention du cinéma, 1832–1897* (Paris: Denoël, 1946), 288, 295, 300–301, 334–35. Related conversations in David Robinson, *The History of World Cinema*, 2nd ed., rev. and updated (New York: Stein and Day, 1981), 32–33, as well as Jacques Deslandes and Jacques Richard, *Histoire comparé du cinema II* (Paris: Casterman, 1968), 375, 286.

36. Sadoul, *Histoire du cinema mondial*, 20.

37. Sadoul, *Histoire du cinema mondial*, 21.

38. Vincent Pinel, *Louis Lumière: Inventeur et Cinéaste* (Paris: Nathan, 1994), 46—and quoted in Loiperdinger, "Lumiere's Arrival of the Train," fn 39.

39. Loiperdinger, "Lumiere's Arrival of the Train," 105.

40. Elsaesser, *Early Cinema*, 18.

41. Elsaesser, *Early Cinema*, 18.

42. Philippe Dubois, "Le Gros Plan Primitif," *Revue belge du cinéma*, no. 10 (1984–85): 11–34.

43. See Frank Gray in *The Silent Cinema Reader*, ed. Lee Grieveson and Peter Krämer (London: Routledge, 2004); and Christian Hayes, "Phantom Rides," *Screenonline*, http://www.screenonline.org.uk/film/id/1193042/index.html. See also Jordan Schonig, "Contingent Motion: Rethinking the 'Wind in the Trees' in Early Cinema and CGI," *Discourse* 40, no. 1 (2018): 30–61.

44. Film History Essentials: Passage d'un Tunnel en Chemin de Fer (1898), https://moviegoings.com/2023/03/27/film-history-essentials-passage-dun-tunnel-en-chemin-de-fer-1898/.

45. 1898—Panorama from Top of a Moving Train | Silent French Actuality | Georges Melies | HD Remaster, https://youtu.be/qkQg92RVvPM?si=RQeUdrLufiNyqgFQ

46. Baer, "Transnational Imaginaries," 224.

7. Scale: The World as Close-Up

1. André Gardies, "Cinema on Show in the Work of the Lumière Brothers," in *Echoes of Narcissus*, ed. Lieve Spaas (New York: Berghahn Books, 2000), 111–21.

2. "J'estime que le cinématographe n'a pris son essor qu'à partir du moment où l'on a créé les gros plans, c'est-à-dire à partir du moment où l'on permit au public de voir les acteurs, les vedettes, sous un angle beaucoup plus grand que d'habitude, et de saisir sur leur physionomie des finesses d'expression qu'on ne voit pas au théâtre, parce qu'on voit sous un angle trop petit. Je crois que c'est un des éléments importants du succès du cinématographe." See "Témoignage de Louis Lumière devant la commission Renaitour," in Jean-Michel Renaitour, *Où va le cinéma français?* (Paris: Éditions Baudinière, 1937), 455; Groupe du Cinématographe à la Chambre des Députés, 14e séance, 7 May 1937.

3. See "Theater and Cinema Part 1–2," in André Bazin et al., *What Is Cinema?* ed. and trans. Hugh Gray (Berkeley: University of California Press, 2005).

4. See Conrad Schick, "Notes and News," *Quarterly Statement* 31 (London: Palestine Exploration Fund: 3–4, January 1899), 116.

5. Naomi Schor, *Reading in Detail* (New York: Methuen, 1987). Jonathan Crary on maps in *Techniques of the Observer: On Vision and Modernity in the Nineteenth Century* (Cambridge, MA: MIT Press, 1990).

6. Pascale Casanova, *World Republic of Letters*, trans. Malcolm DeBevoise (Cambridge, MA: Harvard University Press, 1999).

7. Casanova, *World Republic of Letters*, 3.

8. Casanova, *World Republic of Letters*, 2.

9. Casanova, *World Republic of Letters*, 3.

10. Casanova, *World Republic of Letters*, 3.

11. See Robert Stam, *World Literature, Transnational Cinema, and Global Media: Towards a Transartistic Commons* (London: Routledge, 2019); Lúcia Nagib et al., *Theorizing World Cinema* (Place: I. B. Tauris, 2012): and Shekhar A. Deshpande and Meta Mazaj, *World Cinema: A Critical Introduction* (New York: Routledge, 2018).

12. Nirvana Tanoukhi, "The Scale of World Literature," *New Literary History* 39, no. 3 (2008): 614.

13. Tanoukhi, "The Scale of World Literature," 614.

14. Anne-Marie E. McManus, "Scale in the Balance: Reading with the International Prize for Arabic Fiction ('The Arabic Booker')," *International Journal of Middle East Studies* 48, no. 2 (2016): 219.

15. Mary Ann Doane, "The Close-Up: Scale and Detail in the Cinema," *differences: A Journal of Feminist Cultural Studies* 14, no. 3 (2003): 90.
16. Doane, "The Close-Up: Scale and Detail in the Cinema," 91.
17. Doane, "The Close-Up: Scale and Detail in the Cinema," 91.
18. Doane, "The Close-Up: Scale and Detail in the Cinema," 97–99.
19. I refer here to studies addressing the face in cinema. See, for example, Noa Steimatsky's brilliant book *The Face on Film* (New York: Oxford University Press, 2017); as well as Igal Bursztyn, "Faces as Idea, Faces as Object: A Cinematic History (1911–1967)," *Studies in Zionism* 10, no. 2 (1989): 139–54; Paul Coates, *Screening the Face* (London: Palgrave Macmillan, 2012); Jennifer González, "The Face and the Public: Race, Secrecy, and Digital Art Practice," *Camera Obscura: Feminism, Culture, and Media Studies* 24, no. 1 (2009); and Jean-Marie Samocki, "Nouvelle fictions du visage," *Trafic* 38 (Summer 2001): 93–113.
20. Katherine Groo, *Bad Film Histories: Ethnography and the Early Archive* (Minneapolis: University of Minnesota Press, 2019), 65.
21. Groo, *Bad Film Histories*, 65.
22. Groo, *Bad Film Histories*, 66.
23. Groo, *Bad Film Histories*, 66. See also Laura Marks, *The Skin of the Film: Intercultural Cinema, Embodiment, and the Senses* (Durham, NC: Duke University Press, 2000).
24. I allude here to some of the arguments in Harun Farocki's *Bilder der Welt und Inschrift des Krieges*, especially in regard to Marc Garanger's colonial photographs, and to "What Is a Camera?" in Kaja Silverman's *Male Subjectivity at the Margins*, which offers parallel instances. See Ingo Kratisch et al., *Bilder der Welt und Inschrift des Krieges = Pictures of the World and Inscriptions of the War*, ed. Harun Farocki (New York: Video Data Bank, 2011); and Kaja Silverman, *Male Subjectivity at the Margins* (London: Routledge, 1992).
25. This film can be found in a collection curated by the Cinemathèque in Jerusalem: https://www.youtube.com/watch?v=GjK8euMLMPQ.
26. Roland Barthes, *Camera Lucida*, trans. Richard Howard (New York: Vintage Classics, 1993).
27. Harun Farocki, "Commentary from *Bilder der Welt und Inschrift des Krieges* (*Images of the World and Inscription of the War*)," *Discourse: Journal for Theoretical Studies in Media and Culture* 15, no. 3, article 4 (1993).
28. For more on *photogénie*, see Sarah Keller and Jason N. Paul, eds., *Jean Epstein: Critical Essays and New Translations* (Amsterdam: Amsterdam University Press, 2012).
29. As Palestinian cinema has emerged, this early Lumière film has receded from most accounts and been replaced with the basic components of a national film history: beginning with Sirhan's film in 1935, the silent films of 1948–67, the films of the Palestinian Revolution (1968–82), and feature-length films of the contemporary period (1980–present) dominated by auteurist cinema: Michel Khleifi, Rashid Masharawi, Hany Abu-Assad, Nizar Hassan, Mai Masri and Elia Suleiman. See, for

example, Livia Alexander, "Is There a Palestinian Cinema? The National and Transnational in Palestinian Film Production," in *Palestine, Israel, and the Politics of Popular Culture*, ed. Rebecca L. Stein and Ted Swedenburg (Durham, NC: Duke University Press, 2005), 150–72; and Terri Ginsberg, *Visualizing the Palestinian Struggle: Toward a Critical Analytic of Palestine Solidarity Film* (London: Palgrave Macmillan, 2016).

30. Italo Calvino, *Invisible Cities* (New York: Harcourt Brace Jovanovich, 1978).

31. Barthes, *Camera Lucida*, 36.

32. Barthes, *Camera Lucida*, 36.

33. Barthes, *Camera Lucida*, 37.

34. Nurith Gertz and George Khleifi, *Palestinian Cinema: Landscape, Trauma and Memory* (Edinburgh: Edinburgh University Press, 2008).

35. Lina Khatib, *Filming the Modern Middle East: Politics in the Cinemas of Hollywood and the Arab World* (London: I. B. Tauris, 2006).

36. Mary Ann Doane, *Bigger Than Life: The Close-up and Scale in the Cinema* (Durham, NC: Duke University Press, 2021), 17.

37. Doane, *Bigger Than Life*, 17.

38. Doane, *Bigger Than Life*, 234. In addition to Hito Steyerl, Doane references Mark Dorrian and Frédéric Pousin, eds., *Seeing from Above: The Aerial View in Visual Cultural* (London: I. B. Tauris, 2013); and Laura Kurgan, *Close Up at a Distance: Mapping, Technology, and Politics* (New York: Zone Books, 2013). I have been inspired by the brilliant work of Vera Tollman, *Sicht von oben*, "Powers of Ten" und Bildpolitiken den Vertikalität (Leipzig: Spector Books, 2022); and Geert Lovink, "Interview with German Media Theorist Vera Tollmann on *View from Above*" https://networkcultures.org/geert/2023/10/11/interview-with-german-media-theorist-vera-tollmann-on-view-from-above/.

39. Homay King, *Virtual Memory: Time-Based Art and the Dream of Digitality* (Durham, NC: Duke University Press, 2015), 3.

40. Doane, *Bigger Than Life*, 235, with references to Kurgan, *Close Up at a Distance*.

41. King, *Virtual Memory*, 56.

Epilogue. Planet: Otherworldly Futures

1. Fabienne Servan-Schreiber et al. *Lumière et Compagnie = Lumière & Company*, ed. Roger Ikhlef and Timothy Miller, directed by Sarah Moon et al. (Fox Lorber Home Video, 1995).

2. G.-Michel Coissac, *Histoire du cinématographe de ses origines à nos jours* (Paris: Éditions du "Cinéopse," 1925), vii.

3. Coissac, *Histoire du cinématographe*, vii.

4. Georges Méliès, *Le Voyage dans la lune* (Star Film Company, 1902).

5. See, for example, the entry on "Jules Janssen" in Hermann Hecht et al., *Pre-Cinema History: An Encyclopaedia and Annotated Bibliography of the Moving*

Image before 1896, (Place: Bowker Saur, 1993). See also Stephen Herbert's entry in *Who's Who of Victorian Cinema* (https://www.victorian-cinema.net/janssen).

6. For greater detail, see Françoise Launay and Peter D. Hingley, "Jules Janssen's 'Revolver Photographique' and Its British Derivative, 'the Janssen Slide,'" *Journal for the History of Astronomy* 36 (2005): 57–79.

7. Frédéric Neyrat, "Celestial Democracy: From Geocentric Ecology to Planetary Philosophy," *Comparative Literature* 76, no. 3 (Winter 2024): 269. See also Frédéric Neyrat, *The Unconstructable Earth* (New York: Fordham University Press, 2018).

8. Neyrat, "Celestial Democracy," 271.

9. Neyrat, "Celestial Democracy," 271.

10. Gayatri Chakravorty Spivak, *Death of a Discipline*, 20th anniv. ed. (New York: Columbia University Press, 2023).

11. Spivak, *Death of a Discipline*, xv.

12. Gayatri Chakravorty Spivak, "How the Heritage of Postcolonial Studies Thinks Colonialism Today," *Janus Unbound* 1, no. 1 (Fall 2021): 26–27.

13. Spivak, *Death of a Discipline*, xv.

14. Spivak, *Death of a Discipline*, xv.

15. Larissa Sansour, *A Space Exodus* (Mec Film, 2008).

16. Jacques Deslandes and Jacques Richard, *Histoire compareé de cinéma* (Paris: Casterman, 1968).

Bibliography

Films

Abounaddara. *In Search of the Syrian Fanatic*. https://vimeo.com/819559793.
Allouache, Merzak. *Bab El Oued City*. Médiathèque des Trois Mondes, 1994.
Chaplin, Charlie. *Modern Times*. United Artists, 1936.
Duvivier, Julien, et al. *Pépé Le Moko*. Criterion, Janus Collection, 1937/2006.
Farocki, Harun. *Arbeiter verlassen die Fabrik*. Werner Dütsch, 1995.
Farocki, Harun. *Bilder der Welt und Inschrift des Krieges = Pictures of the World and Inscriptions of the War*. New York: Video Data Bank, 2011.
Lumière! Le cinématographe, 1895–1905. Seven 7, 2015.
The Lumière Brothers' First Films. New York: Kino on Kino, 1997.
Lumière and Company. Videorecording. Fox Lorber, 1995.
Méliès, Georges. *Le Voyage dans la lune*. Star Film Company, 1902.
Palestine en 1896. https://vimeo.com/86980049?share=copy/.
Pontecorvo, Gilles. *Battle of Algiers*. Casbah Films, Kanopy Streaming, 1966.
Sansour, Larissa. *A Space Exodus*. Mec Film, 2008.
Sansour, Larissa, and Søren Lind. *Nation Estate*. Mec Film, 2012.
Sansour, Larissa, and Søren Lind. *In the Future They Ate from the Finest Porcelain*. Sci-Fi Trilogy, 2015.
Straub, Jean-Marie, and Danièle Huillet. *Too Early, Too Late*. Grasshopper Film, 1982.
Vertov, Dziga. *A Sixth Part of the World*. Film & Kunst GmbH, 2010.
Wilkinson, David, et al. *The First Film*. Content Media Corporation, 2015.

Articles and Books

Abel, Richard. *The Ciné Goes to Town: French Cinema, 1896–1914*. Updated and expanded edition. Berkeley: University of California Press, 1998.

Abel, Richard, ed. *Encyclopedia of Early Cinema*. London: Routledge, 2005.
Abel, Richard, Giorgio Bertellini, and Rob King, eds. *Early Cinema and the "National."* Bloomington, IN: John Libbey, 2008.
Abounaddara. "Dignity Has Never Been Photographed." *Documenta 14*, June 2017. https://www.documenta14.de/en/notes-and-works/15348/dignity-has-never-been-photographed.
Abounaddara. "Fanaticism on Screen." Institute for Ideas and Imagination of Columbia University, May 2021. https://ideasimagination.columbia.edu/events/abounaddara.
Agamben, Giorgio. *The State of Exception*. Chicago: University of Chicago Press, 2005.
Alexander, Livia. "Is There a Palestinian Cinema? The National and Transnational in Palestinian Film Production" In *Palestine, Israel, and the Politics of Popular Culture* edited by Rebecca L. Stein and Ted Swedenburg, 150–72. Durham, NC: Duke University Press, 2005.
Allan, Michael. "Deserted Histories: The Lumière Brothers, the Pyramids and Early Film Form." *Early Popular Visual Culture* 6, no. 2 (2008): 159–70.
Allan, Michael. "Picturing Other Languages: Reflections on Photography and Philology." *College English* 82, no. 1 (2019).
Allan, Michael. "Youssef Chahine's Iskandariyya . . . Leh?" In *Global Encyclopedia of Lesbian, Gay, Bisexual, Transgender, and Queer History*, 847–51. New York: Charles Scribner's Sons, 2019.
Alloula, Malek, and Barbara Harlow. *The Colonial Harem*. Translated by Myrna Godzich and Wlad Godzich. Minneapolis: University of Minnesota Press, 1986.
Alsdorf, Bridget. *Gawkers*. Princeton, NJ: Princeton University Press, 2022.
Amad, Paula. *Counter-Archive: Film, the Everyday, and Albert Kahn's Archives de la planète*. New York: Columbia University Press, 2010.
Andrew, Dudley. "An Atlas of World Cinema." *Framework* 45, no. 2 (Fall 2004): 9–23.
Andrew, Dudley. "Time Zones and Jet Lag in World Cinema." In *World Cinema/Transnational Perspectives*. London: Routledge, 2009.
Arondekar, Anjali. *Abundance*. Durham, NC: Duke University Press, 2023.
Askari, Kaveh. *Relaying Cinema*. Oakland: University of California Press, 2022.
Aubert, Michelle, et al. *La production cinématographique des Frères Lumière*. Librairie du Premier Siècle du Cinéma. Paris: Editions Mémoires de cinéma, 1996.
Auclair, Clara. "In Focus: The Treasures of the Francis Doublier Collection." From the Eastman Museum, April 9, 2021. https://www.youtube.com/watch?v=khiiz1RoVGc.
Aumont, Jacques. "Lumière Revisited." *Film History* 8, no. 4 (1996): 416–30.
L'Aventure du cinématographe: Actes du congrès Mondial Lumière. ALEAS: Université Lumière, Lyon 2, 1995.

Azoulay, Ariella Aïsha. *Potential History: Unlearning Imperialism.* London: Verso Books, 2019.
Baer, Nicholas. "Transnational Imaginaries: The Place of Palestine in Gershom Scholem, Franz Kafka, and Early Cinema." In *Transnational German Studies*, edited by R. Braun and B. Schofield, 224. Liverpool: Liverpool University Press, 2020.
Ballerini, Julia. "Orientalist Photography and Its 'Mistaken' Pictures." In *Picturing the Middle East: A Hundred Years of European Orientalism*, edited by Henry Krawitz, 22–23. New York: Dahesh Museum, 1995.
Bao, Weihong. "In Search of a 'Cinematic Esperanto': Exhibiting Wartime Chongqing Cinema in Global Context." *Journal of Chinese Cinemas* 3, no. 2 (2009): 135–47.
Barak, On. *On Time: Technology and Temporality in Modern Egypt.* Berkeley: University of California Press, 2013.
Barak, On. *Powering Empire: How Coal Made the Middle East and Sparked Global Carbonization.* Oakland: University of California Press, 2020.
Barthes, Roland. *Camera Lucida.* Translated by Richard Howard. London: Vintage Classics, 1993.
Baudry, Jean-Louis, and Alan Williams. "Ideological Effects of the Basic Cinematographic Apparatus." *Film Quarterly* 28, no. 2 (1974): 39–47.
Bayoumi, Moustafa. "The Civil War in Syria Is Invisible—but This Anonymous Film Collective Is Changing That." *The Nation*, June 29, 2015. https://www.thenation.com/article/archive/the-civil-war-in-syria-is-invisible-but-this-anonymous-film-collective-is-changing-that/.
Bazin, André. *What Is Cinema?* Edited and translated by Hugh Gray. Berkeley: University of California Press, 1967.
Behdad, Ali. *Camera Orientalis.* Chicago: University of Chicago Press, 2016.
Belisle, Brooke. "Nature at a Glance: Immersive Maps from Panoramic to Digital." *Early Popular Visual Culture* 13, no. 4 (2015): 313–35.
Belloï, Livio. "Lumière and His View: The Cameraman's Eye in Early Cinema." *Historical Journal of Film, Radio & Television* 15, no. 4 (October 1995): 461–74.
Benali, Abdelkader. *Le cinéma colonial au Maghreb.* Paris: Éditions du Cerf, 1998.
Benjamin, Roger. *Orientalist Aesthetics: Art, Colonialism, and French North Africa, 1880–1930.* Berkeley: University of California Press, 2003.
Best, Stephen, and Sharon Marcus. "Surface Reading: An Introduction." *Representations* 108, no. 1 (2009): 1–21.
Bhabha, Homi. *The Location of Culture.* London: Routledge, 1994.
Birchard, Robert. "Kalem Company, Manufacturers of Moving Picture Films." *American Cinematographer* 65 (1984).
Bjorli, Trond, and Kjetil Jakobsen, eds. *Cosmopolitics of the Camera: Albert Kahn's Archives of the Planet.* Bristol: Intellect Books, 2020.
Bordwell, David. *On the History of Film Style.* Cambridge, MA: Harvard University Press, 1997.

Bottomore, Stephen. "She's Just Like My Granny." In *Celebrating the Centenary of Cinema*, edited by John Fullerton. London: John Libbey, 1998.
Burch, Noël. "Primitivism and the Avant-Garde: A Dialectical Approach" in *Narrative, Apparatus, Ideology: A Film Theory Reader*, edited by Philip Rosen. New York: Columbia University Press, 1986.
Burch, Noël. *Theory of Film Practice*. Princeton, NJ: Princeton University Press, 1981.
Burch, Noël, and Ben Brewster. *Life to Those Shadows*. Berkeley: University of California Press, 1990.
Bursztyn, Igal. "Faces as Idea, Faces as Object: A Cinematic History (1911–1967)." *Studies in Zionism* 10, no. 2 (1989): 139–54.
Byg, Barton. *Landscapes of Resistance*. Berkeley: University of California Press, 1995.
Calvino, Italo. *Invisible Cities*. New York: Harcourt Brace Jovanovich, 1978.
Caron, Didier. "L'in(ter)vention Lumiere." *Revue de la Cinémathèque*, no. 5 (Spring 1994): 104–16.
Casanova, Pascale. *World Republic of Letters*. Translated by Malcolm DeBevoise. Cambridge, MA: Harvard University Press, 1999.
Chardère, Bernard. *Lumières sur Lumière*. Lyon: Presses universitaires du Lyon, 1987.
Chardère, Bernard, Guy Borgé, and Marjorie Borgé. *Les Lumière*. Lausanne: Payot, 1985.
Cheah, Pheng. *What Is a World? On Postcolonial Literature as World Literature*. Durham, NC: Duke University Press, 2016.
Coates, Paul. *Screening the Face*. London: Palgrave Macmillan, 2012.
Coissac, G.-Michel. *Histoire du cinématographe de ses origines à nos jours*. Paris: Éditions de Cinéopse, 1925.
Colla, Elliott. *Conflicted Antiquities*. Durham, NC: Duke University Press, 2007.
Colla, Elliott. "The Measure of Egypt." *Postcolonial Studies* 7, no. 3 (2004): 271–93.
Conley, Tom. *Film Hieroglyphs*. Minneapolis: University of Minnesota Press, 1991.
Cooke, Paul. *World Cinema's "Dialogues" with Hollywood*. Basingstoke: Palgrave Macmillan, 2007.
Cosandey, Roland. "Le catalogue Lumière (1896–1907) et la Suisse: Éléments pour une filmographie nationale." *1895, revue d'histoire du cinéma*, no. 15 (1993): 3–30.
Cotterell, Paul. *The Railways of Palestine and Israel*. Abingdon: Tourret, 1984.
Crary, Jonathan. *Techniques of the Observer: On Vision and Modernity in the Nineteenth Century*. Cambridge, MA: MIT Press, 1990.
Curran, Brian. "Review of *Egyptomania: Egypt in Western Art 1730–1930*." *Art Bulletin* 78, no. 4 (1996).
Curtis, Scott. *The Shape of Spectatorship: Art, Science, and Early Cinema in Germany*. New York: Columbia University Press, 2015.
Damisch, Hubert, and John Goodman. *The Origin of Perspective*. Cambridge: MIT Press, 1994.

Daney, Serge. "The Tracking Shot in *Kapo.*" In *Postcards from the Cinema*, translated by Paul Grant, 17–35. London: Berg / Bloomsbury, 2007.
Deleuze, Gilles. *The Fold: Leibniz and the Baroque.* Translated by Tom Conley. Minneapolis: University of Minnesota Press, 1993.
Demurger, Manon, and Musée Albert Kahn, *Les Archives de la Planète.* Edited by Valérie Perlès. Musée départemental Albert Kahn: LienArt, 2019.
Dennison, Stephanie, and Song Hwee Lim, eds. *Remapping World Cinema: Identity, Culture and Politics in Film.* New York: Wallflower Press, 2006.
Derrida, Jacques. "The Pit and the Pyramid: Introduction to Hegel's Semiology." In *Margins of Philosophy*, translated by Alan Bass. Chicago: University of Chicago Press, 1984.
Deshpande, Shekhar, and Meta Mazaj, eds. *World Cinema: A Critical Introduction.* New York: Routledge, 2018.
Deslandes, Jacques, and Jacques Richard, *Histoire compareé de cinema.* Paris: Casterman, 1968.
Deutelbaum, Marshall. "Structural Patterning in the Lumière Films." In *Film before Griffith*, edited by John L. Fell, 299–310. Berkeley: University of California Press, 1983.
Diba, Layla. "Images of Power and the Power of Images: Intention and Response in Early Qajar Painting." In *Royal Persian Paintings: The Qajar Epoch, 1785–1925*, edited by Layla S. Diba et al. Brooklyn Museum of Art in association with I. B. Tauris Publishers, 1998.
Didi-Huberman, George. "People Exposed, People as Extras." *Radical Philosophy* 156 (July/August 2009): 16–22.
Di Ioro, Sam. "Three Tracking Shots." *Contemporary French Civilization* 32, no. 2 (July 2008): 85–112.
Doane, Mary Ann. *Bigger Than Life: The Close-up and Scale in the Cinema.* Duke University Press, 2021.
Doane, Mary Ann. "The Close-Up: Scale and Detail in the Cinema." *differences: A Journal of Feminist Cultural Studies* 14, no. 3 (2003): 89–111.
Doane, Mary Ann. "Film and the Masquerade." *Screen* 23, no. 3–4 (1982): 74–87.
Dorrian, Mark, and Frédéric Pousin, eds. *Seeing from Above: The Aerial View in Visual Culture.* London: I. B. Tauris, 2013.
Dubois, Philippe. "Le Gros Plan Primitif." *Revue belge du cinéma*, no. 10 (1984–85): 11–34.
Dyer, Richard. "Zineb Sedira: Saphir." *Nka: Journal of Contemporary African Art* 24 (2009): 56–61.
The Egyptian Railway; or, The Interest of England in Egypt (London: Hope and Co., 1852).
Eisenstein, Sergei. *Film Form: Essays in Film Theory.* Edited and translated by Jay Leyda. 1949. San Diego: Harcourt Brace, 1977.
Elhaies, Karim. "When Old Cinema Was New: The Media Making of Modern Egypt and Its Early Cinema." PhD diss., New York University, forthcoming.

Elias, Chad. "Emergency Cinema and the Dignified Image: Cell Phone Activism and Filmmaking in Syria." *Film Quarterly* 71 (2017): 18–31.

Elsaesser, Thomas, and Adam Barker. *Early Cinema: Space, Frame, Narrative*. London: British Film Institute, 1990.

Elsaket, Ifdal. "Projecting Egypt: The Cinema and the Making of Colonial Modernity 1896–1952." PhD diss., University of Sydney, 2013.

El Shakry, Hoda. "Palestine and the Aesthetics of the Future Impossible." *Interventions* 23, no. 5 (2021): 669–90.

Esmeir, Samera. "On Becoming Less of the World." *History of the Present* 8, no. 1 (April 2018): 88–116. https://doi.org/10.5406/historypresent.8.1.0088.

Fairfax, Daniel. "Straub, Jean-Marie & Huillet, Danièle." *Senses of Cinema*, no. 52 (September 2009). https://www.sensesofcinema.com/2009/great-directors/jean-marie-straub-and-daniele-huillet/.

Farid, Samir, ed. *Tarikh Al-Cinema Al-Arabiyya Al Samita*. Cairo: General Union of Arab Artists, 1994.

Farocki, Harun. "Commentary from *Bilder der Welt und Inschrift des Krieges* (Images of the World and Inscription of the War)." *Discourse: Journal for Theoretical Studies in Media and Culture* 15, no. 3 (1993): article 4.

Farocki, Harun. "Workers Leaving the Factory." Translated by Laurent Faasch-Ibrahim. *Senses of Cinema*, no. 2 (July 2002). https://www.sensesofcinema.com/2002/harun-farocki/farocki_workers/.

Fay, Jennifer. "A Portal to Another World: On Cinema, Climate Change, and a Good Apocalypse." In *What Film Is Good For: On the Values of Spectatorship*, edited by Julian Hanich, 13–23. Oakland: University of California Press, 2023. https://doi.org/10.1525/9780520386822-004.

Fowzy, Fatma, and Doaa Kandil, "Re-Constructing Old Mahmal Procession Route through Consulting Contemporary Visual Sources." *Journal of Arts, Architecture, and Humanistic Sciences* 8, no. 8 (2023): 160–76.

Foucault, Michel. *This Is Not a Pipe*. Berkeley: University of California Press, 1983.

Frei, Hans. *The Eclipse of Biblical Narrative: A Study in Eighteenth- and Nineteenth-Century Hermeneutics*. New Haven, CT: Yale University Press, 1974.

Friedberg, Anne. *The Virtual Window: From Alberti to Microsoft*. Cambridge, MA: MIT Press, 2006.

Fullerton, John. "Creating an Audience for the *Cinématographe*: Two Lumière Agents in Mexico, 1896." *Film History: An International Journal* 20, no. 1 (2008): 95–114.

Fullerton, John, ed. *Celebrating 1895: The Centenary of Cinema*. Sydney: John Libbey, 1998.

Galt, Rosalind, and Karl Schoonover. *Global Art Cinema: New Theories and Histories*. New York: Oxford University Press, 2010.

Ganguly, Debjany. *This Thing Called the World*. Durham, NC: Duke University Press, 2016.

Ganguly, Keya. "World Literature, World Cinema, and Dialectical Criticism." In *The Cambridge Companion to World Literature*. Cambridge: Cambridge University Press, 2018.

Garcia, Edgar. *Signs of the Americas*. Chicago: University of Chicago Press, 2020.

Gardies, André. "Cinema on Show in the Work of the Lumière Brothers." In *Echoes of Narcissus*, edited by Lieve Spaas, 111–21. New York: Berghahn Books, 2000.

Gaudreault, André. "Showing and Telling Image and Word in Early Cinema." In *Early Cinema: Space, Frame, Narrative*, edited by Thomas Elsaesser and Adam Barker, 274–84. London: British Film Institute, 1990.

Gaudreault, André, et al. *The End of Cinema?: A Medium in Crisis in the Digital Age*. New York: Columbia University Press, 2015.

Gauthier, Christophe. "Comment les Frères Lumière devinrent les pères du cinéma: La querelle des inventeurs." *Bibliothèque de l'École des chartes* 167, no. 1 (2009): 155–78.

Geduld, Harry. *Filmmakers on Filmmaking*. Blooomington: Indiana University Press, 1967.

Gertz, Nurith, and George Khleifi. *Palestinian Cinema: Landscape, Trauma and Memory*. Edinburgh: Edinburgh University Press, 2008.

Ginsberg, Terri. *Visualizing the Palestinian Struggle: Toward a Critical Analytic of Palestine Solidarity Film*. London: Palgrave Macmillan, 2016.

Ginzburg, Carlo. "Carlo Ginzburg: 'In History as in Cinema, Every Close-Up Implies an Off-Screen Scene.'" *Verso Books*, June 6, 2023. https://www.versobooks.com/blogs/news/5536-carlo-ginzburg-in-history-as-in-cinema-every-close-up-implies-an-off-screen-scene.

Glass, Joseph. "The Biography in Historical-Geographical Research: Joseph Novon Bey—A Case Study." In *The Land That Became Israel*, edited by Ruth Kark, 77–89. New Haven, CT: Yale University Press, 1990.

Goedert, Nathalie, and Ninon Maillard. "Culture visuelle du territoire (I): *Pépé le Moko* et l'invention de la frontière." October 1, 2016. https://imaj.hypotheses.org/1229.

González, Jennifer. "The Face and the Public: Race, Secrecy, and Digital Art Practice." *Camera Obscura: Feminism, Culture, and Media Studies* 24, no. 1 (2009).

Gott, Michael, and Thibault Schilt, eds. *Cinéma-monde*. Edinburgh: Edinburgh University Press, 2018.

Stephen Grant Collection. "The Stephen Grant Postcard Collection Digitization Project." *National Museum of African Art*, February 2020. https://africa.si.edu/2020/02/the-stephen-grant-postcard-collection-digitization-project/.

Gray, Frank. "The Kiss in the Tunnel." 1899. "G. A. Smith and the Emergence of the Edited Film in England," in *The Silent Cinema Reader*, edited by Lee Grieveson and Peter Krämer. London: Routledge, 2004.

Gregory, Derek. *The Colonial Present: Afghanistan, Palestine, and Iraq*. Malden, MA: Blackwell, 2004.

Griffiths, Alison. *Wondrous Difference: Cinema, Anthropology, and Turn-of-the-Century Visual Culture*. New York: Columbia University Press, 2002.
Groo, Katherine. *Bad Film Histories: Ethnography and the Early Film Archive*. Minneapolis: University of Minnesota Press, 2019.
Gunning, Tom. "An Aesthetic of Astonishment: Early Film and the (In)Credulous Spectator." *Art and Text* 34 (1989): 31–45.
Gunning, Tom. "Camera Movement." In *Encyclopedia of Early Cinema*, edited by Richard Abel. London: Routledge, 2005.
Gunning, Tom. "The Cinema of Attractions: Early Cinema, Its Spectator, and the Avant-Garde." *Wide Angle* 8 (1986).
Gunning, Tom. "Moving Away from the Index: Cinema and the Impression of Reality." *differences* 18, no. 1 (2007): 29–52.
Gunning, Tom. "Never Seen This Picture Before: Muybridge in Multiplicity." In *Time Stands Still: Muybridge and the Instantaneous Photography Movement*, edited by Phillip Prodger, 222–72. New York: Oxford University Press, 2003.
Gunning, Tom. "New Thresholds of Vision: Instantaneous Photography and the Early Cinema of Lumière." In *Impossible Presence: Surface and Screen in the Photogenic Era*, edited by Terry Smith. Sydney: Power, 2001.
Gunning, Tom. "'Primitive' Cinema: A Frame-up? Or the Trick's on Us." *Cinema Journal* 28, no. 2 (1989).
Gunning, Tom. "The Whole World within Reach." In *Virtual Voyages*, edited by Jeffrey Ruoff. Durham, NC: Duke University Press, 2006.
al-Hadari, Ahmed. *Tarikh al-sinima fi Misr*. Cairo: Nādī al-Sīnimā bi-al-Qāhirah, 1989.
Hamzaoui, Hamid. *Histoire du cinema égyptien*. Paris: Autres Temps, 1997.
Hassan, Ilhami. *Tarikh al-Cinema al-Masriyya (1896–1970)*. Cairo: Ministry of Culture, 1995.
Heath, Stephen. "Narrative Space." *Screen* 17, no. 3 (Autumn 1976): 68–112.
Heberle, Helge, and Monika Funke Stern. "Das Feuer im Inneren des Berges: Gespräch mit Danièle Huillet." *Frauen und Film*, no. 32 (1982).
Hecht, Hermann, et al. *Pre-Cinema History: An Encyclopaedia and Annotated Bibliography of the Moving Image before 1896*. Bowker Saur, 1993.
Helmy, Samy. *Bidayat al-Cinema al-Misriyya*. Alexandria: General Organization of Cultural Palaces, 2013.
Helmy, Samy. *Madrasat al-Iskandariyya lel-Tasweer al-Cinema'i*. Alexandria: Bibliotheca Alexandrina, 2013.
Helmy, Samy. "Start Up City: Alexandria, The Cradle of Egyptian Cinema." *Rawi*, no. 9, 2018. https://rawi-publishing.com/articles/startup-city?lang=en
Hennebelle, Guy. *Les Cinémas Africains en 1972*. Paris: Société africaine d'édition, 1972.
Higbee, Will, and Song Hwee Lim. "Concepts of Transnational Cinema: Towards a Critical Transnationalism in Film Studies." *Transnational Cinemas* 1, no. 1 (2010): 7–21.

Higson, Andrew. *The Instability of the National*. London: Routledge, 2000.
Hjort, Mette, and Scott Mackenzie, eds. *Cinema and Nation*. London: Routledge, 2000.
Hochberg, Gil. *Becoming Palestine: Toward an Archival Imagination of the Future*. Durham, NC: Duke University Press, 2021.
Howe, Kathleen Stewart. *Excursions along the Nile: The Photographic Discovery of Ancient Egypt*. Santa Barbara: Santa Barbara Museum of Art, 1994.
Huhtamo, Erkki. *Illusions in Motion: Media Archaeology of the Moving Panorama and Related Spectacles*. Cambridge, MA: MIT Press, 2013.
al-Jabarti. *'Abd al-Rahman al-Jabarti's History of Egypt. 'Aja'ib al-Athar fi 'l-Tarajim wa 'l-Akhbar*. Edited by Thomas Philipp and Moshe Perlmann. Stuttgart: Franz Steiner Verlag, Stuttgart, 1994, vol. 3, part II, section 31.
Jackson, William Henry. *Algiers—The Embankment and Boulevard de la République Photograph*. Published as halftone in *Harper's Weekly*, 1895.
Jacquier, Philippe. "Un opérateur de la Maison Lumière, Gabriel Veyre." In *Le Cinéma Francais Muet Dans le Monde, Influences Réciproques*: : Symposium de la FIAF. Paris: Cinematheque de Toulouse/Institut Jean Vigo, 1988.
Jacquier, Philippe, and Marion Pranal. *Gabriel Veyre, Opérateur Lumière: Autour du monde avec le Cinématographe, Correspondance (1896–1900)*. Lyon/Arles: Institut Lumière/Actes Sud, 1996.
Jaikumar, Priya. *Where Histories Reside*. Durham, NC: Duke University Press, 2019.
Kantorowicz, Ernst. *The King's Two Bodies: A Study in Mediaeval Political Theology*. Princeton, NJ: Princeton University Press, 1957.
Keating, Patrick. *The Dynamic Frame: Camera Movement in Classical Hollywood*. New York: Columbia University Press, 2019.
Keller, Sarah, and Jason N. Paul, eds. *Jean Epstein: Critical Essays and New Translations*. Amsterdam: Amsterdam University Press, 2012.
Kepley, Vance, Jr. "Whose Apparatus? Problems of Film Exhibition and History." In *Post-Theory: Reconstructing Film Studies*, edited by David Bordwell and Noel Carroll. Madison: University of Wisconsin Press, 1996.
Kessler, Frank. "Images of the 'National' in Early Non-Fiction Films" *Early Cinema and the "National,"* edited by in Richard Abel, Giorgio Bertellini, and Rob King. Bloomington, IN: John Libbey, 2008.
Khatib, Lina. *Filming the Modern Middle East: Politics in the Cinemas of Hollywood and the Arab World*. London: I. B. Tauris, 2006.
Khatib, Lina. *Storytelling in World Cinemas*. Vol. 1–2. London: Wallflower Press, 2012.
Khouri, Malek. *The Arab National Project in Youssef Chahine's Cinema*. Cairo: American University in Cairo Press, 2010.
King, Homay. *Virtual Memory: Time-Based Art and the Dream of Digitality*. Durham, NC: Duke University Press, 2015.
Kirby, Lynne. *Parallel Tracks: The Railroad and Silent Cinema*. Durham, NC: Duke University Press, 1997.

Kurgan, Laura. *Close Up at a Distance: Mapping, Technology, and Politics*. New York: Zone Books, 2013.
Landau, Jacob M. *Studies in the Arab Theater and Cinema*. Philadelphia: University of Pennsylvania Press, 1958.
Lant, Antonia. "The Curse of the Pharaoh, or How Cinema Constructed Egyptomania." *October* 59 (1992).
Lehmbeck, Leah. "Fine Art on Film." *City of Cinema: Paris 1850–1907*, eds. Lehmbeck, Salvesen, and Schwartz. Los Angeles: Delmonico Books, 2022.
Lahmbeck, Leah, Britt Salvesen, and Vanessa Schwartz, eds. *City of Cinema: Paris 1850–1907*. Los Angeles: DelMonico Books, 2022.
Launay, Françoise, and Peter D. Hingley. "Jules Janssen's 'Revolver Photographique' and Its British Derivative, 'the Janssen Slide.'" *Journal for the History of Astronomy* 36 (2005): 57–79.
Lenssen, Anneka. "The Filmmaker as Artisan." *Third Text* 34 (2020): 159–71.
Leprohon, Pierre. *L'exotisme et le cinéma: Les "chasseurs d'images" à la conquête du monde*. Paris: J. Susse, 1945.
Leyda, Jay. *Kino: A History of Russian and Soviet Film*. Princeton, NJ: Princeton University Press, 1983.
Lim, Bliss Cua. *Translating Time: Cinema, the Fantastic, and Temporal Critique*. Durham, NC: Duke University Press, 2009.
Lindberg, David C. *Theories of Vision from Al-Kindi to Kepler*. Chicago: University of Chicago Press, 1976.
Lindsay, Vachel. *The Art of the Moving Picture*. New York: Macmillan, 1915.
Lockman, Zachary. *Comrades and Enemies: Arab and Jewish Workers in Palestine, 1906–1948*. Berkeley: University of California Press, 1996.
Loiperdinger, Martin, and Bernd Elzer. "Lumiere's Arrival of the Train: Cinema's Founding Myth." *Moving Image* 4 (2004): 89–118.
Lovink, Geert. "Interview with German Media Theorist Vera Tollmann on *View from Above*." *Geert Lovink Blog*, October 11, 2023. https://networkcultures.org/geert/2023/10/11/interview-with-german-media-theorist-vera-tollmann-on-view-from-above/.
Lumière, Louis. "The Lumiere Cinematograph." In *A Technological History of Motion Pictures and Television: An Anthology from the Pages of the Journal of the Society of Motion Picture and Television Engineers*, edited by Raymond Fielding. Berkeley: University of California Press, 1967.
Ma, Jean. *Melancholy Drift: Marking Time in Chinese Cinema*. Hong Kong: Hong Kong University Press, 2010.
Malkmus, Lizbeth, and Roy Armes. *Arab and African Film Making*. London: Zed Books, 1991.
Mannoni, Laurent. *The Great Art of Light and Shadow: Archaeology of the Cinema*. Exeter: University of Exeter Press, 2000.
Marinone, Isabelle, et al. *Un Monde et son double: Regards sur L'entreprise visuelle des Archives de la Planète (1919–1931)*. Presses Universitaires de Perpignan, 2019.

Marks, Laura. *Hanan al-Cinema: Affections for the Moving Image*. Cambridge, MA: MIT Press, 2015.
Marks, Laura. *The Skin of the Film: Intercultural Cinema, Embodiment, and the Senses*. Durham, NC.: Duke University Press, 2000.
Marshall, Bill. "Cinéma-monde? Towards a Concept of Francophone Cinema." *Francosphères* 1, no. 1 (2012): 35–51.
Mast, Gerald. "On Framing." *Critical Inquiry* 11, no. 1 (1984): 82–109.
Mathias, Nikita. "Between Immersion and Media Reflexivity: Virtual Travel Media in the 19th Century." *International Journal of Film and Media Arts* 1, no. 2 (2016): 22–33.
Maurice, Alice. *The Cinema and Its Shadow*. Minneapolis: University of Minnesota Press, 2013.
McAllister, Melanie. *Epic Encounters: Culture, Media, and US Interests in the Middle East since 1945*. Berkeley: University of California Press, 2005.
McManus, Anne-Marie. "On the Ruins of What's to Come, I Stand." *Critical Inquiry* 48, no. 1 (2021): 45–67.
McManus, Anne-Marie E. "Scale in the Balance: Reading with the International Prize for Arabic Fiction ("The Arabic Booker")." *International Journal of Middle East Studies* 48, no. 2 (2016): 217–41.
Megherbi, Abdelghani. *Les Algériens au miroir du cinéma colonial: (Contribution à une sociologie de la décolonisation)*. Alger: E.D., 1982.
Merrill, Selah. "The Jaffa Jerusalem Railway." *Scribner's Magazine* 13, no. 3 (March 1893).
Mesguich, Félix. *Tours de manivelle: Souvenirs d'un chasseur d'images*. Paris: B. Grasset, 1933.
Mesguich, Félix. "Felix Mésguich's *Tours de manivelle*." Translated by Kevin Riordan and Corbin Treacy. *Modernism/modernity* 18, no. 2 (2011): 447–48.
Mestyan, Adam. "Khedive." *Encyclopaedia of Islam, Three*. Leiden: Brill, 2020.
Metz, Christian. *The Imaginary Signifier: Psychoanalysis and the Cinema*. Bloomington: Indiana University Press, 1982.
Miller, Angela L. "The Panorama, the Cinema and the Emergence of the Spectacular." *Wide Angle* 18, no. 2 (1996): 34–69.
Miller, Jacques-Alain. "Sovereign Image." *Lacanian Review: Hurly Burly*, no. 5 (Summer 2018): 39–52.
Mirzoeff, Nick. *The Right to Look: A Counterhistory of Visuality*. Durham, NC: Duke University Press, 2011.
Mitchell, Timothy. *Colonising Egypt*. Berkeley: University of California Press, 1991.
Mitry, Jean. *Histoire du Cinéma*. Paris: Éditions universitaires, 1967.
Miyao, Daisuke. *Japonisme and the Birth of Cinema*. Durham, NC: Duke University Press, 2020.
Moretti, Franco. *Distant Reading*. London: Verso, 2013.

Morgan, Daniel. *The Lure of the Image*. Oakland: University of California Press, 2021.
Morgan, Daniel. "Rethinking Bazin: Ontology and Realist Aesthetics." *Critical Inquiry* 32, no. 3 (2006): 443–81.
Moustacchia, Dominique, and Béatrice de Pastre. "De la solitude des premiers opérateurs à la mise en œuvre des équipes de tournage: Le cas des opérateurs Lumière." *La Revue Documentaires*, no. 26–27 (2016): 19–29.
Mulvey, Laura. *Visual and Other Pleasures*. London: Palgrave Macmillan, 2009.
Musser, Charles. "A Cinema of Contemplation: A Cinema of Discernment: Spectatorship, Intertextuality and Attractions in the 1890s." In *The Cinema of Attractions Reloaded*, edited by Wanda Strauven, 161–78. Amsterdam: Amsterdam University Press, 2006.
Musser, Charles. *The Emergence of Cinema: The American Screen to 1907*. New York: Charles Scribner's Sons, 1990.
Naficy, Hamid. "Theorizing 'Third-World' Film Spectatorship." *Wide Angle* 18, no. 4 (1996): 3–26.
Nagib, Lúcia, et al. *Theorizing World Cinema*. London: I. B. Tauris, 2012.
Nagib, Lúcia. *World Cinema and the Ethics of Realism*. New York: Continuum International, 2011.
Nakassis, Constantine V. *Onscreen/Offscreen*. Toronto: University of Toronto Press, 2023.
Naremore, James, ed. *An Invention without a Future: Essays on Cinema*. Berkeley: University of California Press, 2014.
Neyrat, Frédéric. "Celestial Democracy: From Geocentric Ecology to Planetary Philosophy." *Comparative Literature* 76, no. 3 (Winter 2024).
Neyrat, Frédéric. *The Unconstructable Earth*. New York: Fordham University Press, 2018.
Ngai, Sianne. *Ugly Feelings*. Cambridge, MA: Harvard University Press, 2005.
Oleksijczuk, Denise. *The First Panoramas: Visions of British Imperialism*. Minneapolis: University of Minnesota Press, 2011.
Panofsky, Erwin. *Perspective as Symbolic Form*. Translated by Christopher S. Wood. New York: Zone Books, 1991.
Parks, Lisa. *Cultures in Orbit: Satellites and the Televisual*. Durham, NC: Duke University Press, 2005.
Peretz, Eyal. *The Off-Screen: An Investigation of the Cinematic Frame*. Stanford, CA: Stanford University Press, 2017.
Peterson, Jennifer Lynn. *Education in the School of Dreams*. Durham, NC: Duke University Press, 2013.
Petricioli, Marta. *Oltre il mito: l'Egitto degli italiani*. Milan: B. Mondadori, 2007.
Pinel, Vincent. *Louis Lumière: Inventeur et Cinéaste*. Paris: Nathan, 1994.
Potenza, Daniela. "Literary Trajectories of Sulaymān al-Ḥalabī, a Hero Who Was Born a Criminal." *Annali di Ca' Foscari. Serie orientale* 56 (2020): 81–104.

Promio, Alexandre. "A Travelogue." Translated by Gerard-Jans Claes. *Sabzian*, May 27, 2020. https://www.sabzian.be/text/a-travelogue,
"Railway to Jerusalem." Conrad Schick. Accessed October 23, 2025. https://conradschick.wordpress.com/geography/railway-to-jerusalem/.
Rancière, Jacques. *The Future of the Image*. London: Verso, 2009.
Redrobe, Karen, and Jeff Scheible, eds. *Deep Mediations: Thinking Space in Cinema and Digital Cultures*. Minneapolis: University of Minnesota Press, 2020.
Regnault, Félix. *L'Illustration*, May 30, 1896, 446–47.
Renaitour, Jean-Michel. *Où va le cinéma français?* Paris: Éditions Baudinière, 1937.
Rhodes, John David, and Elena Gorfinkel. *Taking Place: Location and the Moving Image*. Minneapolis: University of Minnesota Press, 2011.
Rittaud-Hutinet, Jacques. *Le cinéma des origines : les frères Lumière et leurs opérateurs*. Seyssel: Champs Vallon, 1985.
Robert, Valentine. "La part picturale du *tableau-style*." In *The Image in Early Cinema*, edited by Scott Curtis, Philippe Gauthier, Tom Gunning, and Joshua Yumibe. Bloomington: Indiana University Press, 2018, 15–25.
Roberts, David, et al. *David Roberts*. Oxford: Phaidon Press and Barbican Art Gallery, 1986.
Roberts, Mary. "The Limits of Circumscription," In *Photography's Orientalism: New Essays on Colonial Representation*, edited by Ali Behdad and Luke Gartlan. Los Angeles: Getty Research Institute, 2013.
Roberts, Mary. "Ottoman Statecraft and the 'Pencil of Nature': Photography, Painting, and Drawing at the Court of Sultan Abdülaziz." *Ars Orientalis* 43 (2013): 10–30.
Robinson, David. *The History of World Cinema*. 2nd ed., rev. and updated. New York: Stein and Day, 1981.
Rony, Fatimah Tobing. *The Third Eye: Race, Cinema, and Ethnographic Spectacle*. Durham, NC: Duke University Press, 1996.
Rosen, Philip. *Change Mummified: Cinema, Historicity, Theory*. Minneapolis: University of Minnesota Press, 2001.
Rosen, Philip. "Document and Documentary: On the Persistence of Historical Concepts." In *Theorizing Documentary*, edited by Michael Renov. London: Routledge, 1993.
Royal Collection Trust. "Abbas II Hilmi (1874–1944), Khedive of Egypt." Accessed October 20, 2025. https://www.rct.uk/collection/search#/8/collection/403802/abbas-ii-hilmi-1874-1944-khedive-of-egypt.
Ruoff, Jeffrey, ed. *Virtual Voyages*. Durham, NC: Duke University Press, 2006.
Sadoul, Georges. *Les cinémas des pays arabes*. Beirut: Centre interarabe du cinéma et de la télévision, 1966.
Sadoul, Georges. *Histoire du cinéma mondial, des origines à nos jours*. Paris: Flammarion, 1949.
Sadoul, Georges. *Histoire générale du cinéma. Tome 1: L'invention du cinéma, 1832–1897*. Paris: Denoël, 1946.

Sadoul, Georges. Interview with Louis Lumière in *Sight and Sound* 17, no. 66 (Summer 1948): 68–70.
Sadoul, Georges. *Louis Lumière*. Paris: Seghers, 1964.
Said, Edward. *Orientalism*. New York, Vintage, 1979.
Salazkina, Masha. "World Cinema as Method." *Canadian Journal of Film Studies / Revue canadienne d'études cinématographiques* 29, no. 2 (2020): 10–24. https://muse.jhu.edu/article/776863.
Samocki, Jean-Marie. "Nouvelle fictions du visage." *Trafic* 38 (Summer 2001): 93–113.
Sansour, Larissa. "Time, Nationhood, Resistance: Larissa Sansour's Latest Film *In the Future They Ate from the Finest Porcelain*." Interview. *Art Radar Journal*. February 1, 2016. http://www.artradarjournal.com/2016/02/01/palestinian-artist-larissa-sansours-interview.
Schaaf, Larry. "Charles Piazzi Smyth's 1865 Conquest of the Great Pyramid." *History of Photography* 3, no. 4 (October 1979): 331–54.
Schick, Conrad. "Notes and News." *Quarterly Statement* 31 (January 1899): 3–4. London: Palestine Exploration Fund.
Schonig, Jordan. "Contingent Motion: Rethinking the 'Wind in the Trees' in Early Cinema and CGI." *Discourse* 40, no. 1 (2018): 30–61.
Schonig, Jordan. *The Shape of Motion: Cinema and the Aesthetics of Movement*. Oxford: Oxford University Press, 2021.
Schoonover, Karl, and Rosalind Galt. *Queer Cinema in the World*. Durham, NC: Duke University Press, 2016.
Schor, Naomi. *Reading in Detail: Aesthetics and the Feminine*. New York: Methuen, 1987.
Schwartz, Vanessa. "On the Move: Seeing the World in Early Transport Films." In *Paris: City of Cinema*, 120–53. Los Angeles: DelMonico Books, 2021.
The Scottish Arts Council. *Artist Adventurer David Roberts*. Edinburgh: Ivanhoe, 1981.
Sedgwick, Eve Kosofsky. *Touching Feeling*. Durham, NC: Duke University Press, 2002.
Seguin, Jean-Claude. *Alexandre Promio, ou, Les énigmes de la lumière*. Paris: Harmattan, 1999.
Seguin, Jean-Claude. "Aux origines du cinéma en Algérie: Alexandre Promio." *Le Documentaire dans l'Algérie coloniale*, 2014.
Shafik, Viola. *Arab Cinema: History and Cultural Identity*. Cairo: American University in Cairo Press, 2007.
Shafik, Viola. "A Chronology of Firsts in Alexandria." In *Encyclopedia of Early Cinema*, edited by Richard Abel. London: Routledge, 2005.
Shafik, Viola, ed. *Documentary Filmmaking in the Middle East and North Africa*. Cairo: American University in Cairo Press, 2022.
Shafik, Viola. *Resistance, Dissidence, Revolution: Documentary Film Esthetics in the Middle East and North Africa*. London: Routledge, 2023.

Shaheen, Jack. *Reel Bad Arabs*. New York: Olive Branch Press, 2012.
Sheehi, Stephen. *The Arab Imago*. Princeton, NJ: Princeton University Press, 2016.
Shimi, Sa'id. *Tarikh al-taswir al-sinima'i fi Misr, 1897–1996*. Giza: Cinefilm, 1997.
Shohat, Ella, and Robert Stam. *Unthinking Eurocentrism: Multiculturalism and the Media*. New York: Routledge, 1994.
Siegrist, Hansmartin. *Auf der Brücke zur Moderne Basels erster Film als Panorama der Belle Epoque*. Basel: Christoph Merian Verlag, 2019.
Silverman, Kaja. *The Acoustic Mirror: The Female Voice in Psychoanalysis and Cinema*. Bloomington: Indiana University Press, 1988.
Silverman, Kaja. *Male Subjectivity at the Margins*. New York: Routledge, 1992.
Silverman, Kaja. *The Subject of Semiotics*. New York: Oxford University Press, 1983.
Sitney, P. Adams. "A Cinema of Resistance." *Artforum*, May 2016.
Soueid, Mohamad. "Documenting Lebanon." In *Documentary Filmmaking in the Middle East and North Africa*, edited by Viola Shafik, 33–46. Cairo: American University in Cairo Press, 2022.
Spivak, Gayatri Chakravorty. *Death of a Discipline*. 20th anniversary ed. New York: Columbia University Press, 2023.
Spivak, Gayatri Chakravorty. "How the Heritage of Postcolonial Studies Thinks Colonialism Today." *Janus Unbound* 1, no. 1 (Fall 2021): 19–29.
Stam, Robert. *World Literature, Transnational Cinema, and Global Media: Towards a Transartistic Commons*. London: Routledge, 2019.
Steimatsky, Noa. *The Face on Film*. New York: Oxford University Press, 2017.
Steinhart, Daniel. *Runaway Hollywood: Internationalizing Postwar Production and Location Shooting*. Oakland: University of California Press, 2019.
Stone, Rob, et al., eds. *The Routledge Companion to World Cinema*. Abingdon: Routledge, 2018.
Sunya, Samhita. *Sirens of Modernity: World Cinema via Bombay*. Oakland: University of California Press, 2022.
Tamari, Salim. *The Great War and the Remaking of Palestine*. Oakland: University of California Press, 2017.
Tanoukhi, Nirvana. "The Scale of World Literature." *New Literary History* 39, no. 3 (2009): 599–617.
Taussig, Michael T. *Mimesis and Alterity: A Particular History of the Senses*. London: Routledge, 1993.
Thiong'o, Ngũgĩ wa. *Globalectics: Theory and the Politics of Knowing*. New York: Columbia University Press, 2012.
Tollmann, Vera. *Sicht von oben: "Powers of Ten" und Bildpolitiken der Vertikalität*. Leipzig: Spector Books, 2022.
Trumpener, Katie, and Tim Barringer, eds. *On the Viewing Platform: The Panorama between Canvas and Screen*. New Haven, CT: Yale University Press, 2020.
Turquety, Benoît. *Inventing Cinema: Machines, Gestures and Media History*. Amsterdam: Amsterdam University Press, 2019.

Vaughan, Dai. "Let There Be Lumière." In *Early Cinema: Space, Frame, Narrative*, ed. Thomas Elsaesser. London: British Film Institute, 1990.

Veyre, Gabriel. *Dans l'intimité du sultan, au Maroc 1901–1905*. Paris: Librairie Universelle, 1905.

Virilio, Paul. *War and Cinema: The Logistics of Perception*. Translated by Patrick Camiller. London: Verso, 1989.

Vitali, Valentina, ed. *Theorising National Cinemas*. London: Routledge, 2019.

Waley, Muhammad Isa. "Images of the Ottoman Empire: The Photograph Albums Presented by Sultan Abdülhamid II." *British Library Journal* 17, no. 2 (1991): 111–27.

Wasson, Haidee. *Everyday Movies: Portable Film Projectors and the Transformation of American Culture*. Oakland: University of California Press, 2020.

Watson, Ryan. *Radical Documentary and Global Crises*. Bloomington: Indiana University Press, 2021.

Wells, Sarah Ann. "At the Shores of Work." *Comparative Literature* 73, no. 2 (June 2021): 166–83.

Whitehead, Alfred North. *The Concept of Nature, Tarner Lectures Delivered in Trinity College, November, 1919*. Cambridge: The University Press, 1920.

Williams, Linda. "Film Body: An Implantation of Perversions." *Cine-Tracts* 12 (1981): 19–35.

Young, Damon R. *Making Sex Public, and Other Cinematic Fantasies*. Durham, NC: Duke University Press, 2018.

Zivie-Coche, Christiane. *Sphinx: History of a Monument*. Ithaca, NY: Cornell University Press, 2002.

Index

'Abbas al-Hilmi II (Khedive), 19, 87–91, 92–95, 173; at Abu al-Abbas al-Mursi Mosque, 92; sovereignty and, 90, 91
Abdul Hamid II (Sultan), 2, 89
Abel, Richard, 21
Abounaddara, 87, 99–103, 167
Abu al-Abbas al-Mursi Mosque, 92
Abu-Assad, Hany, 161
adjacency, 20, 26–28, 38, 41, 42. See also "beside" (term)
al-Ahram (newspaper), 5, 87
Alexandria, 4, 5, 12, 85–87, 92, 105–6, 111, 130, 133, 136, 167
Algeria, 2, 4–5, 18–19, 52–53, 56, 60, 62, 65, 80, 83–84, 133, 159
Algiers, 4–5, 12, 18–19, 52–54, 56, 60–61, 62, 65, 75–79, 82–83, 167, 169. See also specific topics
Algiers—The Embankment and Boulevard de la République (Jackson), 82
Allouache, Merzak, 75–77, 83, 167
Alloula, Malek, 54
Alsdorf, Bridget, 47
alterity, 54, 60, 73–74, 76, 177
Amad, Paula, 41, 103
amateur filmmakers, 100
American Mutoscope, 128
anachronism, 9–10, 21, 30, 59, 130, 157, 158
Andrew, Dudley, 30–31
Ânes (film), 53, 65, 67
Les Annales politiques et littéraires (Parville), 16

Apollo Mission, 19, 42
Approach of the Simoon, Desert of Gizeh (Roberts), 108, 111, 112
Apter, Emily, 30, 173
Arab cinema, 4, 26, 41; question of, 13–15
Arab Film Company Production Studio, 161
Arago, François, 107
archive, counter-archive, 2–3, 10–11, 18–19, 31–35, 41, 99–103, 137–38, 163, 169; world cinema and, 31–35
"Archive de la planète" (Kahn), 41
Archives françaises du film (AFF), 192n3
al-Arḍ (film), 26
Arendt, Hannah, 164, 172
Armes, Roy, 41, 161
Arrivée d'un train à La Ciotat (Arrival of the Train at La Ciotat) (film), 19, 124, 126, 126, 130, 133, 135
Asad, Talal, 174
Assassinat de Kléber (The Assassination of Kléber) (film), 95–97, 96, 98, 99–102
atlas, 30–31, 40, 86
Atlas of the European Novel (Moretti), 30
"An Atlas of World Cinema" (Andrew), 30
audience, 5–6, 9, 13–17, 47–60, 129–32
Aumont, Jacques, 153
Azoulay, Ariella Aïsha, 3, 45, 55, 104

Bāb al-Ḥadīd (film), 26
Bab El Oued City (film), 75, 77, 78, 83
Bad Film Histories (Groo), 41
Baer, Nicholas, 135, 143

231

Balázs, Béla, 153
Bandarli, Aziz, 92
Barak, On, 133–34, 137
Barker, Henry Aston, 81
Barker, Robert, 80
Barque sortant du port (A Boat Leaving Harbour), 71
Barthes, Roland, 103, 154, 159, 160
Battle of Algiers (film), 83
Baudry, Jean-Louis, 66
Bayoumi, Mohammed, 203n29
Bayoumi, Moustafa, 100
Bazin, André, 21, 82, 83, 109, 114–18, 122, 146, 206n23; Egypt as metaphor, 115; "The Ontology of the Photographic Image," 108, 114; theory of realism and duration, 116–19
Behdad, Ali, 72, 81, 107
Belloï, Livio, 47–48, 54, 58–59, 69–70
Belton, John, 116
Benjamin, Roger, 81
"beside" (term), 28
Bilder der Welt und Inschrift des Krieges (film), 159, 159, 211n24
Blue Marble, 19, 42, 164–66, 166, 169
A Boat Leaving Harbour. See *Barque sortant du port* (A Boat Leaving Harbour)
Bordwell, David, 88
Bottomore, Stephen, 93
Brewster, Ben, 21
bricks, 35–36, 39–40; as metaphor for montage, 40
Britain, 1, 90, 91, 93, 94, 133
Burch, Noël, 21, 66, 68–71

Cairo, 5, 12, 81, 85–87, 88, 92, 105, 111, 134, 167, 169, 173
Calvino, Italo, 160
Camera Lucida (film), 159, 160
capture, 3, 9, 17, 21, 34, 39, 44–46, 50, 52, 54, 58, 84, 88, 92, 102–3, 164; aesthetics of, 44–46, 167, 175. See also projection
Campion, Jane, 23
Carpentier, Jules, 6, 189n19
Casanova, Pascale, 148–50, 163–66
Casby, William, 160–61
Cassin, Barbara, 173
Chahine, Youssef, 23, 26–27, 27, 41, 119–22, 120, 167, 169
Champollion, Jean-François, 108
Chaplin, Charlie, 37

Charif, Mehdi, 23
The Cheat (film), 154
chronophotography, 6
Church of the Holy Sepulchre, 124
cinema: Arab cinema, 41; of attractions, 43, 45, 60; national cinema, 91, 92, 102, 104, 179; planetary cinema, 169–73, 179. See also early cinema; specific topics
Cinéma-monde (Gott and Schilt), 30
cinematograph: 7; invention and patent, 6–8; weight and specifications, 6, 181. See *specific topics*
cinema of attractions, 43, 60
Citadel, 88, 91, 137
Clercq, Louis de, 107
close-up, 10, 145–47, 151–58, 152, 155, 158, 160; development and significance, 153–54; historical scale and detail, 150–51, 163–66; theoretical reflection, 147
Coissac, Georges-Michel, 1, 20, 169, 174, 175, 179
colonialism, 13–14, 18, 35–39, 54–55, 102; decolonial optics, 38; postcolonialism, 57–58; power, 99; tropes, 101, 106
Colonising Egypt (Mitchell), 13
comparative literature, 4, 104, 149, 175, 179
The Concept of Nature (Whitehead), 117
conceptual cartography, 17–18, 30–31
Congress of Photography, 7, 9, 14, 43, 46–47, 51, 52, 56, 59, 168, 171–72
Conley, Tom, 34
conquest, 56, 85, 169
Cooks Travel, 54
Cooppan, Vilashini, 30
Copernicus, 172
Cortège arabe (film), 13, 14
culture: criticism, 60; difference, 39; film, 50, 89; multiculturalism, 24, 26, 35, 40, 168; production, 30; visual, 33, 42, 91
Curtis, Scott, 49

Damrosch, David, 30
Danse Egyptienne (film), 13, 15
Death of a Discipline (Spivak), 173
Le Débarquement du congrès de photographie à Lyon (The Photographical Congress Arrives in Lyon), 43–48, 44, 52, 68, 158, 170, 170, 172
decolonial optics, 21–22, 36–38, 72–74
Delacroix, Eugène, 54
Deleuze, Gilles, 117, 118, 153

INDEX 233

Dello-Strologo, Henri, 201n5
DeMille, Cecil B., 154
Départ de Jérusalem en chemin de fer (film), 124–25, 125, 128, 133, 135, 136, 138, 158
Deray, Jacques, 23
Derrida, Jacques, 118
Descente de la grande pyramide (film), 106
Deshpande, Shekhar, 30, 149
Deslandes, Jacques, 178
Deutelbaum, Marshall, 139
Dickens, Charles, 111
Dictionary of the Untranslatables (Cassin), 173
Diegues, Carlos, 23, 28
Direct Cinema, 139
Discussion de Monsieur Janssen et Monsieur Lagrange (film), 171
Djebar, Assia, 54
Doane, Mary Ann, 153–54, 163–65
Documenta, 99
documentary, 9, 99
Dolan, Xavier, 23
Dorès, Umberto, 92
double observation, 58–59
Doublier, Francis, 8, 33–34, 36, 38, 41, 173, 193n22
Dreyer, Carl, 154
Dubois, Philippe, 19, 139
Du Bois, W. E. B., 55
Le Duel après le bal (film), 97
Duras, Marguerite, 175
duration, image of, 114–18
Duvivier, Julien, 76–77, 83

early cinema, 6, 17, 33, 39, 47, 128, 132; anachronism in, 21; exceptionalism of, 66; global dissemination of, 52; global trajectories of, 12; illusion in, 16; Japonisme in, 11; national cinema and, 93; objectification in, 58; optics of, 38; Orientalist travel in, 4; semiotic ideology of, 123; sovereigns in, 90–91, 94; tableau style in, 97, 99; train motif in, 130; travel in, 4, 45. *See also specific topics and films*
Edison, Thomas, 6, 15, 16, 193n19
Edison Company, 83, 85, 90, 153
Egypt, 5, 14, 26, 37, 85–87, 92, 94, 105–8, 116, 134. *See also specific topics*
Eisenstein, Sergei, 10, 40, 118
Elhaies, Karim, 89
ellipsis, 1–3, 11–12, 97, 143, 167, 179

Elsaesser, Thomas, 21, 139
empire, 23–24, 35–39, 54, 88–89; world cinema and, 35–39
enchantment, 53–54, 58, 60–61
The End of Cinema (Gaudreault), 21
enframing, versus emplotting, 69, 70–72
England, 1, 90, 91, 93, 94, 133
Epstein, Jean, 153
Esmeir, Samera, 28–30, 40
Esperanto, 4
estrangement, 3, 12, 60, 173
ethics of world cinema, 102, 166, 172. *See also* world cinema
ethnography, 53, 55, 156
ethnographic mirage, 13–17
Eurocentrism, 13, 190n39
excess, as method, 10–13
Exposition Universelle, 80

face, in cinema, 47–48, 145–48, 151–54, 160–62, 165
"The Face of Garbo" (Barthes), 154
Fanon, Frantz, 55
Farag, Alfred, 96
Farid, Samir, 89
Farocki, Harun, 37, 39, 41, 159, 159, 211n24
Fay, Jennifer, 198n45
"The Figure in the Carpet" (James), 148
Filming the Modern Middle East (Khatib), 162
films: Ashanti films, 59, 156; ethnographic films, 156; "original" film, 18; silent films, 161. *See also specific topics and films*
The Film Sense (Eisenstein), 10
framing, 62–84; de-centering, 65–68; enframing, 69, 70–72; mis-framing, 63; theatricality and, 70
France, 24, 25, 28, 60
Frei, Hans, 113–14
Friedberg, Anne, 66, 70
Friese-Greene, William, 6
Frith, Francis, 107
Fromentin, Eugène, 54

Galt, Rosalind, 207n41
Ganguly, Debjani, 34
Garanger, Marc, 159, 211n24
Garbo, Greta, 153, 154
Garcia, Edgar, 34
Gaudreault, André, 21, 97, 139
Gawkers (Alsdorf), 47

Germany, 1, 33, 93
Gérôme, Jean-Léon, 97, 98, 99
Gertz, Nurith, 161
Ginzburg, Carlo, 10
Ginzburg, Natalia, 10
Girel, François-Constant, 8, 36
Glissant, Edouard, 174
globe, 174; scale and, 162–66
Gorfinkel, Elena, 44
Gorky, Maxim, 130
Gott, Michael, 30
Great Pyramid, 106–7, 117, 118, 173
Gregory, Derek, 83
Griffiths, Alison, 4, 55
Groo, Katherine, 41, 59, 132–33, 156–57
Guillaumet, Gustave, 54
Gunning, Tom, 13, 21, 59, 109, 115, 130–31;
    Burch and, 69–70; cinema of attractions
    and, 43; image-making and, 54;
    postcolonialism of, 57–58; travel and, 54

al-Hadari, Ahmed, 4, 89
Haghe, Louis, 110
al-Halabi, Suleiman, 95–97, 99–102
Hammam Schneider, 167
Hamp, M., 169
Hanan al-Cinema (Marks), 190n35
Hanoi, 18, 35–39, 86
Harper's Magazine, 80
Hassan, Ilhami, 89
Hassan, Nizar, 161
Hatot, Georges, 96
The Haverstraw Tunnel (film), 128
Hayakawa, Sessue, 154
Heath, Stephen, 66
Hegel, Georg Wilhelm Friedrich, 118
Heidegger, Martin, 172
Hejaz railway, 133
Helmy, Samy, 4
Hennebelle, Guy, 41
Histoire comparée de cinéma (Deslandes), 178
Histoire du cinéma mondiale (Sadoul), 138
Histoire du cinématographe de ses origines à nos jours (Coissac), 1, 20, 169
history, 206n17; historical reconstruction, 114; historicism, 147; historicity, 206n17; local, 47–51; microhistory, 5, 10–13, 21; world, 51–56
Hitchcock, Alfred, 154
Hobbes, Thomas, 94

Hochberg, Gil, 122
Holmes, Burton, 54
The Holy Land, Syria, Idumea, Arabia, Egypt, and Nubia (Roberts), 111
Howe, Kathleen Stewart, 107
Huillet, Danièle, 37, 41
human bodies: motion of, 107; study of, 73
Hungary, 8, 33
Hunt, William Holman, 111
Hussein, Mahmoud, 37
Husserl, Edmund, 172

ibn Husayn, Bey Ali, 90
Ibrahim, Sonallah, 96
illusion, absolute, 15–17
Imaginary Signifier (Metz), 48
immobility, 127, 128
imperialism, 24, 56–58, 168
In Search of the Syrian Fanatic (short film), 101
indexicality, 4, 20, 34, 172
India, 24, 26, 28
institutional mode of representation, 66
internationalism, cinematic, 18, 90
interplanetary communication, 175
Invisible Cities (Calvino), 160
Italy, 1, 8

al-Jabarti, 95
Jackson, William Henry, 80, 82
Jaffa, 2, 124–29, 132–35, 138, 141
Jaffa Gate, 4, 19, 137, 143, 144–47, 151–57, 160–62, 165–66, 179
Jaffa-Jerusalem railway, 124, 133, 138
Jaikumar, Priya, 45
Jambon, Marcel, 96
James, Henry, 148, 149, 163, 165
Janssen, Jules, 19–20, 170, 171, 172–73, 175
Janus Unbound (journal), 174, 175
Japan, 8, 36, 170, 174–75
Japonisme, 11
Jerusalem, 2, 4, 19, 123, 124–29, 131–39, 140–44, 145–46, 151, 158, 161, 167, 176–78, 179
"Jet Lag and Time Zones" (Andrew), 30
juxtaposition, 24, 27, 31, 140–41, 179

Kahn, Alfred, 41
Kalem Film Companies, 85
Kantorowicz, Ernst, 94
Kennedy, William, 193n19

INDEX 235

Kepley, Vance, 49
Kessler, Frank, 93
Khatib, Lina, 83, 162
Le Khédive et son escorte (film), 88, 89, 92, 104, 137
Khleifi, George, 161
Khleifi, Michel, 161
Kiarostami, Abbas, 168
al-Kilani, Ahmad Hilmi, 161
kinetoscope, 6, 15
King, Homay, 164–65
King Kong (film), 55
The Kings Two Bodies (Kantorowicz), 94
Kirby, Lynne, 130–31, 133, 134
Kiwan, Charif, 100
Kléber, Jean-Baptiste, 86, 87, 95–97, 99, 102
Koehler, Madeleine, 130
Kubrick, Stanley, 176
Kuleshov, Lev, 40
Kurgan, Laura, 165

labor, 26, 33; of factory life, 32; globalized practices of, 25, 39; juxtaposition and, 31; leisure and, 35; of Lumière factory workers, 24–25; mechanized, 39; mimesis and, 73; representation of, 31, 34; routinization of, 37; standardization of, 40; translation and, 175; visualizing, 37; of world cinema, 35–39, 168
landscape, 78–79, 107, 110, 128–29, 133–37, 141–42, 151, 156, 173
Lant, Antonia, 116–17
Lavanchy-Clarke, François-Henri, 14
law, international, 28
Lehmbeck, Leah, 97
Lenssen, Anneka, 100
Lessing, Gotthold Ephraim, 97
Likavčan, Lukáš, 172
Lim, Bliss Cua, 207n41
Lindsay, Vachel, 118
local, 92, 130, 133, 141, 161, 169, 172, 177; local history, 52, 61, 172; versus foreign, 3, 44–46
location, 24, 44–46, 48–49, 60–61
Loiperdinger, Martin, 129–31, 139
looking, at the camera, 47–48, 58–59, 157; masking and, 158–62
Louis-Philippe (King), 108
Lumière, Auguste, 6, 7, 52, 80
Lumière, Louis, 6–7, 43, 52, 71, 80, 130, 145, 153

Lumière, Marguerite, 130
Lumière, Rose, 130
Lumière, Suzanne, 130
Lumière and Company, 168
Lumière Brothers: camera operators and, 8–10, 33–34, 36, 52–53, 56, 80, 169; centenary celebration (1995), 18, 23–31, 168; global network, 7–10, 110, 168; as inventors, 6–7. See also specific topics.
Lumière Brothers Film Company, 8, 25, 31, 52, 61, 86–87, 90, 141
The Lumière Brothers' First Films, 62, 191n1
Lumière et compagnie (film), 119, 120, 121
Lumière Institute, 26, 62, 105, 168
Lvoff, John, 23
Lynch, David, 168
Lyon, 6, 18, 23–24, 31–32, 34–35, 37, 39–40, 42–47, 51–54, 56, 86, 93, 108–9, 127, 141, 163, 168, 171–72
Lyon républicain, 129

Ma, Jean, 207n41
Magritte, René, 63
Maḥmal, 88
Mamoulian, Rouben, 154
Mannoni, Laurent, 6
Marché arabe (film), 46, 52, 53, 54, 57, 59, 62, 158
Marks, Laura, 157, 190n35
Marshall, Bill, 30
La Martiniere, 196n23
Martinique, 36
Masharawi, Rashid, 161
mask, 158–62, 165, 179
Masri, Mai, 161
Maud of Wales (Princess), 90
Mazaj, Meta, 30, 149
McManus, Anne-Marie, 150
Méliès, Georges, 69, 141, 169
Mesguich, Félix, 8, 11, 36, 56
Metz, Christian, 48–49, 51
Mexico, 8, 36
Michals, Duane, 159
microhistory, 5, 10–13, 21
Middle East, 1–4, 11–13, 41, 83, 85, 89, 102, 124, 127, 133–34, 141, 151, 167, 178. See also specific topics
Miller, Angela, 81
Miller, Jacques-Alain, 103
mimesis, 34, 72–75

mirror: as metaphor for world cinema, 59, 165–66, 172–73; as reflection for audience, 46, 47–51. See also window

Mirzoeff, Nicholas, 36, 45, 55

mise-en-scène, 25, 44, 70–72, 74, 96, 102, 119

Mitchell, Timothy, 13

Mitry, Jean, 128

Miyao, Daisuke, 11

Modern Times (film), 37

Moisson, Charles, 6, 8, 33, 189n19

Le Monde (newspaper), 101

montage, 31, 39–40, 76, 96, 153; as conflict, 40; versus movement, 139–40

Moon, Sarah, 168

Moretti, Franco, 30

Morgan, Daniel, 115, 129

motion, 17; capture of, 16; cinematic, 129; continuous, 6, 31; embodiment of, 143; of human bodies, 107; intermittent, 6; locomotion, 140; photography, 4, 6, 24, 86, 104, 170, 171; studies, 73, 118; thematization of, 45; in time, 33; world in/as, 138–40

multiculturalism, 24, 26, 35, 40, 168

"mummy complex," 115

al-Muqtataf (journal), 109

"Le Mur des Cinéastes," 168

La Musée de l'homme, 95, 99

Musser, Charles, 21, 54, 97, 128

Muybridge, Eadweard, 73, 118

Nadeem, Aida, 176

Naficy, Hamid, 49

Nagib, Lúcia, 149

national cinema, 4–5, 23–25, 26–31, 40–42, 87, 89–95, 102–4, 161–62, 179

Navon, Yosef, 124

Neuville-sur-Saône, 18, 43–44, 51, 52, 60, 167

Neyrat, Frédéric, 172

Nicholas II (Czar), 90

Niépce, Nicéphore, 116

objectification, 58, 167

off-screen space, 10, 65–66, 70, 72, 77–78, 97, 119, 153–54, 156, 160

Oleksijczuk, Denise, 81

"On Becoming Less of the World" (Esmeir), 28

One World broadcast, 41

"The Ontology of the Photographic Image" (Bazin), 108, 114

Orientalism, 73, 83–84, 86, 107, 150; artifice, 65, 75, 79; clichés, 65, 72, 76; conventions of, 65; in early cinema, 4; fantasy, 12, 13; realism, 17; Said on, 74; stereotypes, 100; travelogues, 133, 138; tropes, 14; visual culture of, 91

Orientalism (Said), 13, 73

Oscar II (King of Norway), 90

Ottoman Empire, 2, 10, 19, 104, 133, 187n3

Ottoman Palestine. See Palestine

Palestine, 3, 8, 148, 158, 161–62, 176–78, 211n29; Promio's trip to, 13, 19, 124, 141, 145, 168; Sansour and, 122; Studio Palestine, 161; Tamari on, 137. See also specific topics

Palestinian Cinema (Gertz and Khleifi, G.), 161

Palestinian Revolution (1968–1982), 161, 211n29

Panorama en chemin de fer (collines) (film), 141, 142

Panorama en chemin de fer (film), 141, 142, 144

panorama, 81–83

Park, Lisa, 41

Parville, Henri de, 16

Pascal, M. François, 196n23

Passage d'un tunnel en chemin de fer (pris de l'avant de la locomotive) (film), 141

The Passion of Joan of Arc (film), 154

Pathé, 30, 85, 97

Pépé le Moko (film), 76, 79, 83

perception (audience), 5–6, 9, 13–17, 47–60, 129–32

perceptual paradigm, 129–32, 133, 138

Peterson, Jennifer Lynn, 56

phantom ride, 70, 128, 141

Pheng Cheah, 34

photogénie, 153, 160

The Photographical Congress Arrives in Lyon. See *Le Débarquement du congrès de photographie à Lyon*

photography, 24, 50, 103, 115–16; archival, 137; chronophotography, 6; Congress of Photography, 7, 9, 14, 43, 46–47, 51, 52, 56, 59, 168, 171–72; motion, 4, 6, 24, 86, 104, 170, 171; portrait, 88; Société Française de la Photographie, 172

photorama, 19, 80–82, 83
Pinel, Vincent, 71, 138, 139
planetarity, 165, 173–76, 178–79
planetary cinema, 169–73, 177, 179
Pontecorvo, Gilles, 83
portal, 28, 60–61, 137, 170, 198n45
Porte de Jaffa (film), 145–47, 146, 151, 152, 155, 157, 162, 165
postcolonial pivot, 56–60
postcolonialism, 56–60, 174
potential history, 3, 17, 42, 84, 104, 129, 138, 173, 178, 179
Prière du muezzin (film), 62–66, 64, 67, 69–73, 76, 78
primitive mode of representation, 66
Procession du tapis sacré (film), 88
Le Progrès (newspaper), 15
projection, 3, 9–10, 12, 17, 25, 39, 44, 48, 57, 84, 87, 94, 99, 167, 169, 179; reenactment and, 99–103. *See also* capture
Promio, Alexandre: as camera operator, 1–2, 7–10; ellipsis in travelogue, 1–3, 11, 167; North Africa/Middle East journey, 1–3, 52–57, 65, 80, 85–86, 105–6, 124–29, 145; travelogue account, 1–3, 7–10, 52, 127, 128, 167. *See also specific topics*
Les Pyramides (vue générale) (film), 105–6, 106, 108, 118, 123

Queen Christina (film), 153, 154
Queer Cinema in the World (Schoonover and Galt), 207n41

The Railway Journey (Schivelbusch), 128
realism, 113, 116–17, 130, 138, 206n23; cinematic, 114; naïve, 115; Orientalist, 17
reenactment, theoretical reflections on, 99, 102, 103–4; *La Sortie de l'usine* and, 18, 25; *Assassinat de Kléber* and, 95
La Réforme (newspaper), 5, 87
Regnault, Félix-Louis, 55, 126, 130
Renaissance perspective, 66, 81, 164
Repas de bébé (film), 130
representation, 60, 99, 113; global, 123; institutional mode of, 66; of labor, 31, 34; primitive mode of, 66
Rhodes, John David, 44
Robert, Valentine, 97
Roberts, David, 108, 110–14, 112, 116, 121–22
Rony, Fatimah Tobing, 4, 49, 55
Rosen, Philip, 111, 116, 206n17

Rosetta Stone, 108
Ross, Kristen, 30
Rouch, Jean, 23
Roy, Arundhati, 198n45
Ruoff, Jeffrey, 4

Sabotage (film), 154
Sadoul, Georges, 41, 71, 89, 128, 161, 179, 193n19, 198n9; audience perception and, 16; Dubois and, 139; *Histoire du cinéma mondiale*, 138; Lumière, Louis and, 70
SAF. *See* Société Astronomique de France
Said, Edward, 13, 73–74
ElSaket, Ifdal, 89
Salazkina, Masha, 29–30, 40
Salon Indien, 6, 130
Salt, Barry, 21
Sander, August, 161
Sansour, Larissa, 20, 122, 176–78
scale, 107, 113, 140, 145–47; faces and, 153–54, 157; globe and, 164–66; world literature and, 150–51
Schatzberg, Jerry, 23, 28
Schilt, Thibault, 30
Schivelbusch, Wolfgang, 128, 130, 134
Schonig, Jordan, 16, 129
Schoonover, Karl, 207n41
Schwartz, Vanessa, 21
science fiction, 121–22
Screen (Bazin), 116
The Sea Wall (Duras), 175
Sedgwick, Eve Kosofsky, 28
Seguin, Jean-Claude, 189n20, 196n22
Sen, Mrinal, 23, 27, 27, 28, 31, 168, 169
seriality, 19, 32, 87, 88–91; sovereignty, and 90–91, 94
Sestier, Marius, 8
Shafik, Viola, 4, 41, 89, 161, 203n29
El Shakry, Hoda, 122
Shohat, Ella, 13
Silverman, Kaja, 211n24
Sirhan, Ibrahim Hassan, 161, 211n29
Sixth Part of the World (film), 41
Skladanowsky, Max, 6
Sloane, John, 108
Sloterdijk, Peter, 163
Smyth, Charles Piazzi, 106
Société Astronomique de France (SAF), 172
Société Française de la Photographie, 172
Society for the Development of National Industry, 6, 32

Sortie de la briqueterie Meffre et Bourgoin à Hanoi (film), 36
La Sortie de l'usine (Workers Leaving the Factory) (film), 18, 23, 25, 32, 35, 41, 47, 129; commemorative photograph from, 24; Doublier and, 34, 38; Farocki on, 37; global proletariat and, 37; location of, 24; restaging of, 26; threshold visualization and, 32; visual culture and, 33
sovereignty: 'Abbas al-Hilmi II and, 90, 91; afterlives, 99–103; cuts, 95–99; in early cinema, 90–91, 94; image, 101–4; serial, 88–91, 89; visualizing, 87, 91
A Space Exodus (film), 176, 177, 178
Spain, 1, 33, 90
spectatorship, 38, 48–49, 130, 133, 138, 141
Sphinx (at Giza), 105, 109–11, 114
Spivak, Gayatri Chakravorty, 20, 173, 174–75, 179
Sputnik, 164
Stam, Robert, 13, 30, 149
statecraft, 2, 90–91. *See* sovereignty
Steyerl, Hito, 164
Stock Market of Toussoun-Pasha, 86
Stoddard, John L., 54
Straub, Jean-Marie, 37, 41
Studio Palestine, 161
Suite d'un bal masqué (Gérôme), 98
Suleiman, Elia, 161
Sultan Hasan Mosque, 88
Swinton, Tilda, 23
Swiss National Exhibition, 13
Switzerland, 14, 15, 133
Syria, 2, 3; Abounaddara in, 87, 99–103, 167; colonial tropes around, 101

Tabareau, Henry, 196n23
tableau style, in early cinema, 97, 99
Tamari, Salim, 137
Tanoukhi, Nirvana, 150
Tarzan (film), 49, 55
Tavernier, Bertrand, 23, 62, 63, 105
Thaddeus, Henry Jones, 91
theatricality, 70–72, 73; enframing and, 70
Theorizing World Cinema (Nagib), 149
Thompson, Kristin (film historian), 21
Too Early, Too Late (film), 37
Toro, Guillermo del, 23
Toth, André de, 23
Toussoun Stock Exchange, 5, 167
tracking shot, 9, 124–29, 132, 140–44; as movement and method, 140
trains, 130, 132–38; in film theory, 128, 130–32, 138–40; La Ciotat and Jerusalem, 125; in the Lumière catalogue, 130, 132; in the Middle East, 132–35
Transit of Venus (Janssen), 171
translation, 21, 49, 149–50; as translating, 173–76
travel, 56; in early cinema, 4, 45; Gunning and, 54
travelogues, 93, 99; *Marché arabe* and, 54; Orientalist, 133, 138; of Promio, 1–3, 5, 7–9, 52, 127, 128, 167
Tsai Ming-Liang, 198n45
Turkey, 1, 3, 10, 11, 53

United States, 1, 8, 9, 24, 26, 28, 36, 53
Unthinking Eurocentrism (Shohat and Stam), 13

Vaughan, Dai, 15, 16, 71–72, 176
Vecchiali, Paul, 23
Vedder, Elihu, 108
Venus, 170, 171, 172
Vertov, Dziga, 41
Veyre, Gabriel, 8, 11, 25, 35–40
Via Dolorosa, 124
Victoria (Queen of England), 90, 91, 93, 94
Vietnam, 8, 175
Villa Lumière, 23, 25
Virilio, Paul, 129
Virtual Memory (King), 164
The Virtual Window (Friedberg), 66
visagefication, 153
visualization, 8, 45, 60, 92, 111, 121–22, 141, 179; of labor, 37; macrohistory and, 12; of sovereignty, 87, 91; of threshold, 32
Le Voyage dans la lune (Méliès), 169

Warhol, Andy, 159
Wasson, Haidee, 49
What Is Cinema? (Bazin), 114
Whitehead, Alfred North, 108, 117, 118, 122
Wilhelm II (Kaiser), 93, 146
Williams, Linda, 73, 74
window, 46, 51–56, 59. *See also* mirror
Wondrous Difference (Griffiths), 55
Wong Kar-Wai, 23
Workers Leaving the Factory. *See La Sortie de l'usine*

world cinema: as archive, 31–35; as atlas, 26–31; concept of, 1–5, 23–26; as empire, 35–39; ethics of, 102, 166, 172; future of, 169, 172, 178–79; microhistory of, 11–13; as movement, 127, 140–42; as question of scale, 147, 164, 165; sovereignty and, 87, 91. *See specific topics*
World Cinema (Deshpande and Mazaj), 30, 149
world literature, 30–31, 34–35, 148–51, 165

World Literature, Transnational Cinema, and Global Media (Stam), 149
The World Republic of Letters (Casanova), 148
world system, 19, 26–27, 38, 129, 149, 163

Zaghlul, Saʿad, 203n29
Zhang Yimou, 168
Zweig, Stefan, 93, 94

MICHAEL ALLAN is Associate Professor of Comparative Literature and Cinema Studies at the University of Oregon. He is the author of *In the Shadow of World Literature: Sites of Reading in Colonial Egypt* (2016, winner, MLA First Book Prize) and serves as editor of the journal *Comparative Literature*.

www.ingramcontent.com/pod-product-compliance
Lightning Source LLC
Chambersburg PA
CBHW020404080526
44584CB00014B/1163